# "A PUNISHMENT ON THE NATION"

CIVIL WAR IN THE NORTH

Series Editor: Lesley J. Gordon, University of Akron

*Broken Glass: Caleb Cushing and the Shattering of the Union*
John M. Belohlavek

*Banners South: A Northern Community at War*
Edmund J. Raus

*"Circumstances Are Destiny": An Antebellum Woman's Struggle to Define Sphere*
Tina Stewart Brakebill

*More Than a Contest between Armies: Essays on the Civil War*
Edited by James Marten and A. Kristen Foster

*August Willich's Gallant Dutchmen: Civil War Letters from the 32nd Indiana Infantry*
Translated and edited by Joseph R. Reinhart

*Meade's Army: The Private Notebooks of Lt. Col. Theodore Lyman*
Edited by David W. Lowe

*Dispatches from Bermuda: The Civil War Letters of Charles Maxwell Allen, U.S. Consul at Bermuda, 1861–1888*
Edited by Glen N. Wiche

*The Antebellum Crisis and America's First Bohemians*
Mark A. Lause

*Orlando M. Poe: Civil War General and Great Lakes Engineer*
Paul Taylor

*Northerners at War: Reflections on the Civil War Home Front*
J. Matthew Gallman

*A German Hurrah! Civil War Letters of Friedrich Bertsch and Wilhelm Stängel, 9th Ohio Infantry*
Translated and edited by Joseph R. Reinhart

*"They Have Left Us Here to Die": The Civil War Prison Diary of Sgt. Lyle G. Adair, 111th U.S. Colored Infantry*
Edited by Glenn Robins

*The Election of 1860 Reconsidered*
Edited by A. James Fuller

*"A Punishment on the Nation": An Iowa Soldier Endures the Civil War*
Edited by Brian Craig Miller

# “A Punishment on the Nation”

*An Iowa Soldier Endures the Civil War*

Edited by Brian Craig Miller

THE KENT STATE UNIVERSITY PRESS

*Kent, Ohio*

ISBN 978-1-60635-144-4
Manufactured in the United States of America



Cataloging information for this title is available at the Library of Congress.

16 15 14 13 12 5 4 3 2 1

*For Brent*

Kathryn Walker (1983–2011)

It is with deep sadness I report that Kathryn Walker has passed away at the age of 28. She brought me the letters you are about to read. She had an inquisitive mind, a generous spirit, and a kind heart. I am so very grateful to have known her and hope that this book will serve as a lasting legacy to her generosity.

# Contents

# Cast of Historical Characters

| | |
|---|---|
| Private Silas W. Haven | Soldier, Company G, 27th Iowa |
| Sarah "Jane" Haven | His wife |
| Ella Haven | His daughter |
| Emmett Haven | His son |
| Laura Olivia "Kitty" Haven | His youngest daughter |
| Fred Muhm | His best friend, 27th Iowa |
| Susan Muhm | Fred's wife |
| Sylvester Haven | His brother, 21st Iowa |
| Laura and Inez Haven | His sisters |
| Jacob Knapp | Sarah's brother, Third Iowa Battery |
| Solomon Haven | His father |
| Charlotte Elizabeth Haven | His mother |

# Acknowledgments

THE READING, transcribing, and editing of the letters of Silas W. Haven has been one of the most rewarding experiences of my historical career. As a self-professed historian of the Confederacy during the Civil War, I have found my journey northward to be enlightening, engaging, and rather fun. Yet, I have not taken this walk alone and my thanks go out to several people who have made this book possible. The project began with Kathi Walker, a student from my History 111 course, who e-mailed me one day, asking me if I would like to see some family Civil War letters. A quick reading of five letters turned into a meeting that resulted in the publication of this book. I am grateful to all the family members, particularly Sharlene Madouras. It is my hope that you are happy with the final product, and that you take as much joy from reading these letters as I did.

I would like to thank the archivists and workers I encountered across Iowa, particularly Mary Anne at the Floyd County Historical Society; the local people of Rockford, Iowa, who allowed me to pick their brains about cemeteries and their histories (or missing histories); the staff at the Floyd County Courthouse in Charles City, Iowa, and the staff of the State Historical Society in Des Moines, Iowa. I thoroughly enjoyed my very first trip to Iowa and left the state with not only a better understanding of Silas Haven and his place in history but also that of Iowa. Thanks also to the staff at the National Archives in Washington who assisted me in getting Haven's pension file.

My life has been enriched by extraordinary friendships, both within and outside the historical community. At Emporia State University, I am grateful for my supportive colleagues Ellen Hansen, Darla Mallein, Phil Kelly, and Greg Schneider. Greg, you have become a model scholar for me to emulate, and I am blessed by our friendship and your willingness to mentor me on walks for coffee three days a week. I am honored to have the support and friendship of the following people who help make each day a better one: Paul Beazley, James

Ehlers, Ross Guthrie, Matt Johnson, Alice Lachassee, Matt Mosley, Courtney Roy (who housed me in Washington), Chris Stacey, Minoa Uffelman, Mike and Carol Upton, Brian Van Norman, and Chuck and Jen Westmoreland. Thanks to John Neff for always chatting and providing source hints, especially from a cemetery in Iowa. Special thanks to Terry Bax, who provided me with a "home away from home" in Kansas City, where I edited and transcribed most of this manuscript.

In addition, I am grateful to the tireless efforts of the staff at Kent State University Press, especially Mary Young and the incomparable Joyce Harrison. Dan Sutherland read the entire manuscript and offered superb suggestions and feedback, which assisted me in producing a stronger product. Lesley Gordon, the editor of this series, is a true shining gem, and I appreciate her faith in me, her feedback, and, more importantly, her friendship. Thank you all for pushing me to create a better book that does justice to the legacy that an ordinary man left behind.

I am grateful for Nick Messing, who makes each day better than the previous. Thank you for your own passion, your friendship, Starbucks, breakfast with Pooh, the endless laughs, and the conversations with Bear and Max. Finally, to my parents, Craig and Linda Miller, and my sister Brooke, who revolved each of our family vacations around a Civil War battlefield. In particular, on our trip to Shiloh, we discovered a database computer that revealed the location of the grave of Philip B. Spotts, a relative who died at Antietam. Later on that trip, we stopped in Sharpsburg to place a small American flag amid an endless sea of headstones at the Antietam National Cemetery. The memory of that evening, a pivotal one in my own personal development as a historian, flooded back to me one afternoon when I stood placing another small American flag on a grave, this time in Rockford, Iowa. I am thankful to have a family who loves and supports me and have even, dare I say, joined my historical entourage.

This book is dedicated to my brother, Brent Darwin Miller, who played the Union soldier in our Civil War battles in the backyard. My parents had plenty of woods (to do Shiloh), a pond (Shiloh, again), peach trees (Shiloh and Gettysburg), a makeshift log cabin (Chickamauga), a big field (Gettysburg), lots of big rocks (Gettysburg), an old barn (Gettysburg), and a cornfield in the summer—well, the corn section of our family garden (Antietam), where we fought out the bloodiest day in American history, much to the chagrin of our parents. You are an incredible human being, a model gentleman, a devoted public servant, and a brother who has always loved me unconditionally. It has been a true pleasure to watch my little bro grow over the years, and I hope this book dedication is a reminder of how important you are in my life.

INTRODUCTION

# Private Silas W. Haven's Civil War

On May 30, 1895, future Supreme Court Justice Oliver Wendell Holmes Jr. delivered an address on the significance and importance of Memorial Day before a graduating class at Harvard University. Holmes reflected on the Civil War, noting, "As for us, our days of combat are over. Our swords are rust. Our guns will thunder no more. The vultures that once wheeled over our heads must be buried with their prey. Whatever of glory must be won in the council or the closet, never again in the field. I do not repine." He then added, "We have shared the incommunicable experience of war; we have felt, we still feel, the passion of life to its top."[1]

In the midst of the American Civil War, soldiers and civilians picked up their pencils and pens in an attempt to share their thoughts, feelings, opinions, and experiences of a generation immersed in conflict. With a literacy rate of more than 90 percent, white Union soldiers left behind a wealth of correspondence in which they conveyed their experience of war.[2] The letters, newspaper clippings, and diary entries remain the only viable way for future generations to peer through the windows of the past in order to assess and communicate to a reader that "incommunicable" experience of war. In recent years, a flurry of letter collections and diary entries have been published from the era of Civil War America, representing soldiers and civilians from the mountains of Vermont to the piney woods of Mississippi and from the plains of Kansas to the coastal plains of Louisiana.

Despite the wealth of recent publications, we still know very little about the experiences of United States soldiers and civilians from the heartland of the Midwest, particularly Iowa.[3] Iowa emerged as one of the late entries into the United States before the Civil War. Settlement for white Americans started in June 1833, mostly residents from neighboring Illinois and Missouri and nearby Indiana. Iowa officially entered the nation as a state on December 28, 1846.

By 1860, the fledgling state had a population of more than 670,000 people. According to enlistment records, 75,474 Iowans served in the United States Army during the Civil War, including 440 African Americans, who marched as part of the 60th United States Colored Troops. The state produced forty-four regiments, two battalions, and nine cavalry units. Out of the thousands who served from Iowa, 13,001 soldiers perished during the war, most of them from disease. Iowa suffered only about 2,000 deaths in combat, and nearly 1,500 men died from their wounds during the war.[4]

One of the several thousand Iowa soldiers who enlisted is Silas W. Haven, born on March 3, 1826 in Ludlow, Vermont.[5] He grew up and received his education in Vermont before moving to Pennsylvania at the age of twenty-one. In 1848, Haven relocated to Winnebago County, Illinois, where he married twenty-year-old Sarah Jane Knapp in 1849. A year later, Jane, as Haven affectionately called her, gave birth to the couple's first daughter, Ella, followed by a son, Emmett, in 1854. The Havens remained in Illinois until 1855 before deciding to move to Rockford, Iowa. In 1860, the family welcomed a second daughter, Laura, whom Haven affectionately called Kitty.[6]

The town of Rockford, founded in the spring of 1856 by John Platt, S.P. Brittain, George Wyatt, and Willard Bowdoin, appeared where Lime Creek and the Shell Rock rivers converged with one another. The men selected the name Rockford because they were from Rockford, Illinois, and the name fit, especially with "the rocky bottom and sides of the ford in use before any bridge was built." After the initial settlers constructed a dam, a sawmill quickly began operation, run by Samuel Pearson on one side of town and George Brentner on the other. The sawmill prompted community expansion and allowed for more settlers to move into this Floyd County community, including Silas Haven, who built a home in 1856 from some of the first lumber produced at the sawmill. Haven's home initially stood on a large tract of land that operated as a family farm. He sold off two forty-acre sections in 1856, according to county land records. With more and more settlers moving to Rockford weekly, the community stabilized as shipments of goods started arriving in the fall of 1856, prompting the construction of a temporary store. The first hotel was built in 1856, one year prior to the construction of a steam-powered sawmill.[7]

George Wyatt, one of the first settlers and the postmaster, got a ferry license in 1858 and helped move people and animals across the river. It cost thirty-five cents for a double carriage drawn by two animals, twenty-five cents for a single carriage, and an individual on foot cost three cents, but the rate increased to ten cents if the person was accompanied by a horse. In addition to the ferry service, the town built a flour mill in 1858, but the foundation gave way in

1861, and the mill crumbled into the water. The community built a new dam across Lime Creek and then a new mill. In 1858, the town included twenty-six homes, a hotel, three stores, two sawmills, a blacksmith, and a schoolhouse, which two of the Haven children attended. The town also created the First Baptist Church in 1858, under the direction of Rev. D. D. Meade, inside a small village schoolhouse. Haven and his wife are listed among the original seven members of the church. Rev. H. H. Burrington, pastor of the church in 1859, also taught at the schoolhouse in town.[8]

By 1860, the town of Rockford contained three hundred residents, who staunchly voted Republican. The county paper, the *Republican Intelligencer,* endorsed Republican candidate Abraham Lincoln on May 24, 1860. Haven is among the fifty-one residents who cast their vote for Abraham Lincoln in 1860 versus the twenty who voted for the northern Democrat, Stephen Douglas. Floyd County overwhelmingly voted for Lincoln as the Republican captured 560 votes, with Douglas coming in second with 201 votes. John Breckenridge, representing the southern Democrats, got twenty-one votes, while John Bell, the constitutional Union candidate, received only one vote. The county voted in a similar fashion in 1864, when Lincoln won 587 votes, compared to the Democrat George B. McClellan, who won only 185 votes. The political and social culture of Rockford, Iowa, reflected the historical roots of many of the settlers who arrived from New England and neighboring Illinois. The republican, religious, and antislavery sentiments fostered by several settlers in the region helped shape Silas Haven and his worldview as he prepared to enter the Civil War as a volunteer soldier.[9]

Most historians traditionally begin any collection of letters with a discussion as to why the soldier enlisted and fought in the Civil War. Historians continue to disagree as to the main motivational force for warfare. Bell Wiley argued that soldiers took up their musket originally for "material considerations and a mere craving for excitement to profound idealism and hatred of traitors." Wiley viewed the main interests that sustained and continued to motivate soldiers as quite similar to World War II, in that men fought for "physical comfort, food, drink, girls, furloughs, mail and gambling, in about that order." He saw some soldiers enlisting to destroy slavery, but at a rate of about 10 percent among Union soldiers. Wiley argued, "A considerable number originally indifferent or favorable to slavery eventually accepted emancipation as a necessary war measure, but in most cases their support appeared lukewarm."[10]

Other historians concentrated on a different set of motivations that filled the ranks. Samuel L. A. Marshall argued that "a man fights to help the man next to him." In other words, soldiers do not necessarily fight "for a cause, but because they do not want to let their comrades down." Reid Mitchell noted, "Men may well have fought during the Civil War for reasons having less to do with ideology than masculine identity." While Gerald Linderman pointed out that "even 'The Cause' reduced itself to a manifestation of courage" as a motivational factor, James McPherson called on historians not to dismiss ideology. He stated, "Unionists fought to preserve the nation created by the founders from dismemberment and destruction." Both sides entered the war with an ideological framework as a motivational force for participation in the Civil War. Gary Gallagher recently reinforced the idea that the conception of Union and its maintenance drove men to enlist. In a recent study concentrating on the role of slavery in the Civil War, Chandra Manning argued that soldiers did not enlist for the money or because they had no choice, as a vast majority volunteered and experienced irregular pay schedules, at best. Instead, ideology drove them to enlist, whether it was to "eradicate slavery" or to "preserve the Union." She concluded, "Yet in spite of these and countless other reasons that sent individual Northerners and Southerners into the ranks, broad consensus existed within each army as to why a war needed to be fought in the first place. Whatever else occupied their minds, ordinary Union and Confederate soldiers recognized slavery as the reason for the war."[11]

Therefore, where does Pvt. Silas W. Haven fit within the realm of Civil War scholarship, especially with regard to why he fought? Haven never directly answered that question, though he offered several clues throughout his letters. He never expressed his desire to fight for the man next to him, other than his best friend Fred. Overall, there are limited references to other soldiers, except in cases of injury or death. Haven's limited combat experience may explain why he did not mention his comrades in arms as motivation for his service. He explained his disdain for slavery throughout his correspondence, and seemed to indicate that he joined the war effort in order to help eradicate the immoral sin of slavery. He wrote extensively about his faith and how churches across the North needed to remain strong and dedicated in order to ensure victory. His drive to see the war fought to a successful conclusion instilled within him an elevated sense of patriotism and he unconditionally supported the Union, even when he faced unbearable health difficulties, grueling marches, and weeks without pay. Although he enjoyed the southern landscape and weather, throughout his letters he revealed much disdain toward the Confederate population for creating the war and routinely labeled the "secesh," as he called them, as traitors. Thus, Haven fought for his family, a religious rebirth in America, and a patriotic desire to support the idea of a nation rid of the sin of slavery.

In a recent conference paper, historian Jason Phillips called on Civil War historians to move beyond the debate on why soldiers fought and explore how they thought. Soldiers routinely used their letters and diaries to hash out their own internal conflicts about issues of race, gender, religion, politics, as well as their varied opinions about different elements of the war. At the same time, the writers entered into an external conversation with a loved one, dear friend, or themselves about some of the most important societal issues of the day.[12] In many ways, Pvt. Haven emerged as an excellent example of a soldier who constantly thought about complex issues in the body of his correspondence. He tackled the causes of the war, the blight that slavery had inflicted upon the nation, and the role of bloodshed in the remission of sin. He examined religion, especially how it shaped both soldier and civilian life, as he wondered how civilians back home had used the church during this time of national crisis. Haven conveyed his opinions about African Americans, women, antiwar Democrats, and the southerners who utilized guerrilla warfare as a mechanism for fighting the war. He read any newspaper he could get his hands on and kept an eye on the main political races of the day, including ones that he actively participated in by exercising his right to vote.

Within the realm of Civil War letter collections, the letters of Pvt. Silas W. Haven stand out for a number of historically relevant reasons. Firstly, with no major published collections from the 27th Iowa in print, the experience of these men has vanished from the historical record. Most of the soldiers in the regiment moved to Iowa from New York, Vermont, or Illinois in the preceding five to ten years. Men reared in New England, like Haven, entered the war with stronger feelings about religion and abolitionism.

Secondly, Haven did not see many military engagements, having fought only during the Red River campaign and the Mobile invasion. For the rest of his three-year enlistment, Haven guarded railroads, moved up and down railroads and rivers, and spent his time worrying about guerrilla attacks. Without the constant threat of battle and since he entered his military service as a literate man, Haven had ample time to express his strong views on a host of issues pertinent to Americans living in the 1860s. With a lack of military campaigns, Haven witnessed many experiences away from the battlefield, including southern women taking an oath of loyalty and hundreds of former slaves flocking to steamships and Union lines in order to gain their freedom.

Thirdly, Haven wrote extensively about the daily grind of the common soldier. He provided a wealth of detail about picket duty, the behavior of soldiers, clothing and food rations, and his frustration with waiting for the arrival of mail deliveries and his pay. He regularly filled his letters with updates about his health (sometimes in vivid detail), the decisions made by officers, army rumors, ways to pass the time, and the bonds of brotherhood and friendship forged in the midst of war. Since a majority of Civil War soldiers spent most their time in camp away from combat, Haven's daily experiences accurately reflect those of thousands of other Union soldiers.

Finally, the series of letters portrayed the strong bond between a husband and wife, a father and his children, and a son and his parents. Haven constantly asked for details on local elections, the status and health of the church, and how the family coped with the war, particularly with regard to the health and condition of his wife and children. He continually promised them that he would return home on a furlough, only to be disappointed time and time again. He remained the perennial optimist as he insisted that the war would soon draw to a close. He ended most letters with a request to kiss his children. The family survived the war without any major episodes of trauma, illness, or tragedy, which ensured a joyous homecoming in the summer of 1865.

The collection of letters you are about to read comes from Pvt. Silas Haven, written over the course of four years to his wife, his children, and, from time to time, his parents and members of his extended family. Surprisingly, the collection contains only a few letters written back to Haven, as the soldier readily admitted that he destroyed several of the letters, except for those that he mailed to other family members to read. Haven remained an active writer during the war, trying to draft a letter at least once a week or writing daily diary entries, which he included as part of the weekly correspondence back home. He wrote anytime and anywhere, including on board steamships, while lying on his back, sitting on the ground at camp, standing during guard duty, and, on a few occasions, sitting at a desk, which he found agreeable. He preferred to express his thoughts in pencil, using ink on a few occasions, on paper either acquired from the U.S. Sanitary Commission or purchased from local cities and army camps. Haven also wrote on behalf of others, such as his best friend Fred, who remained illiterate throughout the war.

Haven's regiment, the 27th Iowa, organized on July 2, 1862, in Dubuque, Iowa, started the war in Minnesota and Iowa. However, Company G, Haven's company, detached from the regiment to oversee payment from some Native Americans in Mille Lacs, Minnesota, while the rest of the regiment moved south back into Iowa. The mission among the Native Americans lasted until the end of October 1862, when Company G reunited with the rest of the regiment in Cairo, Illinois, then traveled down the Mississippi River to Memphis,

Tennessee. Throughout the final months of 1862 and most of 1863, the Iowans, based in Memphis, protected supply lines and the Memphis & Charleston Railroad, and fought Confederate guerrillas throughout Arkansas, Tennessee, and Alabama. However, Company G saw no military action during this time as the soldiers spent their time guarding trains and protecting supplies, rather than actively engaging the guerrillas. On August 27, 1863, the regiment joined the 3rd Iowa in Little Rock, Arkansas, where they stayed until November and then returned to their base of operations in Memphis.

In 1864, the regiment found themselves part of General Sherman's raid on Meridian, Mississippi, and an integral part of the Red River expedition, under the command of Maj. Gen. Nathaniel Banks and Brig. Gen. Andrew J. Smith. The plan, conceived by Gen. Henry Halleck, called for the Union forces to capture Shreveport, Louisiana, the base of operations for Confederate forces in the west, control the Red River, and move into east Texas. Although Smith had early success in taking Fort DeRussy, Louisiana, on March 14, 1864, the Union army ran into a snare at Mansfield, not far from the Texas border, and fell back to Pleasant Hill, Louisiana, where the Confederates attacked them on April 9, 1864. Although the Union had some early success in the battle, the Iowans soon found themselves flanked and had to fall back as the Confederates inflicted severe casualties on Company G. Banks eventually abandoned the campaign, which cost the Union precious time away from focusing on Mobile, a more important city in the grand scope of Union strategy. The Iowans retreated to Grand Ecore, Louisiana, and then back up the Red River, all the way to Vicksburg. The battle at Pleasant Hill emerged as the only major military action that Haven saw during the entire war, even though his regiment would engage in several fights near Vicksburg and Memphis throughout the latter months of 1864.

With Confederate Gen. John Bell Hood's invasion of Tennessee in the late fall of 1864, the 27th Iowa joined with Union forces in Nashville, Tennessee, under the command of Gen. George Thomas. Thomas easily defeated Hood over the course of two days, but the Iowans suffered some casualties on December 16, 1864. Haven remained in camp during the battle due to another bout with illness and pain in his side, which plagued him for the rest of his life. He did accompany his regiment in early 1865, when the Iowans moved into Alabama, invaded Mobile, resided in Montgomery, and remained there for the rest of the war until they were mustered out at Clinton, Iowa, on August 25, 1865.[13]

Historian James McPherson, in a book that examined why soldiers fought in the Civil War, wrote that after reading hundreds of letters, he concluded that "in their personal letters written in a time of crisis that might end their lives at any moment they revealed more of themselves than we do in our normal everyday lives."[14] The letters contained in this volume, largely intact, revealed the heart, soul, and mind of a common soldier caught in the most traumatic moment in American history. They are currently in the possession of the Madouras family, of Overland Park, Kansas, tucked away in a small metal box. After meeting with the family, I spent an afternoon photocopying the entire collection. Then the process of transcription commenced over the course of several months.

As an editor, I corrected some minor spelling and grammatical errors. I also removed any sections of the letters that are illegible or damaged, which was rare, considering their pristine condition and Haven's impeccable penmanship. At times, the letters contained some sections that were rather repetitive, as they had appeared in other letters. I have removed those passages, along with any passing vague references that I could not track down through additional research. In the end, the editorial decisions removed only what encompassed a few dozen paragraphs over the span of nearly two hundred letters. Any corrections or deletions have been done with the utmost care without diminishing the value or integrity of the letters. His wartime correspondence revealed an abundant amount of information that painted a complete portrait of the man, the soldier, his army, his country, and his family. In many ways, Haven had successfully attempted to share that "incommunicable experience of war."

CHAPTER 1

# Kiss the Children for Me

## *1862*

THE COLLECTION OF letters that encompass 1862 included an early letter that Silas Haven wrote to his parents before his enlistment in the Civil War. The letter described the state of the war for Union forces in 1862. Haven not only explains why the war has emerged but also why the nation must continue to endure the trials of war. The United States had struggled early on in the Civil War, with a humiliating defeat at Bull Run on July 21, 1861, and stalled efforts in the West. His personal convictions against the institution of slavery did not waver as he entered the war. In fact, as the correspondence revealed, Haven's hatred deepened for an institution that he deemed immoral and a "punishment on the nation." As historian James McPherson noted, "Experience in the South reinforced the convictions of most antislavery soldiers."[1]

—

Rockford, Iowa, February 28, 1862

Dear Father and Mother

We are all pretty well at present. I am so that I have kept school all the time, but some days it has been quite a task to go to my school through the snow and storm, when I did not feel well. My side has troubled me a great deal more than it would probably if I could have got things together so as not to have had to carry on my back, but I have had to be on the run about every night this winter to get feed for cow and pigs and also for myself to try to get wood, and I have had to back up a good share of what I have burnt this winter. God will revive his work in this place. I have engaged/bought wood of two different men, and one disappointed me and the other went to the falls last week and left me without any and also without hay, so I have had to back my hay about 50 rolls and pick up my wood, and we have been out of pork and had nothing but flour to live on, so you see that your letter and contents came in good time for which I thank you.[2] I don't know what they are going to do with that judgment, but think they will let it out as a bad job for them and conclude to pay the costs for the sake of what they can get. I will inform you as soon as I find out; one thing is certain, I am not going to pay any costs and am going to stand up for my rights.

First, this war is a punishment on the nation. This nation has long upheld some of the most glaring sins, and God punishes national as well as individual sins and as in ancient times. God let them go till their times of inequity were full, so it is now. We have harbored the hydra monster of slavery till there seemed no way to escape from it all, knowing it an evil and great sin, but could do nothing to do it away, and all the time the cries of the innocent have ascended to him who has said vengeance is mine and I will repay; our time has come now, I think, and I do not believe that this war will close till the death blow is struck to slavery, neither will it close without bloodshed. For there is no remission without the shedding of blood and the sooner this war is conducted on the principle of freedom to all, the sooner it will cease.[3] The North will have to suffer as well as the South. Many who have offered their sons and brothers to the service of the country, it will prove to [be] a sacrifice also; God grant that in our case it may not prove so, but if it does, let us bow submissive to his will. I believe that this nation will come out of this war better off in some respects than when it was before. The death blow will be given to slavery.[4] The North and South will have a better knowledge of each other, and therefore understand their dependence on each other and the bounds of religious liberty will be extended, and the way opened for the extension of the kingdom of Christ for civil wars never go backward. There will be probably a large national debt to provide for, but that will have a tendency to teach us economy. The North have been given too much to making money and have not heeded the precept that this is not our abiding place and have been trying too much to lay up those treasure that corrupt it. I do not like the way the war has been carried on so far. I think our government has been too careful or afraid of hurting slavery and have been mild in dealing with traitors.[5] I am well aware that the departments were and still are full of traitors, but it is time that they were cleaned out and others put in their place. The fact is the war so far has been carried on by the East and has been a money-making concern, and if there is not something done soon, I believe the West will take out of it their hands and close up the thing at once. Our generals about all have a chronic disease of hunting slaves for the benefit of the South and if there is any of the go ahead, and would strike when they could, they are either removed or superseded for fear they will do something.

I hope they have got a new set of books opened, as Lane said at Washington, and are going to do something.[6] I don't believe we shall lose as many men by a vigorous prosecution of the war as by the waiting do nothing policy. That it may close soon is my prayer. We are going to have a series of meetings next week. The Baptist church is waking up and now we have Baptist preaching every other Sunday. I hope that God will revive his work in this place. We would like to see you very much. Our school is out, but there is a woman who wants to teach two months a one dollar a scholar is she does. The folks here are all pretty well at present and feel pretty well about the war news. Give my love to all. Good bye for this time. From Silas[7]

—

ON AUGUST 21, 1862, Silas W. Haven joined Company G of the 27th Iowa Regiment. A carpenter born in Windsor, Vermont, he stood five feet five inches tall, had brown hair and blue eyes and a light complexion. At the age of thirty-six years and five months, Haven had been listed on his enlistment document as "Samuel," but the name had been scratched over with "Silas" written over it. Throughout his enlistment record, the names Samuel and Silas are used interchangeably. He signed his name as Silas, concurring that he had attained a lawful age, enlisted as a sober man, and was physically able to complete his three-year enlistment as a soldier in the Union army.[8]

At the time of his enlistment, the fortunes of the United States had ebbed and flowed in some dramatic fashion. Ulysses S. Grant had won significant victories at Fort Henry and Fort Donelson in Tennessee, and also defeated Albert Sydney Johnston at Shiloh. Union forces in the west triumphantly captured several cities, including New Orleans, Memphis, Baton Rouge, and Nashville. In the east, Union Gen. George McClellan marched very, very slowly during his Peninsula campaign, which took his army to the outskirts of the Confederate capital in Richmond, only to be beaten back by Robert E. Lee. Lee looked northward, where his army would clash with Union forces once again at Bull Run in late August 1862.

After his enlistment in August, Haven used his early letters home to detail the daily grind of camp life, his expedition to Minnesota, and his movement into Tennessee. Haven's early correspondence included a wealth of daily camp life details and his perceptions of the people he encountered. He used the letters to explore his religious views and how they applied to the war. Haven wrote his first letter to his wife Jane from St. Charles, Iowa, on August 27, 1862, and then wrote her again once he arrived in Dubuque, Iowa.

—

Dubuque, Iowa, September 6, 1862[9]

Dear Jane,

I seat myself this morning to inform you of my health and how we are getting along. We left St. Charles Wednesday morning and went to Cedar Falls the same day. The next day we came through Dubuque. We stop in town, as the barracks are all full. The 21st regiment is still here will leave next week and then we will take their place. We were inspected yesterday and about all of the co. passed. George Ball is going home.[10] It is pretty lively times here now; there must be as much as 20 companies here besides the 21st regiment and more coming every day. There was four or so companies came in Thursday and there yesterday and more expected today. I expect we shall go into the 32nd regiment, but don't know [for] certain. We expect to go into camp next week if we do expect to get some pay. Fred is well and does well.[11] He says he will write next week, but I must hurry as the mail closes at 9 o'clock and I have got to be on hand for drill. You must try to keep your courage up and look on the bright side, and remember that I am in the care of one that doeth all things well. Kiss the children for me and write soon.[12] From your affectionate husband, Silas W. Haven.

Camp Franklin, Dubuque, September 8, 1862

Dear Jane,

I seat myself to write what we have been doing and how we get along. I am going to try to keep a regular journal after today so that when I get a chance to send it off, I will have it ready. We came into camp last Saturday morning and had to build our barracks. Our barracks are 16 feet wide and 50 feet long and have three tiers of bunks on each side, eight in a tier. Fred and I occupy one on the upper tier; they are calculated to hold 98 men. The 21st regiment is here yet, but expects to leave this week. There are nearly two regiments quartered in town and more coming every day. I see a number of men every day that I am acquainted with. Raymond that married one of the Crowell girls is here.[13] I expect our regiment will be sworn in today, but don't know. I am in hopes that we shall draw our pay as soon as sworn in, but don't know whether we shall or not. I can buy good calico here for ½ a yard cotton cloth for 15 cents. Our barracks or camp is 1½ miles from town and I don't expect to go in very often as it takes up so much time that we can't stay but a few minutes in town. We have to be here at roll call or else have to stand guard. The guard are on duty 24 hours. Two hours on and four off. We drill from 10 to 11½ Battalion drill from 2 till 4, dress parade at five. We did not drill yesterday, only went on dress parade. I went to town to meeting in the early morning. We had two services in camp in the afternoon. Elder Butley from Independence preached. We draw plenty of rations such as bread, meat, sugar, coffee, etc. I have been well all the time since I left home, but quite a number of our men are sick with dysentery caused by change of diet and eating too much. Most of them are well enough for dress today. I was detailed to go to town as guard, but as there was men enough without, I got clear for today. They have to guard the river and see that no one goes off to escape the draft. I shall try to do my guard, but there our Captain is officer of the day today. There is about everything going on. Some of them in the company got to gambling. He [the captain] came along and put a stop to it, which suited the most of our company first rate, but I must go and drill.

September 10, 1862

I must close this as to have it go out today. We hear a mail brought to camp every night. I want you should write all how you get along. I have not seen any [of] Father's folks, but expect that they will be along today. The 21st drew their bounty money yesterday and are out mostly out on furloughs. We expect to be mustered in to the regiment sometime this week. I don't expect that we will draw our clothes till Saturday. They are not here yet, but are expected every day. I got a quilt of Emily till we get our blankets. A lot of us are going to make up a mess to eat together. I have plenty to eat and give part of my rations away to others to eat when we get in to a mess together. I stand the drill without getting tired, but some of them that would be called tough get pretty tired, but I must close. Give my love to all, kiss the children for me and remember that I am in God's care and that he will take care of me when I am in the path of duty. Have faith in him and all will be well, goodbye for this time. From your affectionate husband, Silas W. Haven.

Tell Ella to write for I want to hear from her. Tell Emmett to hurry and learn to write for I want to hear from him. Tell Kitty to be a nice lady, and kiss them all for me. For I love you all, and think of you all the time. I shall try to write some every day so as to have it ready to send off as often as one allows.[14]

Camp Franklin, September 11, 1862

Dear Jane,

Last night we come very near of having a mess. A company from Guttenberg had a notion of leaving on account of not receiving blankets, but got quieted down. Their captain promised them blankets, but only got a few. We were sworn into the regiment this morning and expect to get our clothes soon. I am on guard today, on two hours, and then four hours off. Fred is on guard to the 21st regiment. Their men have all most all on furlough.

September 12

We had a pretty nice time standing guard last, although it was cold. The fore part of the night was dark and quite a number run the guard and then it cleared off and we had quite a time of running to catch them. We got some, six or eight, and three run into the water up to their necks. I expect that Laura and Inez will be down with Sylvester tomorrow.[15] I don't go out on drill, only dress parade after standing guard.

September 13

Nothing of any particular interest today. The colonel told us that we should have our clothes as soon as they could come from Davenport. I am afraid that we shall lose our captain for I think they will make a field officer of him. Col. Brodtbeck says our company is the best in the regiment.[16] We are going to divide into messes today. The 21st left about ten today.[17] It commenced raining just as they left camp. I have stood guard at the Quarter Master's quarters since 9½ o'clock. I shall stay about one hour longer and then will get rid of standing when my turn comes till next time, which won't be for two weeks. I get a pair of boots and a hat that were left. I have not got any money nor don't know when we shall get any but pretty soon. Fred has got some postage stamps so I borrowed one from him. Give me all information that you can and I think I can manage with the aid of any court and in order to have everything to proceed to suit me. It would be necessary. I did not get relieved last night so I had to stand guard till this morning. They forgot that I was on outpost duty and I sent word to the sergeant major and he came at 9 o'clock, and I sent by him to our barracks and got a quilt and some bread and a dish to get water in and they brought me some supper, and Fred came and stayed with me. We was as well off as if we had been in barracks, as we slept in the house and it rained and our barracks leaked. I am free from guard duty for two or three weeks. Our regiment has (or is) moving into the quarters of the 21st, which is a better place than ours was, but we are afraid of lice. Our barracks appears clean and I am in hopes that our fears are vain. I got your letter last night and was glad to hear from you. Fred got one the same time from Susan.[18] I redid them. The first thing I did you had better believe. I was sorry that you entertained hopes that I would not be accepted for I felt sure all the time that I should. I felt that it was my duty to go and I feel that I have the approbation of providence, and I believe that he will sustain and protect me as he has already so far, and I believe that he will return me once more to my family that I love so well. No one knows what a trial it was for me to leave my family, nor what I did undergo before I made up my mind to enlist. I tried to give up thinking of coming, but it would not do, for I would dream of it nights and since I enlisted, my mind has been clear and there is only one thing to make me perfect by contented and that is that you should feel that I am in the path of duty and could take courage to do the best that you can; if you could feel so you would have help from on high to sustain you, and all trials and sacrifices would come easy; go to Christ for strength. Go with faith believing and go frequently and he will hear and answer you. My prayers to God are for my family and that I may be permitted to return to them soon. Goodbye for this time. From your husband, Silas W. Haven.

The Sergeant Major thinks I will make a good soldier as I take things and they come along with grumbling. Kiss the children for me and tell them to be good children till I come home.

September 17

Dear Jane,

Our regiment is busy fixing up so that we don't go out to drill. I got my bunk fixed up all straight and quite convenient but don't know but what we shall have to take another when we get divided into sections. The first time I stood on guard was that cold night. My turn came the next day but one and I did not feel very well, so Fred volunteered to stand in my place, which he did through the day and then was discharged from further duty. His turn came the next day and he stood through the day and I stood through the night. It rained very hard, but on both my two hours. It was pleasant and moonshiney; then I was detailed to guard the quartermaster stores yesterday, which brought me into notice of the Adjutant and Sergeant Major, which will be a great advantage to me, but I must close for Fred wants me to write for him.[19] Silas W. Haven

Camp Franklin, September 18, 1862

Dear Jane

We have been very busy today. We divided our company into sections and the barracks is divided off the same so we had to move to another bunk, which kept us pretty busy. Our captain got back last night and our clothes are in Dubuque and we expect to get dressed up this week, but I don't expect to draw any money till next week. We had quite a time; just at dark the news came in that the whole rebel army north of the Potomac was taken and such hallowing you never heard as there was for a few minutes.[20] I received your letter tonight and was about to hear from you, but I must blow out my light.

September 19

Nothing of any importance has transpired today; part of our clothes, I expect, will be distributed tomorrow, but it is uncertain whether we get our money before next week. I am short of everything, such as paper, postage, and tobacco. I had to stop for a call for dress parade. The regiment were out; our captain says we have got to go to town tomorrow morning for our clothes. J. M. Dennis is in the 38th Iowa.[21] Fred has got a bite on his shin.

September 21

I did not write yesterday as we expected to go to town to get our clothes, but our captain went in the morning and it was night before he could get them and it was after 11 o'clock before I got mine. The clothes are very good, better than I expected, but we only got part of our clothes. We got an overcoat, a dress coat, two pairs of drawers, a blanket, a cap and a pair of shoes. The blanket was not the first quality, but the rest are extra. Our company is all pretty well; only one or two on the sick list. We only went out today on inspection in the morning and dress parade at 4 o'clock.

September 22

I found a prayer meeting last evening and they are going to hold them every night. They have a good attendance.

September 23

It has been raining this afternoon so that we did not go out on battalion drill. So I have been round to the barracks to see what they are doing. Some are reading, some writing, some playing cards, others singing, dancing and most everything going on; the most of our company are reading and writing, some drilling and some playing cards. Our company is the best drilled in the regiment. Fred sends his love to all. Direct care of Capt. Slocum, Camp Franklin, Dubuque, Iowa.[22]

Camp Franklin, September 23, 1862

Dear Jane,

I don't know but what I shall have to go on guard tomorrow and if I do, I shall have no time to write, and as I shall have to have this go out tomorrow night to have it reach you in time, I thought I would get it ready for fear. We have to stand on guard two hours and off four, but according to the new regulations, we have to stay at the guard house all the time and the corporals have to fetch our dinner or meals to us. We are divided up into messes. There is 20 in our mess. We draw a loaf of bread a day to a man and have plenty of coffee and meat. We have potatoes part of the time and beans, rice and molasses part of the time and sugar every day. I have enough to eat and am getting fat. Camp life appears to agree with me. We have to get up at five and drill an hour and a half before breakfast, then we drill from half past nine till eleven, then we go on battalion drill from two till four, dress parade at five, about half an hour, and we have to clean our bunks and keep it clean around the barracks, which keep us busy. I have been out to prayer meeting twice. We have to be present at half past eight at roll call or be put on extra duty. Fred keeps well and stayed September 24. I was called out on dress parade so that I had to stop writing yesterday, and now I have just got in from battalion drill and have only just got one hour before dress parade. Our captain is just distributing shirts and stockings. 1 shirt and 1 pair stockings. The talk is that we won't get any pay this week; some think that we won't get any till we get to St. Louis, but I think we will get it when we are mustered in. We had a very good drill today, our co. still haves the praise of doing the best of any in the regiment. My turn to stand guard will probably come on tomorrow. I have not been to town this week, but shall go as soon as I have stood guard. I want to see you very bad. I wish I had your pictures, it would do me so much good to look at them. I think of you often and my love grows stronger every day for you. Kiss the children for me and goodbye for this time from your affectionate husband, Silas W. Haven.[23]

By the way the war is now going, I should not be surprised if I come home next spring or summer. Keep up good spirits and write often.

Camp Franklin, September 25, 1862

Dear Jane,

I received a letter from you tonight and was very glad to hear from you. I was on guard at the time and have only just came off and got my supper, and it is now eight o'clock and I have got to blow out my light at nine, so what I write will have to be done in a hurry. I am very lucky in standing guard. I have had good weather to stand in and today and my beat came on a place that was guarding prisoners, and as there was two places that had prisoners, they moved them all to one place and so they dismissed me at seven o'clock. It seems that everything is made easy for me. I feel that I am under the protection of providence and I feel to thank God for his mercies and blessings, which is extended towards me. We have a prayer meeting every night. Tomorrow we are going out of town somewhere to drill and are going to be gone all day. There is not room enough to drill all three regiments at once so we are going to take our rituals with us and stay till night. Out regiment looks very nice with their new clothes. I have got two pair of stockings and a shirt. Our clothes are all good, but our blanket is not of the best quality. I will give you a description of the camp as soon as I get time. I keep well, but this morning I did not know but what I was going to have a touch of the Mississippi quick step, but it passed off.[24] I got a letter from Mr. Graham, but don't know how soon I can tend to it, probably not before next week.[25] Tell him that I will tend to it as soon as I can get leave of absence. The postage stamp came in good play, as I am out of paper and stamps. The last stamp I had to borrow, and I have to get this paper from Fred, but I must close. Give my love to all the folks and tell them to write. Tell the children that I think of them often and that they and you have my best love. With love to you all, I close this. From your affectionate husband, Silas W. Haven.

Fred is on guard and cannot write. I am going over at nine o'clock to read his letter to him, as when the letters came, I was on my beat and when I came off so I could not read it to him till he came off. The reason that you did not get your letters before Saturday was when I went to the Captain's tent to have them mailed, there was a man there that was going right through to St. Charles and I let him take them and did not think that you would not get them till noon instead of in the morning. Kisses for the children, tell them that I love them.

Camp Franklin, September 28, 1862[26]

Dear Jane,

Yesterday I got leave of absence for part of the day and had to step round pretty lively to buy my uniform things. I was surprised to find the things so high and they will be still higher. Good heavy cotton clothes from 25 to 30 cents according to width, calico from 15 to 20 cents. There is lots of fruit in market such as apples, peaches and grapes. I have not had any peaches to eat yet and can't bear to eat any such things; I had some grapes to eat yesterday.

The colonel says we shall get some payment Wednesday. I shall believe it when it comes. The soldiers all appear to feel pretty well. If Emmett was here, he would have plenty of drumming.

September 29, 1862

Dear Jane,

I want you should write what the price of things are in Rockford and whether you have got any from Wyatt, Kimball, Harriman.[27] I sent three spools of thread. I would have sent more. Fred had some books given to him and he sent them to Susan. I expect we shall get thirteen dollars next Wednesday if we could get the whole and I could get a furlough for eight or ten days; I shall try to come home and see you, but I don't know as I can. Our regiment, they say, was lettered yesterday, but I don't know for certain; if so, our letter is G. I am going to send some papers to the children, one to each. There have been two or three men round distributing books among the rest, some that had hymns in them and as a natural consequence, we have had more singing and less card playing. Adjutant General Baker was here and reviewed the three regiments.[28] The talk is that six companies have got to go to Minnesota soon; whether our company will get to go is uncertain; anyway the regiment won't leave here till they get their pay. They are making out the muster roll for our first month's pay today. We get our pay Wednesday.

September 30

I was called on guard today, but my good luck follows me. I am an extra and stay in the barracks (unless called on) all day. Today is the first day of the fair, but it is a rainy day. We were just called to the Adjutant's quarters and General Baker told us that there was six companies wanted for Minnesota and he had talked with the colonel and captains and they did not like to have the regiment divided, but were willing to go. He said he had a dispatch last eve that he might send a whole regiment and he would take the 27th, so we shall leave here soon. I expect we shall go by the way of Cedar Falls, but don't know; we can't go from here till we get our guns and all of our pay if we go by the way of Cedar Falls. I am in hopes I shall see you. The most of the regiment like the idea of going. Our captain has just got back from St. Charles. The talk is that we shall get all of our pay tomorrow. I hope we shall; after that we shall all get a furlough, but for how long I don't know. I don't much believe we shall go north; if we do we shall stay there till we are discharged and not have much to do. I am in hopes that if we do go north we shall go through Rockford so I can see you; if we go to Spirit Lake, we shall have to go through there. It would be quite right for you folks there. I have gained three or four pounds since I came down here. Give my love to the children and save a good share for yourself. Good bye for this time from your affectionate husband, Silas W. Haven.

—

ORDERS CAME THAT the 27th Iowa was to report to Maj. Gen. John Pope, commander of the Department of the Northwest, a demotion he earned after the Union debacle at the battle of Second Manassas at the end of August 1862. Despite Pope's failure at Manassas, the Army of the Potomac, once again commanded by George McClellan, fought Robert E. Lee to a military draw at the battle of Antietam in western Maryland on September 17, 1862. Nearly 23,000 casualties piled up over the course of a day, which resulted in Robert E. Lee withdrawing his Confederate army back into Virginia. Five days later, Lincoln issued the preliminary Emancipation Proclamation. Haven did not offer extensive commentary on his thoughts about the Union victories other than his perennial optimism that the war would end soon. For Silas Haven and his regiment, Col. James Isham Gilbert received the official orders to depart Camp Franklin on October 11, 1862.

—

Camp Franklin, October 3, 1862

Dear Jane,

I have had no time to write for two days. The whole regiment marched down to the fair Wednesday. It was rainy so that it spoilt all the pleasure that would occur to us had it been otherwise. We stayed there about two hours and it rained most all the time. There was quite a lot of cattle, horses, hogs that looked very fine. There was six white goats (three large and three small) that was real nice. There was quite a large quantity of fruit that was nice. I should like to have eat some of it. There was also a lot of plants and flowers that were arranged in splendid style. I should like to have had you seen them. We got home about two and there was quite a number of visitors in camp and it made me feel lonesome, so I got leave from the captain to go to town and stay overnight. I had a good visit. I waited till night before I went so as to get your letter. I was very glad to hear from you. I was sorry to hear that your garden had been destroyed. If I were there, I would make Webster pay for it for he has no business to let his oxen run for he knows that they are unruly.[29] I was very glad to get letters from Ella and Emmett and I will try to answer them. The postage stamps come very handy as I have had to borrow and that I don't like very well. I am going to lay in a supply when I get my money so as not to be bothered, but I must close for this time; I could write all day if I had time for there is much I would like to say, but I generally have to write in such a hurry and in so much noise that I forget what I want to say most till I get my paper all written over. Try and put your trust in God for I feel that I am in his care and shall sometime be restored to your love. To you from your affectionate husband, Silas W. Haven.

PS Kiss Kitty and tell her that pa will come and see her one of these days and maybe fetch her something.

To Ella and Emmett
Dear Children,

As I have not got but a few minutes to write, I will try and answer your letters together. I want to see you very much and I hope that I soon shall have the chance. I want you should be good children and help your mother and go to Sabbath school and learn to love your Savior. There is most everything going on in camp that you can think of. There is drumming from five o'clock in the morning every half an hour till 9 o'clock at night. It has been very rainy for a few days back, but it is a pleasant day today and I soon shall have to go out on battalion drill. We have to go out at 2 o'clock and drill till four and then at five we go out on dress parade. We drill twice in the morning, once before breakfast; we have to get up at five o'clock, so you see we are kept pretty busy, but I stand it very well, but I must bid you good bye for this time. Write again soon. This from your loving father, Silas W. Haven.

Camp Franklin, Sunday night, October 5, 1862

Dear Jane,

We received $13.00 pay yesterday and about 30 of our company took furloughs of five days and went home.[30] I did not take any furlough because I thought I would have a chance after we got our bounty money to get a longer furlough, and I could not any more than get there and stay over night before I would have to start back and that would be a useless waste of money for neither I nor you could enjoy so short a visit. The intention is for those of us that don't have a furlough now to start ahead of the Regiment and make our visit and meet the Regiment somewhere on the line of march, and that, I think, will be at Rockford or near there. I am quite well again; my dysentery did not last only one afternoon to amount [to] anything. I felt pretty weak the next day, but now feel as well and stat as ever. I was very much disappointed in not getting a letter from you Friday, but I shall look for one next Wednesday. It is raining again and I must stop for tonight.

October 7

I was on guard yesterday at the arsenal at town and we did not get a chance to write, and I am on board of the cars going with Mathis to Dyersville and have got to be back Thursday. Our regiment is ordered to St. Paul and we leave or expect to leave here Sunday. We are very much disappointed as we expected to get furloughs to go home. Our captain says we shall have the first chance to go after we get settled down. We receive our bounty Saturday and then I am going to buy a lot of things to send home, but the cars roll so that I can't write. Good bye for this time. Kiss the children for me. From your affectionate husband, to his dear wife, SW Haven.

Camp Franklin, October 10, 1862

Dear Jane,

I got your letter last night. When we got orders to go to St. Paul, the Captain came to see me about it and I told him that I would take time and go out to father's. He said he should have the first chance to go home, but I don't expect that will be before next spring. Have got ten dollars left, which I should have spent for things, but wanted to buy altogether; I shall buy what I can and shall send you some money. I shall save enough to buy me another blanket and some tobacco, paper, postage stamps, etc., for we don't want to carry much money with us. Our next pay day will be the first of January, I expect, and when that comes, you may look for some more. I think that it is all useless for us to go to St. Paul, for we shall have nothing to do only to keep warm and with what clothes I have got, I can keep from freezing. We probably shall go into barracks, stay there, while the cavalry do the fighting.

I don't want you should be any alarmed about my freezing, for you know that I am good to stand cold weather, and the probability is that we shall never see a battle. The way that things are shaping now, it is very probably that this war will be closed by next spring, and probably we shall have a good long furlough. You must try to get along the best that you can and put your trust in God, and he will sustain you. I feel to trust him and to leave you in his care, but sometimes it is hard for me to get along without seeing you. No one knows what a sacrifice it is for a person to leave wife and children that they love as I do mine, even for a short time, till they have tried it. I could get along better if you could feel that I am in the path of duty and I hope you will take courage. Do not expect to get letters as often as you have. We don't know how it will be about sending them regular, but will try to write as often as we can and will try to send once a week if we can, but I must close for I have got to write for Fred yet tonight. Give my love to all. Kiss the children for me and tell them to kiss you for me. This from your affectionate husband, Silas W. Haven.

As I have a little more time I will try and fill up this. I have so much to say that I can't think of anything. I am going to try to send the children all some presents: Ella a pin and earrings, Emmett a drum, Kitty a harp (if I can find one) and a doll, or doll's head. I shall send you a clock (if the money holds out) and a shawl and my picture taken in the position of a soldier at parade rest. I would give a good deal if I had your and the children's pictures. It would be so much comfort for me to look at them and I wish that if you get a good chance to have them taken, you would, and then if I stop long enough in one place, you can send them to me.[31] I was very glad to get letters from Ella and Emmett, and I hope they will continue to write. I was very glad to hear that you were all well. I worried a great deal for fear that you was going to have a sick time. I keep well. I was weighted today and I weighed 142 pounds, so you see I am getting fat. Goodbye for this time. Write soon and tell the rest to write. Silas W. Haven

Camp Gilbert, Fort Snelling, October 14, 1862, Minnesota[32]

Dear Jane,

I am well and have been; we left Dubuque Saturday about four o'clock in the afternoon and had a very pleasant ride up the river and got to St. Paul at 12 o'clock noon on Monday, and at two o'clock we marched to Fort Snelling, 6 miles up the river, and got here at five o'clock. The country is very rough till we got to Hastings, and then the bluffs are not so high. La Crosse, Winonna and Hastings are very pretty places. I had to stand guard the first night and my good luck attended me; I only had to stand from 9 till 11 at night and about an hour after nine o'clock in the morning I had a chance to sleep in the cabin after standing guard. When we got here our baggage came up the river and no tents, so one of the Company that were here invited us to stay with them, and we drawed a barrel of crackers and some bacon, and we eat supper and had a good warm room to sleep in, and it was the first time I had had my overcoat and shoes off since we left Dubuque. We have been putting up the tents today, six stays in a tent. I was on the first look out and got a first-rate crowd for my mates, four co. of our regiment came today, and two more will come tomorrow; they had a row at the camp after we left, and one man was killed. I don't know justly how many troops there are here, but there is 1,800 horses and 300 mules here and quite a number (600) was sent off last week. We did not get our bounty money till noon Saturday and I did not [have] much time to trade, but bought you some things and sent them to Cedar Falls to the care of Mr. Childs; have him get them drawed up and pay him for freight and hauling.[33] I could not find a harp for Kitty in Dubuque, but sent her a doll. Write often for we are anxious to hear from home and write whether you get any money from me till you know that I know or get your letter for if we are on the move, we may [not get] some of your letters.

—

Col. Gilbert received orders from Gen. John Pope to move his soldiers to Mille Lacs, Minnesota, over one hundred miles northwest of St. Paul. The purpose of the mission was to supervise the payment of money to friendly Indians in the region per previous federal treaties. The mission saw no attacks from any Natives in the region. Haven's regiment went to see the Chippewa Indians. The St. Charles City *Republican Intelligencer* detailed the treaty payments to all Natives across the county in the October 2, 1862 edition. The Chippewa were owed money from a treaty signed in 1855.

—

October 16, 1862, Camp Gilbert, Fort Snelling, MN

Dear Jane,

We had orders to start today at seven o'clock and got all ready even to striking our tents, but did not go as the horses wanted shoeing, and I don't believe we shall get away tomorrow as they are going to take two brass cannon with us and we have no knapsacks, and they have got to carry our baggage in wagons. We are going 70 or 80 miles north to the Indian agency. I have been well and enjoy myself well only when I get to thinking about you at home. I hope that this war will soon end so that I can be with you once more. We drew our gun accoutrements last night and forty rounds of ammunition, and today we got another blanket and shirt so you see that it is pretty here mornings, but has been very pleasant days. I was in the fort today and saw one of the Indian prisoners. They had him carrying wood and they made him carry big handfuls too. They are breaking horses here for cavalry service and the way run them is a caution once in a while one gets throwed, but none have got hurt yet; there is quite a large force up here and no Indians to fight, and what in the world they want so many I don't know unless Pope wants a large force under him to do nothing.[34] We did not get our guns changes as the Colonel could not get them in time. Some men in one Company stacked their arms, but they found that the Colonel had gone after the guard; the most of them took them up again, and the colonel arrested the rest. They all took them, I believe, and so that was the end of it, but they are hallowing roll call. So I must close; give my love to all and with love to you, I subscribe myself your husband, Silas W. Haven. Kiss the children for me and I hope to have a chance to kiss you all one of these days. We are only 150 miles from you.

Anoka, MN, October 18, 1862

Dear Jane and all the children,

We left Fort Snelling yesterday about nine or ten o'clock and traveled 13 miles the first day and about eighteen today, through as fine a country as you would want to see, and pretty thickly settled. Minneapolis is quite a large town or city opposite of St. Anthony. I went to see the Minnehaha falls, which is very pretty; they have a perpendicular fall of about sixty feet and a man can go clear across the stream right behind them. The stream is about as big as Shell Rock. I had a very good time of it being guard as I was in the rear guard and the wind was right behind us and blowed the dust away from us. Today it was warm and pleasant but some wind, but I must close for tonight.

October 19

We have just got our tents set up and I have had a good wash in Rum River and I thought I would write a few lines to you. We have marched about 17 miles today and through a poor, sandy country; I would not live here one year for a whole township. We crossed the Mississippi River last night just before we camped. We have got about 60 miles more to go. We are going to Milaca to see about two thousand Chippewa Indians paid, and that will be the amount of our trip up here.[35] I keep well yet and like the business well.

Princeton, MN, October 20

We have marched about 21 miles today, and I would not take a township of the land as a gift if I had to live on it one year. I stood the march well, but some of the men give out and had to fall in the rear. We saw quite a lot of wild geese and ducks, and a lot of deer tracks, which shows that this is a game country and that is all it is fit for. I expect that we shall get Milaca 42 miles from here by Thursday noon. I do not know how long we shall stay there, probably not more than four or five days so you must not worry if you don't hear from me for a week or two. I send you 7 dollars and a certificate of my enlistment before I left the fort. You must try and get all that was promised and the bounty from the Company, and try and get along the best that you can.

Camp at Mille Lacs, MN, October 25, 1862[36]

Dear Jane,

We got to this place yesterday after being three days and a half in the woods. We found the place to consist of three log houses and a big log barn, and any quantity of Indian wigwams and the Indians are half starved and half-naked creatures. We expect to stay here about three or four days and then start back. I don't think much of this country, only as a hunting place; that and Lumbering is all it is fit for, unless it is trading with the Indians, which would not suit me, so I quip I shall not make any claim up here. Fred got a letter from Susan yesterday and I was very much disappointed that I did not have one, as it was an express from Fort Snelling, which we may not get again for some time. I don't know of any news to write, but will try and fill this and with something interesting if I can. I was on guard the second day we came into the woods and the roads were very bad and all of the men had to carry their blankets, but those on guard did not have to carry anything, only an ax and help fix roads, which was no work at all. I am on guard today. We expect the Indian agent along tonight and then we will soon get away from here, I hope. The Indian agent and General Roberts, I believe, has just come; as soon as they pay the Indians, we have got to go back to attend the court martial about killing that man at Camp Franklin, and then as near as I can find out, we shall got to Fort Ridgley to winter.[37] We had pretty hard living in the woods. They drawed flour and the cooks could not cook enough for them to eat for a day or two, but I had saved some of my crackers along and had quite a supply till night before last. I bought five cents' worth, and as we did not get any dinner, they came in handy and our trams did not get here till nine o'clock last night and did not get our supplies till eleven last night. It will cost the government as much as twenty thousand dollars for us to come up here, when one man would have done just as well, but it is all the same to us. We had quite an Indian drum this morning, which Emmett could beat all hollow after the Indians. I wish you could see the Indians; some are white, some red and some are rather black, and if you look in the geography, you will find out how their wigwams are built. I will send a twenty-five cent and a ten-cent stamp in this. Give Ella and Emmett the ten-cent stamp and Kathy five out of the other, and buy something for yourself with the rest. Give my respects to all and with love to yourself and children. I will close this by subscribing myself your affectionate husband, Silas W. Haven.

Camp in the woods five miles from Mille Lacs, October 27, 1862

Dear Jane,

We started yesterday (that is four Companies) at one o'clock and came here on our way back; the other two co. stayed back to wait till the payment is finished and we were to wait here till they came up. They have just got along, but it is raining some. The first we have had on the march and it may prevent our starting today; if it rains much we shall have an awful time of getting out of these woods for it is bad enough in a dry time. I was on guard the other night and had to load my gun, and today I shot it off and was second best in a crowd of ten; the first best had shot his gun before. The regiment is very glad to get out of this place for we all think that we have come up here on a Tom Fool's errand. The Col. says that we are going to Kentucky, but it is doubtful we shall go; our fare has been pretty hard, as we had to bake our own bread, and our appetites have been extra good.[38] Our co. has been very good. One has got the measles and one was taken last night with lung fever. But the order has come to pack up and be ready to start in two hours, and I must stop for this time.

October 29

We left our camping place at 12 o'clock the 27th and went to our old camping ground, about 8 miles. It snowed a little and made the roads pretty bad; yesterday we had rather muddy roads, but we went to our old campout; today it has been froze so we got along pretty well. We are now about two miles below our old camp, waiting for the teams to come up. We have had very fair weather for our trip; one half day more will take us out of the woods; our Col. has gone ahead to make arrangements for our trip down the river. I don't know whether we shall stop in Dubuque or not, but expect to go to Davenport or St. Louis. I have to write with a pencil as it is very inconvenient to write with a pen on my knee.

November 1

We had a little flurry of snow today, but not enough to lay the dust. The weather long back has been quite warm. I was sick with a bad cold and headache for three days back. I came with the advance guard and was relieved about one o'clock for the last two days, but have not carried anything. I expect that we shall start immediately from St Paul to Cairo as the rest of our regiment has already started. You must do the best that you can. I sent you seven dollars and quite a lot of things from Dubuque, which I expect you have got before this time; if you have not, let me know; the things were to be directed to S. W. Haven, care of J. S. Childs, Rockford, Iowa.[39] I did not get time to pay the freight, so I sent you the money. You have Mr. Childs pay the freight and get him for you, and if you don't get the money, I will send you ten dollars, the next payment, which is now due, and hire someone to chop your wood that is not afraid that they won't get their pay.[40] I think you will get the money I sent all safe; if you don't, do not be afraid to run in debt to the amount of 8 or 10 dollars a month as my pay is good. When it comes, I sent you a certificate of my enlistment; if you have got that, get the orders and trade them off to the best advantage you can, but I must close. I did not buy Emmett any clothes for want of time. I hope you will get the things. I did not get you any shoes. I feel well tonight and pray to trust you in the hand of a kind providence, for rest assured that I shall meet you all again. With love to you, I subscribe myself your affectionate husband, Silas W. Haven.

Fort Snelling, November 6, 1862

Dear Jane,

We got here last Monday about noon and stayed till the next night in tents, and then we moved into the barracks, which are very nice. I feel very anxious to hear how the children are getting along and also whether you have got the things that I sent from Dubuque, and the money I sent from here. I expect that we shall start from here tomorrow for down the river, which suits us all very well, as we have had enough of Minnesota. We have been on the go the most of the time since we left Dubuque. The health of the Regiment is pretty good, only bad colds and some few have got the measles. I have not felt very well ever since I left Mille Lacs, but have walked in the ranks and done guard duty all the time, only I was retrieved from guard two nights yesterday and day before. I went to the Doctor and got cough medicine and have kept still so that now I feel pretty well again. I feel in hopes that when you get this, you will all be enjoying good health again. There is nothing going on here, only they are building some more barracks, and repairing the fort. The cavalry regiment has gone to Fort Ripley and the most of the rest have gone to other places.[41] We have men here every day to sell pies, apples, paper and once in a while to sell watches. I bought another package of paper the other day and I got a small locket with it, which I will send to Emmett. I also have another string of beads (the mate to the one I sent to Kitty) that I will send in a paper to Ella as soon as I can get one, so that all can have something that come from here. If I had some more money (I have only got two dollars) I would try and buy one or two blankets to send home as the same boys don't want to take but one. I believe I shall take both of mine as our Lieutenant says we shall need them. Give my respects to all of my friends there (if I have any) and with love and kisses to you and the children. I will close by signing myself your affectionate husband, Silas W. Haven.

I have a very little tamarack gum that I will send in a paper if I can.

Prairie du Chien, Wisconsin, November 11, 1862

Dear Jane,

While we are waiting here for the cars, I will try to mail you a few lines. We started last Saturday from the fort and marched to St. Paul, and got on board of the boat, but did not leave there till Sunday morning, and we got here about two this morning. We did not have any incident worth mentioning; coming down the water was very low and we had to ride on barges the most of the way to Lake Pepin, and have got on them twice since to crop the bars; we laid by the first night on the account of a bar that we had to crop and as the men had got to bed, the Colonel would not have them waked up; they laid by two or three hours last night to Lansing and they had quite a time. The people had come from quite a distance to see their friends and they had a large bonfire so that it was quite light. The Colonel told us all to go ashore, and the most improved it; we are going to leave here at three o'clock for Chicago. I don't know how long we shall stay there. I don't know, but probably not more than two or three days and then for Cairo. Send your next letter to Cairo. I have not had any from you since I was last at St. Francis, and the latest was dated the 20th. I am very anxious to hear from you. I am well pleased at going South, although I can stand it up here first rate. I have not heard much war news yet, nor have had much time to read it. This is the first place we have been to where we could hear anything. I am in hopes that we shall get the war closed up so that I can come home next spring, if I don't before. With love to you and the children. I will close for this time. Good bye, write soon. From your husband, Silas W. Haven.

Write whether you have got a string of beads in one letter and a small [locket in] another. I will send some beads to Ella in this. Kisses to you all. Silas[42]

Memphis Camp, November 23, 1862

Dear Jane,

I have just got my tent up, and I thought I would write up what we have been doing. We left camp the 20th at 6:30 P.M. We was all day getting on the boat. We came a few miles below Columbus and then tied up for the night. The next day we got to Fort Pillow and the next day (22nd at 3 o'clock) we got to Memphis, and today we marched into camp about 3 or 4 miles from the city.[43] It looks pretty dreary along the river as a great share of the houses are vacated and hardly any whites to be seen, but plenty of Negroes. Some whites that we saw on the bank were secesh. One of them made some indecent motions to us, and one of the men shot at him. He made himself scarce pretty quickly. There is lots of them down here, but they dare not show it. I went and got some water to a nice house, where they had the yard fenced up in real nice style. They had lot of evergreen trees such as cedar, English Laurel, pine balsam and some other kind. They also had some nice statuary around the yard. The folks were gone and Uncle Sam takes charge of it. There is some Negroes living in the house. Memphis is a very pretty place. The prettiest on the river, and Cairo is the meanest hole I ever saw. It is all filth, and after a rain, it is awful muddy. Our Col. told the Commander there that if he did not let the men get out of that mud hole, they would leave of their own accord so he sent us to Columbus, and if they wanted any more men there for us to stop; if not, to go on till we found a place. I did not know one but what we should got to Helena, Arkansas. I wish they had. The weather is quite warm today, but coming down the river it was quite chilly. I don't know how long we shall stay here, probably a month, if not more. The report is that the rebels are evacuating Vicksburg; if they are not, they had better. We found the boat with the secesh prisoners on board here when we came marching for orders. There was one shot trying to swim ashore last night. This morning there was one from each company called for as additional guard, and Fred volunteered to go. He will probably be gone a week, if not longer.

Nov. 24

I start in a few moments to go board of the boat to go to Vicksburg with the prisoners. One of our men was sick and so Fred sent for me to come and I told him I would go. We probably shall be gone a week. I am well, and enjoy myself first rate. We are camped in a grove and I have picked about two quarts of hickory nuts and am going to carry on to the boat to crack. I wish I could send you some, also one of my blankets, my old pants and shoes, but I don't dare to send as you was so bothered getting your other hat. I should be afraid that you would not get one sent from there till spring, if at all; there must be as much as one hundred and fifty thousand troops concentrated in this vicinity that is here at Holly Springs, Helena, Arkansas. The weather is about like our September weather but not frost, but I must stop; good bye for this time. From your affectionate husband, Silas W. Haven. Kisses to the Children.

—

DURING THE GAP between Silas Haven's letters, the 27th Iowa joined William Tecumseh Sherman's army. Sherman attempted to outflank Gen. Sterling Price's Confederate army along the banks of the Tallahatchie River near Waterford, Mississippi. Sherman got around Price and headed to Vicksburg. However, his movement halted, as Gen. Earl Van Dorn's Confederate cavalry raided Holly Springs, Mississippi, the main base of supply. The 27th Iowa did not see any military action on the expedition and suffered no casualties, except a few soldiers who got sick and were captured in a hospital. The soldiers were quickly paroled and returned to the regiment. Haven does not seem to have participated in this endeavor, as he remarks in the December 26, 1862 letter that he does not know where the regiment is, but assumes they are down in the Vicksburg area.

—

December 10, 1862

Dear Ella and Emmett

I thought I would try and finish this today as we are steaming up the river, and in two days more we expect to get to Helena. We left Vicksburg on the eighth after sundown and came 6 miles to the gunboat fleet and anchored.[44] There was nine gunboats, and I suppose that they commenced firing on Vicksburg today. The weather is very fine and pleasant and it is very nice riding on the boat. We see some nice plantations, and there is a great many Negroes that want to get on board, but we don't take any. The water in the river is very muddy; looks like the water in a mud puddle after a hard rain, but it is quite good if it has a chance to stand a spell and settle. I want you should write how you get along at school and write all the news that you think will interest me. If you, Ella, have not got your ears pierced over again, you had better not; those earrings are not very good for you to wear, and I will get you another pair as soon as I can. I hope you, Emmett, are suited with your drum and can play me a tune when I get home. Tell your mother that I washed yesterday and raised a blister on one of my fingers. I want to see you all very much and give you a good kissing. Goodbye for this time—write often. From your father in the army to his son and daughter, Silas W. Haven. Kiss your mother for me. I send you a flower I picked.

To Laura Olivia Haven

Dear Little daughter, I would like very much to see you and give you a real kissing. I hope you are a good girl and is suited with your doll and I hope you have got a string of beads that I send to you in a letter. I would like to send you a harp if I could, but when I come home I will try and fetch you one. You must kiss your mother and Ella and Emmett for me and remember your father that is in the army. Good bye for this time from your father, Silas W. Haven

On Board of Steamer *Metropolitan* near Vicksburg, Dec. 5, 1862

Dear Jane,

We got at Vicksburg the 1st and was till yesterday getting rid of our freight, and starting back we got 30 miles up the river last night and found 1600 prisoners going down to be exchanged and we are going back with them. The prisoners we brought down was a hard-looking set, and it appears that they were perfect specimen of the troops at the south, a dirty, ragged, half starved. We have 49 of our men on board that have been prisoners for quite a spell. They say that they had to live on cornbread and meat and not enough of that, and that it was the same that they fed their own soldiers on. They say that the citizens are a moving from Vicksburg, and that they think that the secesh will leave there when we make an attack. The hardest fighting, I think, will be done at Jackson, MS and that will end the fight, except guerrilla fighting in this part. I did not get a chance to see the boys at Helena, but Fred did; they was going down the river on an expedition. They started from there the day before we did. There was about 30,000 in the expedition. I suppose you have read about a new gun that goes by turning a crank and the balls was put into a hopper. I saw one in operation in Cairo and it worked at first rate; it throwed balls about half a mile. I am in hopes that I shall get a chance to see them when we go back.

December 16, 1862

Dear Jane,

We got to Helena yesterday morning. I expect our regiment will go to Helena as soon as we get up here, at least that is the report we heard that they were in Memphis, doing provost guard duty. I expect that we shall join the regiment, but may not; we may have to go to Cairo or down the river again. I am not particular as this is very easy work, and we are in out of the wet and we have a good chance to keep clean. Some of our crowd caught lice, but I have found none on me and I have changed my clothes twice and washed them all clean. I have been quite well with the exception of a cold since I started on this trip. I have given all my pills away, but shall get some more at Memphis, although I have not had occasion to use only three or four since I left home. I can't help worrying about you sometimes, thinking that you will have hard times to do your chore, and getting your wood chopped, but shall my faith is strong that God will watch over and protect and provide for you and also that I shall soon return to you. I have got two dollars that I will try to send you as soon as I can. I think that this war is fast drawing to a close. The South is in pretty close quarters and as soon as Vicksburg falls, they are cut off from their supplies of meat, and that and corn bread is all they have to eat now, and once disperse their army and they cannot organize another as it is hard work for them to keep the one they have got together. We see lots of Negroes on the banks that want to come aboard, but we don't take any on; one night nine come off in a skiff, but we would not take them. Love and kisses to you all, from your affectionate husband, Silas W. Haven.

Fort Pickering, December 26, 1862

Dear Jane

I intended to write you a few lines today, but the tent was so full all day, and it has been so full and so much talking that I have only just got at it, and it is now eleven o'clock, but as I don't feel like sleeping, I will make a commencement. I have had the dysentery for a few days back and have not done anything, only to draw our rations; for two days yesterday and today I have done the cooking, only made the rest fetch the water. We have to fetch our water up the riverbank, which is quite high. I have not heard anything [about] how the expedition against Vicksburg gets along, but I expect they are having a hot time down there. I don't know where our regiment is and don't expect to anyways until the Vicksburg affair is settled. Fred has given up all hopes of being in any battle unless we have one here, which was expected a few days ago when the troops left, but the chance for that grows slimmer every day, as there is a good many troops coming in here every day and before we had enough to hold the place against ten thousand. They had quite a scare in town, and they kept us on the alert in the fort as it was reported that there was from 10 to 15 thousand men out about 6 miles and was going to attack the town. I was none alarmed, for I did not believe they would run the risk of getting in range of the big guns in the fort nor of the gunboat, which lies here. Our pickets take some prisoners every day or two, and we have got one that will probably watch him as a spy.

We did not have a Christmas dinner, as we have only one kettle to cook in and I boiled some rice in that. Last night they throwed up a lot of rockets in town, which looked quite nice. I watched them till I was tired and wished that you could have seen them. The Negroes had a big dance, I believe; there is a great many here to work for Uncle Sam, but I must close for tonight; if you will call in the morning, I will give you some first-rate beef soup of my own cooking. One of our boys (S. Wise) came in from Cairo and tells us that Isaac Fleenor died at Cairo last Friday.[45]

December 27

I can hardly realize that the snow must be as much as a foot deep and blowing every which way in Iowa, and I expect you are having your hardest time doing now, and I hope I can get some money this pay day to send you, but don't know how it will be as I may not get my descriptive rolling time to draw now, but don't know how it will be. Write how you get along. Write everything as it is. I have felt pretty well today. We had to move our tent about 80 rods, and I and Fred built the chimney, and I got supper and tonight I feel about as well as ever.

CHAPTER 2

# Guarding the Rails

## *January–June, 1863*

THE LETTERS THAT cover 1863 included a number of letters to and from Haven's parents that regularly discussed local and national politics and the fears that those against the war would gain political power. For the first six months of 1863, Haven guarded the Memphis & Charleston Railroad. Although the regiment saw no major military action, the protection of Union supply and communication lines proved vital for the success and maintenance of military campaigns. Maj. Gen. Ulysses S. Grant received orders to lead a force to capture the city of Vicksburg, the last major Confederate stronghold on the Mississippi River. Grant's army moved from Tennessee into northern Mississippi in December 1862. On December 20, 1862, Confederate forces under Gen. Earl Van Dorn surprised Grant's army at Holly Springs, Mississippi, capturing nearly fifteen hundred soldiers, burning four hundred bales of cotton, and stealing nearly $1 million worth of supplies. Holly Springs, about forty miles southeast of Memphis, Tennessee, emerged as a major supply center for Grant's maneuvers on Vicksburg, and the successful attack by the Confederates slowed Grant's advance. Haven used the down time to talk about his perceptions of African Americans and Southerners, the state of the war for both the United States and the Confederacy, and how the regiment handled their military obligations.

—

Fort Pickering, Memphis, Tennessee, January 4, 1863

Dear Jane,

I take my pen tonight to let you know that I am well, and enjoying myself as well as I can under the circumstances. I want to see you very bad. I have not had any letters from you since I left Cairo and I expect all my mail was burnt up at Holly Springs. There was a number of our Regiment taken prisoners there, but none of our company. I some expect that we shall go to the regiment soon as they have got the railroad open to that place. There was one division of Grant's army here last week after provisions, and they opened the railroad and are guarding it. The first train came in last night. I was in the city last week and had quite a chance to see it. There are a great number of nice buildings there and is a real pretty place. I was in the park. It is one block and has an iron fence around it and has walks through it every way and has some nice trees and seat to set down on. There was a yard eight squares in the center and Gen. Jackson's monument in it fixed up real nice.[1] The words on one side had been defaced some with a chisel. They were "The Federal Union must be preserved"; the words "the Federal" and the letter *u* were the only ones that were defaced any. There was a tame grey squirrel there running around. I wish you could have seen it. They are quite busy here in the fort finishing it up. I guess they are going to make this quite military post by the actions they are tearing down all the houses in front of the fort and they are going to build a large war house inside and a number of magazines, and I expect that they will build barracks as soon as they can get lumber. Gen. Grant gets his supplies from here and they have a lot on hand and more coming every day. I don't know where our regiment is. It may have gone to either Nashville or Vicksburg; the last we heard of it, it was at or near Holly Springs, guarding railroad; if they are there now, we probably shall go to them soon.[2] I am in hopes to get some letters before we do. I expect that you get the war news before we do, so I will not say much about it. They have had (and I don't know but what they are still having) a big battle at Vicksburg.[3] I suppose you will hear the result before this reaches you. Gen. Smith's body went up the river yesterday and Gen. J. B. Wyman's body is here in town on its way up. They are having a desperate battle there and a heavy loss on both sides.[4] The last report we had was that our forces had twenty-eight thousand prisoners and had got possession of the city. When Vicksburg falls, our fighting in the west is about over, and I think that this war is pretty near to a close and that, I find, is the general impression down here.[5]

Fort Pickering, January 15, 1863

Dear Jane,

I take my pen with pleasure this morning to converse with you awhile. Yesterday was a very rainy day. It rained steady all day. Our Lt. Col. came in from the regiment, which is now at Jackson, Tennessee, guarding railroad and brought us a pile of letters.[6] I don't know as I can answer all of your letters in details as my conveniences for writing are not very good. (I set on a camp kettle and hold a board on my lap, and the tent is full talking.) I did not put much faith in the promises of the people of Rockford. I enlisted because I thought it was my duty to do so, and my faith was in God that he would take care of you, and my faith was strong that this war would not last long and what I have seen down here confirms my faith, and I believe that I shall soon be permitted to return home. Although I see many things in our offices that are painful for a true patriot to see, but still my faith is unshaken. God's ways are past the comprehension of man. He orders all things for the best; put your trust in him and everything will come easy to you if those that promised to give do not. Look to God and he will supply and think of me as being as much in His care here as if I was in Rockford.[7] I stand the hardships of war better than most of the large men, men that were strong and healthy when they enlisted. My health has been middling good, only I catch cold very easy, but I get over it in a day or two and can generally can eat my rations the most of the time, although they are not quite so good as sausages, mince pies, but we occasionally buy a little butter and sometimes trade coffee for it and then we have some warm bread and butter. I bought some onions one day and eat them raw, roasted and fried as I had occasion I have two dollars that I want to send to you, but did not dare to, but if I can get to town before I send this off so as to get some money that will be good up there, I think I shall risk it. I don't know when I shall get my pay. I want to get to the regiment before they are paid off; if I don't, I shall not get it till next pay day, which will make it rather bad for you; as for me, I have got along well so far. My money holds out, and I get along well for money a little does me and I share some with Fred. The barrel of apples I picked out was first-rate winter apples; if there was any rotten ones, they must have changed the barrel.

January 16

I went to town today but did not find any letters, which was quite a disappointment. I did not hear any news, but saw a number of steam boats go up the river, loaded with secesh prisoners taken on while river, I suppose. We have had to back up our wood nearly a mile; for the last two days the government is tearing down houses that are too near the fort. Most of them fine nice buildings and some built with brick. They cost as much as two or three thousand dollars and we get the lumber to burn. Today has been clear but cold. There is about six inches of snow on the ground. Yesterday was a regular snowy, blowy Iowa day and it jumped us up some. Today is the first day I have had to wear my mittens since I came down here. I will send you a dollar in this and will soon send you some more. Write soon and direct to Silas W. Haven. Goodbye for this time. Kiss the children for me and with love to yourself, I close. From your affectionate husband, Silas W. Haven.

Fort Pickering, January 23, 1863

Dear Jane,

My health is not very good, but I am not sick. Our tent has been very crowded and it has been very wet weather, mud both outdoors and in the tent, and as I did not want to crowd to stay by the fire all the time. I caught a cold and had the side ache some, but I have kept quiet and now we only have three in the tent. We are getting along quite comfortable and I am doing my share of the cooking, but don't intend to do any more. I have a pretty easy time of it; I don't have any guard duty to do or in fact anything else. You write that it has not been very cold up there, but I guess it has been rather colder there than here. It has not been down to zero yet, although we had an Iowa snow storm, which stayed on for two or three days for the last week. The "sunny south" has stepped out and we have not seen the sun but once or twice, and today it looks as if we should not see it for a week to come. The river is very high between then and fifteen feet higher than it was when I first got here, and it is still rising. There is no war news in particular. The 27th is at Jackson doing guard duty and are all well. We don't hear anything from the forces down the river. Everything appears very quiet, but there is always a calm before a storm. I hope so. I want this fighting pushed ahead and this war brought to a close so that we all can come home. Fred got letters the same time I did. Also two boxes of pills, but I must close for I have got to write for Fred yet tonight, if I can. With love and kisses to you and the children, I will close. From your affectionate husband, Silas W. Haven.

Ft. Pickering, February 5, 1863

Dear Jane,

I improve this opportunity to write a few lines to you to let you know how I am getting along. I am still in the Fort and don't know but what I shall have to stay here for the next two months. The weather has been quite rainy for some time back, and we have had to move our tents about 40 rods and ten occupy a tent, which makes it pretty crowded and quite disagreeable, especially when there is two or three disagreeable persons in the tent. My health is about as usual, only I have a pain in my side some. I am not troubled with the dysentery and most of the time I feel well enough to do military duty, but there is not much to do here; they have about 30 men to work every day cleaning up camp ground and a few for guards so that my turn does not come very often. Our regiment is still at Jackson, Tenn. and most all in good health and I expect it will stay there for quite a spell. Anyone can go there in a day, but it is almost impossible to get a letter from there short of ten or twelve days. I have not had any letter from you for some time and feel very anxious to hear from you. When we are doing nothing and have nothing to read, I get lonesome and a letter from home cheers me up, and if I don't get any, I am as uneasy as a hog on ice. Kiss the children for me and with love to yourself. I close by subscribing myself your affectionate husband, Silas W. Haven.

Ft. Pickering, February 17, 1863

Dear Jane,

I thought I would try to write you a few lines today to let you know how we get along. My health is middling good at present. I went out on guard duty Sunday and I am so that I keep around my bowels are regular, but I am troubled with the pain in my side. I expect I shall get my discharge, but how soon I don't know. There is a lot of the 27th that are waiting and their papers have been all ready but signing for most four weeks, and there is no knowing when they will get them. I expect know but what I shall have stay here for quite a spell, but hope not. The weather is variable wet and dry, rather more wet then dry, but it has not been very cold and now I expect that the southern spring has set in as we hear the birds sing. I have not had any letters from you for most a month and it makes me feel rather lonesome, and I have not seen Fred for two weeks, but heard from him yesterday. He was pretty well, although his back hurts him some. Tell Susan not to be uneasy about him as he is in a good place. I was in hopes that I should get home by the first of next month. You need not tell the folks that you expect me home soon for I want to take them by surprise. I am in hopes that Fred will soon get an examination soon for I think he will get his discharge. But we must wait patiently for we are in the hands of a just and merciful God and he doeth all things well. I feel that he has been with me and watched and protected me ever since I came into the army and my trust is in him. Tell Susan to direct her letters to Memphis Ward, Overton Hospital.[8] Don't put any regiment or company on it. Kiss the children for me and tell them that I hope to kiss them myself soon. With love to you and the children, I remain your affectionate husband, Silas W. Haven.

PS Times are rather dull here in the fort. It is a wet foggy day, rained all night last night. I feel pretty well today. They are expecting a battle out where the 27th is, but they are ready.[9]

Fort Pickering, February 25, 1863

Dear Jane,

I don't expect to find out anything definite about my care for two or three days, and it may be a week or even a month as quite a lot of the 27th have been waiting for their discharge papers for a month. Have not got them yet and some they say are lost and some have had their descriptive rolls returned and have yet to go through the same rigmarole again. I expect to go before Dr. Allen, the U.S. Inspector, soon.[10] I was intending to have gone to see about it today, but it is raining hard so that I don't venture out much in the wet on account of my health. If I don't get discharged, I think I shall get detailed into some business here to do writing and stay here. I can get in a good position most any day, but I don't know whether I could stand it to write all the time and so I shall try for my discharge first. So don't worry about me and also don't set your mind on my getting my discharge, but leave all in the hands of a merciful God, who has always been our protector and especially since I have been in the service. With love and kisses to you and the children. I close by subscribing myself your affectionate husband, Silas W. Haven.

Ft. Pickering, March 2, 1863

Dear Jane,

I take my pen to write to you to let you know how I am getting along. My health is about the same as it has been. I am so that I can get about and do a little work, but my side and breast troubles me, especially nights. Our Capt. came in yesterday to see how the boys get along. He is trying to find their papers and I expect that they all will go to the regiment if their papers are lost. I and Fred are going anyway. If George Mahoney's papers are found all right, he is going home immediately; if not found, to the regiment, as that is the best place for all of us.[11] I got two letters from you yesterday and it was a great comfort to me to hear from you to know that you were getting along as well as you are. I was sorry to hear that the children had been sick, and that Kitty had got hurt. I was glad to hear that you have been having meetings there. I feel that God has answered my prayers not only for you but also for the place you live in, and my faith is firm that he still will watch over and protect me and mine as long as we walk in the path of duty and put our reliance in him. Put your trust in him and all will be well.

The weather has been quite warm and pleasant for most a week. Troops are going down the river most every day. There is going to be a big battle at Vicksburg unless the secesh run as usual. Our regiment is at Jackson, Tennessee, yet and expects to have to stay there all summer. They are pretty healthy. My side bothers me so that I can't write much longer at present, but will try to write again soon. Give my respects to all inquiring and with love and kisses to you and the children, I subscribe myself, your affectionate husband, Silas W. Haven.

Jackson, Tennessee, March 9, 1863

Dear Jane,

I once more take my pen to write you a few lines to inform you how I get along. I got in last Wednesday night and was pretty tired when I got here. All the boys appeared pleased to see us; most of them are well and hearty, and I think I should have been if I had not gone on the Vicksburg trip, although they have had some pretty hard marching and have tried pretty hard to get into a fight, but could not for Price and Van Dorn could run the fastest.[12] They got to Holly Springs the next day after their battle and then went back to the Tallahatchie River. When they came up here Co. G had to guard the wagon train, but before they got up here, they were most all mounted on confiscated mules and horses.[13] My health keeps about the same, only when the weather is wet and cold I am not so well. For two or three days back it has been rainy and yesterday my side ached a great deal. Today is sunshiny and warm. I don't have any duty to do, and have not had to take any medicine from the doctor yet, and don't much expect that I will have to for a spell and I don't mean to take any of their medicine if I could help it. I was glad to hear that you have been having meetings up there and not only there but in other places. I think it is about time for the church of Christ to awake to their high calling, especially when the nation is engaged in a war like the present. I hope they will keep up prayer meetings and pray for the army for there is a great deal of wickedness in the army, and pray for a termination of the war, pray in faith and wait in hopes. I have enjoyed myself most of the time since I enlisted. My faith is as strong, if not stronger, and I believe that a man can be a Christian in the army as well as at home, although he meets with more temptations, but he has the same helper here and the bible says that he shall not be tempted above his strength if he will rely on Christ for help. I will close for this time. From your affectionate husband, Silas W. Haven.

Camp Reed, Jackson TN, March 15, 1863

Dear Jane,

It was a warm pleasant morning this morning, and I went down to the creek and took [a] good wash and set and hear the bird sing, and I thought I would write you a few lines to let you know how I get along. I keep about the same. The weather affects me some. I am worse in damp and in very hot weather. I stay in the tent at that time, but I walk around the most of the time when it is so that I can. I have not taken any medicine since I came here, only pills to keep my bowels regular, which are the case the most of the time. The weather has been quite warm and pleasant for a few days back, but it has clouded up for a storm this afternoon. The regiment is doing guard duty. They have to go out on picket or out post; every other day they take 14 or 15 out of Co. G at a time; the boys all like it. There is some talk here in camp of a probability of this regiment going to escort the Indians over the Rocky Mountains. The rumor is that the Col. is working for the chance.[14] The boys all would like to go; that is, the well ones and they are the majority. It would be a fit journey for the regiment as they have done some tall marching ever since they left Camp Franklin and have tried pretty hard to meet with the secesh, but have been unable to yet and the boys begin to think that they won't get a chance to. The col. is trying to have the regiment paid off and the talk is that we shall get two months' pay soon. I hope we shall as I want you should have some. I don't need any, only for tobacco and that is very high, about $1.50 a pound. I wish I could send you some of our extra rations, such as coffee, rice, crackers. The boys don't like rice, peas and grits and crackers. You wrote that Graham wanted to trade cows.[15] You can do as you are a mind to, but if he wants to take a cow to pike peak, one cow is worth more to him to take along than his, and anyway, I don't think he had ought to ask or have much, but I would like be there to help to make garden and fix up the farm, but don't know as I can unless the regiment goes north. Tell Ella, Emmett and Kitty that I love them all and would like to see them and kiss them and I hope I shall soon. With love to you all, I close. From your affectionate husband, Silas W. Haven.

—

THIS IS THE FIRST of several private letters that Haven included in his correspondence to his wife. Clearly, Haven knew that his letters passed among several sets of hands within his family and the community. The use of private letters allowed Haven to share personal and intimate thoughts and details meant only for his wife.

—

READ AND BURN THIS

Camp Reed, Jackson, TN, March 15, 1863

Dear Jane,

Fred got a letter this afternoon from Susan and I was sorry to hear that the report got out that I had got my discharge, as I did not remember that I had written that my discharge was all made out but signing. I was only marked for a discharge, but when I was examined, I did not have my descriptive roll, and could not have any papers made out till I got it, and when I got it, there was a new board of examiners and they would not discharge hardly anyone and I was advised to wait till Dr. Allen got back and have him examine me, but the way they were using Iowa soldiers, I intended that if I did not get my discharge or find out something certain about it by the 15th of this month, I would come to the regiment, but we wrote to the Capt. and he came up, but could not stay anytime and thought that we would do better to come down here, and the way that things have turned out, I don't know but what we have I still have turned out.[16] Our captain says that we can get our discharges at the regiment pretty quick after we get here and I still think I shall get mine, but it may be some time first as it will depend on circumstances. Don't set your heart too much on my getting my discharge soon, but pray for it and all will [right] be well. Don't let anyone know about it. Write soon as you get this. From your husband, S.W. Haven.

Sunday Eve, March 15

Dear Jane,

My faith is still strong and, if anything, stronger that this war will soon close. It may look dark to some, but I believe that the South is fast losing their hopes. The soldiers all want to go home bad enough, but when you talk to them [and ask] if they want to give up and let the South go, the response is no, never. There are some Copperheads here in the army, but they are Democrats that enlisted to escape the draft, but they have to keep their mouths shut here.[17] The same they would have to do up there if a few regiments should go that way, but I must close. Keep up good courage and put your trust in God and all will be well. SWH

Camp Reed, Jackson, TN, March 22, 1863

Dear Jane,

My health keeps about the same. I was up to the head doctor day before yesterday and he examined me and wanted to have his assistant examine [me], but he was absent and I don't know yet they will conclude to go with me, but expect they will keep me a spell yet. They are going to try to cure Fred's back. They took him to the hospital last week. I have not had a chance to go to see him yet, but shall hear from him today. The weather has been quite fine for a few days back and also some warm; we had quite a thunderstorm night before last and it has just commenced to rain some today. I have not had any letters from you for a long time, but am in hopes that I shall have some today. We have a mail regular every day, but yesterday it come in rather late as the guerrillas tore up the track to catch a paymaster and they got him, but did not get the money.[18] There was a wood train ahead of the passenger train and that run off the track, and when the passenger train came up, they reversed the steam and it began to run the other way, just as they got among the guerrillas, and the pay master thought it was a collision and jumped off and the rebs nabbed him, but they did not get the money. Help is scarce as about all the Negroes have skedaddled for other parts. I expect before you get this you will hear of fighting at Vicksburg. I have great faith that the fall of that place will be the beginning of the close of the war. It will close very quickly after the fall of Vicksburg. I suppose you would like to know how I spend my time. I spend about half the day in my tent lying down and reading, and I walk around camp out once in the day. I generally go to the creek, about 80 rods, and have a good wash. I am going to try this week to do my washing. I read the St. Louis and Chicago and Memphis papers and from two to twenty chapters in the testament. I am very restless nights; don't very often get any sleep before two or three o'clock. I have not heard but one sermon since I got off the boat at Memphis and have not been inside of a church but once since I left Camp Franklin, and that was at Cairo and that was not on a Sunday, but still I think I enjoy religion and I feel that God has me in his care and I put my trust in him. With love and kisses to you and the children, I remain your affectionate husband, Silas W. Haven.

Camp Reed, Jackson, Tennessee, March 25, 1863

Dear Jane,

I was in town today and as I don't expect I can get to sleep very easily tonight, I thought I would spend the time in writing to you. My health keeps about the same. I got a good long letter from you Monday and was very glad to hear from you, but sorry you had got your heart set on my coming home for I know you must feel very much disappointed. I blame myself that I did not write more fully for all things are uncertain in war times, and discharge papers have so many hands to go through that unless there is some office to look after them, they are very apt to either get lost, mislaid or delayed so long that the war will be over before they will get around. I did not know how they went quite so well then as I do now, but I knew that they were very uncertain. I was in hopes that I should have got some money before this to have sent to you. We have been expecting to be paid this week up to the first of November, but I don't know as we shall get any before the first of May. If we don't get any till then, we shall get paid up to the first of March, and that will be quite a sum to have all at once. If we are paid up to the first of March, I shall send you between 60 and 70 dollars. You must try to get along the best you can till I do send. We shall get our pay any way by the middle of May up to March. Get what the Company gives for you need it. Don't let any false pride stand in the way for it is no more than right that you should have it. Those that promised to pay and did or have not, let them go if their conscience will bear them out in breaking their promises. We will not, or must try not to judge them. I think and feel that you will get along, and that God in his own good time will reunite us again and that to before a great while, it may be not before the war is over. It may be sooner, I think, that this war is about to close that is the fighting parts. I have to go to the Doctor every morning to get excused from duty. I don't know just what the doctor thinks ails me, but the one that examined me at Memphis said my lungs and kidneys were affected. I would get well if I went north, where I could have a chance to take care of myself. Tell Kitty I am glad to hear that she is learning her letters, and I will send her a book as soon as I can get a good one. I am sorry to hear that she burnt her arm. Tell Ella and Emmett I hope they have learnt a lot this winter and I hope they will write to me often. I also hope that they love their savior and obey him.

---

IN THE FOLLOWING letter, Haven again takes up the topic of why the Civil War erupted in America. Haven's rhetoric here about the war emerging as a punishment for the sins of the nation matches what many abolitionists and religious individuals thought about the war. In his second inaugural address, President Lincoln echoed similar sentiment when he noted that every drop of blood from the lash would be atoned with a drop of blood from the sword. Additionally, the duration and horrific amount of bloodshed forced many Americans, North and South, to question their religious beliefs or at least question why God had allowed the war to last so long. Haven remained steadfast in his religious ideology throughout the war.

---

March 26, 1863

Dear Jane,

I got into an argument last night on the war and so I did not finish this so as to send off today and so I would write to you a few things. How I have always looked on this war, but more especially how God has dealt with me. War is a punishment (I think) that God inflicts on a nation for national sins. I will not try to enumerate the sins that this nation has to atone for, but I think that the North as well as South had grievous sins, and this war was brought upon us to atone for them and so soon as they are atoned for, this sacrifice of blood and treasure will be brought to a close. I thought last fall and I my faith grow brighter every day. I felt it my duty to enter the service, but why it was my duty more than others at that time I could not see, but now I think that I see that God so ordered it in his providence that we should be separated for our good, both spiritual and temporal. Were we not in danger of thinking more of each other and the children than we did of our Savior? And I feel that he has sustained and protected me in all of my duties since I have been a soldier, and has helped me in all of my trials. The greatest after I parted from you was when I was in St. Frances when I got your letters informing me of the children's sick[ness] and it was sometime before I could pray. Thy will be done, but when I could, my mind was easier and when I got the next news at Cairo that they were getting better, I felt that God would in his mercy would preserve all of our lives and that we should meet again, and I feel that God has ordered all things for our good, and when I get home, we will try to improve the lessons we have learned, and I think that we shall be better fitted to enjoy his bounties to live more according to his divine will. I was glad to hear that there was a revival in Rockford and was in hopes that it would do a great deal of good and I hope it has, although it may not be seen at present. The churches have got to wake up and cleanse their garments and remove all stumbling blocks out of the way before they can prosper. If church members let pride and petty jealousy stand in the way, causing the church to [be] brought to shame and others to stumble, I am afraid that God will remove them if they do not repent and return to the path that Christ has marked out for them. The war news is quite cheering; you probably will hear it long before this reaches you. The order was read on dress parade tonight for the officers to get their pay rolls ready immediately up to the first of March, and as soon as they do, we shall be paid, probably the fore part of next week. With love and kisses to you and the children, I remain your affectionate husband, Silas W. Haven.

Camp Reed, Jackson, TN, March 31, 1863

Dear Jane,

I received a letter today from you and was glad to hear that you were well, but sorry that Kitty's arm was so bad. It has been quite cold and windy this week so far and we have had to do our cooking in our tents, which makes it rather bad for us as there is none in my tent that can chop wood. I have had a blister on my side, and Mahoney got some tea spilt on his back, and the other occupant has the diarrhea, so we have to pick chips or trade rations to get wood chopped.[19] It doesn't affect me much for I generally eat only toasted bread and sugar and drunk tea or coffee. I trade of one ration of bread for sugar and then have lots of bread left. We draw rations every five or six days and they now draw flour and have it baked. I get half a loaf a day and it will last me two days. We got potatoes, onions, and white fish. The last time we draw, my appetite was very good and all I have to do is to eat and grow fat. My health keeps about the same; as long as I keep quiet, I feel pretty well, but if I stir around too much, I have a severe pain in my side. I don't sleep very well nights or very much. I don't very often get to sleep before two or three o'clock, but still I am not sleepy day times. I am sorry that there is difficulty in the church and I hope it will be settled in a Christian spirit as expeditiously as possible, for the longer it lingers, the harder it will be to settle and the more the church will lose in respect not only from unbelievers, but by church members. This is no time for the church of Christ to be sleeping, but up and doing. I read about a church in Canada that had prayer meeting for the speedy close of this war, and I hope to see the churches take the same course, but the actions of [the] church will be of no avail if quarreling and contention abound in them. Therefore let the church be holy so that God can heed their prayers. I hope and pray that the church at Rockford will speedily examine and remove all stumbling blocks so that it may prosper. There was a rumor a few days ago that this regiment and all the troops around here were going to be mounted.[20] Tell Kitty that I am sorry that she burnt her arm and I will write her and Ella and Emmett a letter one of these days.

Camp Reed, Jackson, TN, April 6, 1863

Dear Jane,

I was in Jackson yesterday. It is quite a pretty place. It is not so huddle up as most of the places are, so they have very nice gardens, yards filled with evergreen shrubbery and flowers and laid out in a tasty manner. The flowers are in bloom and look real nice. My health keeps about the same. I take cough drops and have had one blister on my side. I did expect to have had another, but the Doctor has not seen fit to give me any. I don't have any confidence in the head doctor, so as long as I don't think I need any medicine (that is, such as they have here), I shall not trouble him. The war news is quite cheering, but I suppose you get it before I could write it to you. Our acting quartermaster was taken prisoner at the time of the raid on the railroad, but he managed to get away and has come back. A clerk that the paymaster sent down to examine our pay rolls was taken at the same time. The quartermaster is a going to Memphis in a few days, and says that we can get our pay. I don't know why it need to take so long to get ready to pay us as long as our pay rolls are made out and the money is in Memphis (or reported to be) to pay us. There is some fault somewhere and our families have to suffer for it. I think the pay will come before long, as they won't have any excuse for delaying much longer. There is a great deal of dissatisfaction because they don't pay the families and I think that when they get home, they will talk pretty hard to the supervisors. I am sure that they will long be remembered. I think it is a perfect shame that Floyd County can't do half as well as other company have done. I think that this war is fast drawing to a close and if it had not have been for the action of the Copperheads up north, it would have ended before this, but their time is short and they will have to keep their mouths shut when the soldiers get home. There is a good many things written from here about our regiment, company officers that are far from the truth. Our staff and company officers are, as a general thing, competent and look after their men, but they can't suit everyone and we have some Copperheads in the army. Besides a few grumblers, we draw plenty of rations. We have divided our sugar, tea, coffee and bread to each one and most of them have coffee and some have sugar to sell. I live mostly on bread and sugar and I have as much again bread as I want. I trade part of it off for sugar and sell some for postage stamps and give some away, so if you hear that we are short of rations, don't you believe it. I sold my coffee yesterday that I brought from Memphis for 40 cents a pound, cash, and I got me some paper and envelopes and have got some left to buy stamps with. Stamps are getting scarce here now, but we shall get a supply on from Memphis soon; if we don't, I will send some money for you for some. I forgot to tell you that we have started a prayer meeting again. We have one every Saturday, Sunday and Thursday night. I have not been to but one as my blister bothered me some and I don't like to be out in the evening air too much unless it is very pleasant. I think the regiment has improved a great deal. There is not so much swearing and card playing as there was, and it is the same with most other regiments, so I am told. I hope the churches up north will awaken up. I would like to be there. I could enter into religious matters with more earnestness than before I came down here, believing that God has us all in his kind care and that he will soon reunite us. I close by sending love and kisses to you all. From your affectionate husband, Silas W. Haven.

You must not get discouraged for fear you will not get any money for it will come before long. Give my respects to all inquiring friends and tell them to write. Give Ella and Emmett each one of these pictures. There were a lot of guerrilla prisoners brought into Jackson yesterday. Give each one of the children a kiss for me. Write often.

Camp Reed, April 6, 1863[21]

Dear Jane,

I received a letter from you today and was glad to hear from you that you were all well, and I thought I would commence a letter tonight and fill it up at times so as to see if I could not write something interesting. My health keeps about the same. The captain asked me if I thought I was well enough to do some duty tomorrow. He said I need not unless I was a mind to. The regiment or those that are well are going off on a two days' march, and the convalescents have got to stand camp guard. The regiment is going on the railroad to Humboldt and how much further they don't know, but they expect to have a brush with the guerrillas and they are all anxious to go.[22] The 27th has tried so hard to have a fight that I almost wish that they might be gratified. The whole regiment is down on the head company, and I think that there will be a new order of things in situated soon as a circumstance transpired today that colonel lowered him somewhat in the mind of the officers and it may be the means of losing him his place.

April 9th

I must try and finish this tonight so as to send it off in the morning. I have not seen Fred yet, but hear from him most every day. He keeps about the same. I also am about the same [as] I was. I had some sauerkraut for supper tonight and it tasted real good. Our scare last night did not amount to much. Three men undertook to run the guard. It is supposed that they had stolen some horses. I went out and saw them in line of battle. They got out pretty quick. They catch the 27th Regiment napping. Company G was the first one formed; Company G and B went to the pickets to find out what the firing was for. We don't hear much news. I was in hopes to have got some pay before this time, but it still don't come. You must get along the best you can. There will be a bunch when it does come. With love and kisses to you, I remain your affectionate husband, Silas W. Haven.

Camp Reed, Jackson, Tennessee, April 12, 1863

Dear Jane,

I was downtown Friday and Fred gave me this sheet of paper, so I thought I would commence today so as to fill it out if I could before it was time to send it out. They got a lot of medicines at the hospital and there was a lot of this kind of paper and so they let the boys in the hospital have it. It is a bright, warm sunshiny day today, although it rained last night and I feel pretty well. There is no particular news here on by a man or two got accidentally shot when they were called out in line of battle the other night. They loaded their guns and I told the boys that now there will some of the boys will get shot. They are so careless with their guns. I don't pretend to be a prophet or a son of a prophet, but somehow I felt that such would be the case and Thursday when I heard a gun go off and that a man was shot had [been] hit in the face, but was not hurt as the ball went through a bunk and four thickness of blanket before it struck him. I was in hopes that that would put the rest on their guard, but Friday morning, a man in Company F went to clean his gun and somehow it went off and shot him through his left arm or wrist so that they had to take his arm off just below the elbow.[23] The other man was in Company G. I saw A. R. Prescott [on] Friday.[24] His regiment is down on the railroad between the Junction and Corinth to work, repairing some of the regiment with part of ours, went up to Humboldt towards Columbus to get bridge timbers, and Prescott stayed here while they were gone.

—

In early March 1863, Union forces started construction on a canal across from Vicksburg as a possible avenue for attacking the city. However, Confederate batteries shelled the workers from the batteries located along the shore of the Mississippi River. Grant tried to move on Vicksburg via the Yalobusha River, but Confederate forces inside Fort Pemberton prevented the Union's advance down the river after a six-day gun battle. Union forces failed on two other expeditions to take Vicksburg in March: an attack via Steele Bayou and an attack via Black Bayou. Haven's reference to another canal, in the following letter, is mistaken, as Grant had abandoned the original canal project before he engaged in the bayou expeditions. Union soldiers did need to clear some trees around the Yazoo and Yalobusha rivers, but they never constructed a canal.

—

April 14

I got a letter from you today and was very glad to hear from you. I get your letters pretty regular and I write as often as once a week to you. Did the one you got or have got have a little feather in it for Kitty? I sent one quite a spell ago. I sent a few papers last week with a number of seeds and beans, also a letter with a feather for Emmett. Write whether you get them all safe. Parts of our regiment went up the railroad to Columbus yesterday and are expected back tomorrow. They have not been ordered to Vicksburg and I don't think they will, and our company doesn't know anything about the two women stopping the cars, but I believe that occurrence happened to the nine companies. The doctor at Fort Pickering said my lungs and kidneys were a little affected and that with the diet and the way I had to live, that it would be hard for them to cure me in the service, but if I could go home, I would get well without any trouble. I don't have much opinion of the doctors here and don't take any medicine, only some cough medicine, which is very good as the hospital steward fixed it up for me. I get along very well, only I don't rest good nights. I don't generally get any sleep before two or three o'clock. I have a good appetite and nothing that I eat appears to hurt me. I have had greens two or three times and they set good. We don't get much war news, yet we heard that they were busy at Charleston. All quiet out the Potomac and Vicksburg not taken yet, as they have found another place to dig a canal. I believe I hope when they get that dug, that they will wait till they take Vicksburg before they dig any more. But a better time is coming. Day begins to dawn and soon this fighting will be over and the soldiers will return to their homes, some, I fear, with morals wrecked and many, I hope and believe, better men. Those that have been left at home should be preparing themselves to receive them, prepare themselves by purging their garments from sin and lying in a store of godliness so that they can enter into the work of the Lord with more zeal and with a clear conscience, but I must close for tonight.

April 15[25]

I was to the hospital today and wrote a letter for Fred. He keeps about the same. It is hard work to lay around the way that we are and I get so tired. I don't know what to do. Our regiment was ordered yesterday to be ready with four days' rations to go somewhere (down to Corinth, I guess) and tonight they were ordered to report tomorrow morning ready to start. There was read a communication on dress parade that the colonel had been in communication with the pay department and had been informed that a pay master would be here in two or three days to pay us off; a later dispatch informed him that the pay master was in town and we would probably get our pay tomorrow. So if the regiment doesn't go away tomorrow, we probably shall get our pay. With love and kisses to you, Ella, Emmett and Kitty, I close by signing myself your affectionate husband, Silas W. Haven.

Camp Reed, April 17, 1863

Dear Jane,

Today has been a gaylay day in this Regiment. A pay master did actually come here and better still, he had a few greenbacks and was not afraid to risk some among us and we was not slow to take them, and now we have got them. We are bothering our heads to get some of them up north. I thought I should send ten dollars in this, but I have just heard that our sutler is going to start north in a day or two and if he does, I may conclude to send this letter by him with $25.00 in it. I will send you fifty dollars out of this pay and maybe more. I am going to keep more than I should if I was well for I don't intend to take any more of our Doctor's medicine. I am going to buy some that will do me some good and if I can't get them down here, I shall send away for them. I want you should send me two boxes of Ayers pills and also send three or four postage stamps in each letter you send, and you had better send and get some good newspaper: the *Saturday Post* or *Watchman* and *Reflector* or any other one that would suit you, but spend the money to suit yourself.[26] I don't much expect that we will get any more pay till July, although there is or will be two months' pay due us the first of May. I got $65.75 and I may send you more, but it will depend on circumstances. I keep about the same; my side pains me some, but I don't have hardly any cough. The cough medicine I am now taking has cured it about up. I put another blister on my side today, but shall not try any more at present. The regiment was under marching orders for two or three days, but did not have to go. I suppose they did not know but what Corinth would be attacked and if it had, they would have gone there to reinforce them.[27] They did have some fighting near there, but not with any force. The weather is quite warm here and we have not had any rain for quite a number of days. Write what the date of the letters you get from me with money in them. You had better have Mr. Childs do up the pills for you and direct them the same as you would a letter (27th Regiment, Iowa Volunteers, Cairo, IL) and they will come through safe, but I must close. With love and kisses to you and the children, I remain your affectionate husband, Silas W. Haven.

I shall send ten dollars in this and try to express the rest.

Camp Reed, April 21, 1863[28]

Dear Jane,

I received a letter from you tonight and was very glad to hear that you are all pretty well. I keep about the same. I had another blister on my side and that is pretty sore at present. Our Regiment is down to Corinth. They had orders at eleven o'clock night before last to be ready with two days' rations to go at four o'clock in the morning, and all that were here that was able went, and about 150 that was out on picket went in the afternoon and left the sick and convalescents to take care of the tents, and we was expecting that the guerrillas would make us a visit, so we prepared for them. Every man got a gun handy, so if they had come, they would not have found us napping but would have found out that we could fight but could not run and would not consent to be taken prisoners. The regiment expected to go right to fighting as soon as they could get there, as we heard that they were fighting at Tullahoma, about ten miles from Corinth, but they kept the 27th at Corinth for picket guard.[29] I suppose on account of their guns, but don't know. I don't know how long they will stay there, and don't know certain whether we will have to go there or not. I guess you worry too much about me. I went to stand guard tonight, but was put on supernumerary and won't have to stand unless some of the rest get sick.

April 22, 1863

I felt pretty well today. I got a good sleep and did not have to stand guard at all. I washed my clothes in the forenoon. Besides we have to get our own meals, and I went to town and went about all over it. I got me a portfolio, some ink and had to go into about a dozen stores to find some eggs for one of our men. Eggs are 40 cents a dozen. I wish you could see the yards and flower gardens and also the woods down here. Evergreen trees trimmed up in most all shapes and all kinds of flowers blowed out and lots of large trees in the woods and yards that have flowers on them. I don't know what kind of trees they are, but guess they are Magnolia trees. They look real nice and I will try and send you one, not a tree, but a flower. We drew hams and white fish last week, also potatoes. I don't know what we shall draw tomorrow; we draw five rations at a time. Tell Ella that I got her flowers all safe, and was very glad to see them as it is a sign that winter is over. I expect before this time you have got my big letter, also letters to all of you. Tell the children to write. I close by sending love and kisses to you all from your affectionate husband, Silas W. Haven.

Camp Reed, April 25, 1863

Dear Jane,

I felt as if I wanted to do something tonight so I thought I would commence a letter to you. We are quite lonesome with the boys all gone. We don't have much of anything to do. Today it was quite warm, and we took down our tents and cleaned them all out and let them have the sunshine most all day, and tonight we are having a little bit of a thunderstorm. I went down to the creek today and washed all over and changed my clothes. I feel pretty well most of the time and think that if I could get in a good place to stay, I should get well in a short time. I went about a mile last night and bought a quart of milk; only had to pay 20 cents and had bread and milk and coffee for supper. I did not like the milk in my coffee, but the bread and milk was real good. I had the same for breakfast, only I put a little sugar on the bread before I put the milk in. The cows don't give so much milk down here as up there. I don't intend to buy much milk as it is rather too expensive and most of the folks are secesh. They are just beginning to plant cotton here, and I have a little more seed. We don't hear much war news. We are looking for news from Vicksburg; that is the place we care the most about. We have a large force down near Tullahoma and the rebs have one there, but ours is the largest. We also are not a great ways from Rosecrans, as you will see by the map, but you would be apt to hear what they are doing before we should as all of our news now comes by the Northern papers. They have taken a number of guerrillas prisoners in the course of last week around here and are getting them well thinned out.

---

MAJ. GEN. WILLIAM S. ROSECRANS commanded the Army of the Cumberland during this period, having received high praise at the beginning of 1863 for the Union victory at Murfreesboro, Tennessee. Haven is not referring to his own regiment, the 27th, which continued to guard the railroad until June 1863, but to the other major Union military maneuvers taking place in the spring of 1863.

---

April 26

Today so far has been wet and cloudy. A few of us got together this forenoon in the guard house and had a meeting (prayer and conference) and if it don't rain, we are going to meet tonight at a place in the grove that we have got fixed up for the purpose. One man has come out and joined us and I am in hopes that more will do so. I think good energetic exertions of our ministers both at home and in the army would do much good among the soldiers. There is not near as much swearing and card playing going on as usual. Our regiment is still at Corinth doing picket duty. Give my respects to all inquiring friends and with love and kisses to you, Ella, Emmett and Kitty, I remain your affectionate husband, Silas W. Haven.

---

IN THE FOLLOWING letter, Haven talks about the movement of Union troops to Tuscumbia, Alabama, a major railroad depot along the Memphis & Charleston Railroad. The town, directly west of Iuka, saw a small battle on April 24, 1863, when Union forces, under the command of Gen. Grenville Dodge, held off an attack by Confederate troops. The Union troops had gone to Tuscumbia to destroy the railroad station.

—

Camp Reed, April 27, 1863

Read to yourself first
Dear Jane,

I keep about the same. Have for a few days back done some little work, and if it want for the pain in my side, I could do all duty that is required of any soldier. The pain in my side is a great deal better. I don't have it, only when I do to some work, and then it is not so severe. I am in hopes that it will not trouble me anymore. I am going down to Corinth tomorrow. I don't know how long I shall stay there. The regiment is doing picket duty and may stay there a week or it may come back in a day or two. It is very uncertain how long they will stay in one place, although I rather think they will have to stay here all summer, or as long as they stay down here. They will stay where they are, till the troops or part of them get back from the Tuscumbia expedition. I saw a dispatch in the Memphis paper tonight that our troops had drove the rebels and now hold the place (Tuscumbia) so I think that the 27th will be back to their headquarters here soon. I don't know as it makes much odds to me for one place is as good to stay in as another to me, and I am under the same protective care wherever I am, and my trust is in him, and my faith is stronger every day that we shall soon meet again. I am afraid that you will not have enough to buy that lot and pay what you have been obliged to run in debt and buy what things that you need. Pay all your debt first and then you can make some calculation what you will need to get along with, and then if you can get it cheap enough it will be, buy it, but if you can get along till fall or till I get home, you had better wait. Don't let anyone around there know that you talk of buying it yourself. If Father comes out this spring and collects that order without any trouble, which I think he will, he can buy it for you if you think best. We shall be mustered again for pay in a few days, for two months' pay, but I don't much expect to get any more pay till July. Get that from the country if you can. There is some taxes due on those lots, but don't pay any if you can help it, and don't pay any of my debt (except Gleason if he wants it) for if they find out that you have money, some may pretend that I owe them when I don't and what I do owe, they can wait till I get back.[30] Put your trust in God and try and have faith that he will take care of us (although separate) and will soon reunite us again. Kiss the children for me and save one for yourself, from your affectionate husband, Silas W. Haven.

Corinth, April 29, 1863

Dear Jane,

I was very lucky yesterday in getting a letter from you. The captain got the mail for our company and gave me your letter on the cars. I enjoyed my ride pretty well the most of the way; the road turns through woods with once in a while, a piece of ploughed land. Some had wheat up 6 or 8 inches, corn 4 or 5, cotton just out of the ground and some was yet idle in some places. The Negroes was piling up the logs and rubbish and burning it up. They have any quantity of breastworks, forts and batteries and if the rebs think they want Corinth after the lesson that they received last fall, they will find that there is still room for their graves here. Although there is lots of them buried around here, fifteen thousand men will hold this place against a hundred thousand. I was down in town today to draw rations and had quite a time to look around. Most of the goods in the stores are sutlers goods and military clothing.[31] There is any quantity of military stores here. Uncle Sam looks out pretty well for his boys and don't mean to have them starve. We have first-rate hams and meals. We draw part flour and part crackers. The flour is cooked up on shared and I have had bread enough to eat with eating crackers. We draw plenty of rations and these have been good and would have a lot to sell if we took care of them. There is some talk that our regiment will stay here. I almost hope they will as I think it is a better place to stay as we have barracks to stay in. You write that the table got tipped over and broke a few dishes. If I was in your place, I would give that rickety concern its time and get one that don't want to get the top down so easy. It will be the cheapest in the end. I don't think that I like scolding very well, but I would not care much if I could hear you scold a little at this present time.[32] You write that you want to see me very bad. I think you don't want to see me any worse than I do you, but I don't know how soon that will be, but hope it will be soon. I am in hopes that the war will soon close, and I am in hopes that I am going to get so as to do duty again. I had the best sleep last night that I have had for a great while. Give my respects to all and with love and kisses to you and the children, I remain your affectionate husband, Silas W. Haven.

Camp Reed, Jackson, Tennessee, May 4, 1863

Dear Jane,

I received a letter from you tonight containing eight 3 cent postage stamps and five 1 cent ones and I was very glad to hear from you that you were well. I went to Corinth last week and I felt pretty well the most of the time. I was gone only I had a big bite on my arm. I did not do any duty; only went on dress parade and Saturday was on camp guard and my usual good fortune attended me before I had to go on duty. The guards were dismissed till night to pick up to get ready to leave. We came out about a mile from town and camped in the woods. We camped near the battleground last fall and the marks were all through the woods. The trees were marked with balls and cannonballs and shell and pieces of shell, grapeshot and musket balls were scattered all around and there was a grave of a secesh close by. His feet were sticking out.[33] Some of our regiment covered him up. He was covered up right where he was killed. It looks the most like war of anything I have seen yet. I would like to have gone all over the battleground, but could not. I stood guard four hours at night from 7 to 9 and 1 to 3. We camped just outside of the pickets. I had the best post to stand that there was. Our regiment is or expects to move tomorrow over across the railroad, about a mile from here and a little nearer town. Three regiments, the 52nd IL, 66 IN, 2nd IA came in from the Tuscumbia trip and they look pretty hard, as they had been out for three weeks and slept in open air, rain and mud all the things. They were foul sore ragged and dirty. They captured quite a lot of cotton and burnt some and brought in a lot of Negroes, mostly women and children.[34] We went out on battalion drill this afternoon and it came up a rainstorm, and the colonel told us to break ranks and to our quarters march, and I wish you could have seen the men put for the tents, hollering all the way and again, just as we were forming for dress parade, it commenced raining again and he sent us back the same way, so we have not had only about an hour's duty to do today.

May 5

We had a regular tear up today and moved about a mile. I helped the chaplain move his things and I found a gold pen and as it did not belong to the chaplain or major, I kept it, but I have got to fix it some before I can write with it as the specimen at the head of this page will show.[35] We have a good place and a pleasant one in a grove, but we have got to leave in the morning. The Regiment is going to guard the railroad.[36] The boys appear to like it as we shall yet rid of drilling and won't have any more guard duty to do than we do now.

I have felt first rate today, and am in hopes that I shall get well soon. With love and kisses to you and Ella, Emmett and Kitty, I remain your affectionate husband, Silas W. Haven.

The talk is that we are going to Grand Junction, part of the regiment gone there at a place between there and Corinth.[37]

—

IN THE FOLLOWING letter, Haven refers to Col. Benjamin H. Grierson, a member of the federal cavalry. He received orders to ride from La Grange, Tennessee, through the heart of Mississippi between the Mississippi Central Railroad and the Mobile & Ohio Railroad. Along the way, Grierson was ordered to cut the lines, disrupt enemy communications, and capture any supplies he located along the route. Designed as more of a nuisance raid, Grierson successfully maneuvered two hundred miles to the Southern Mississippi Railroad and captured a trainload full of supplies that was headed to Vicksburg. Confederate Gen. John Pemberton, in charge of the forces at Vicksburg, sent cavalry and artillery after Grierson, which is exactly what Gen. U. S. Grant wanted. Grierson arrived in Baton Rouge, Louisiana, on May 2, 1863, fifteen days after the expedition began a few hundred miles to the north.

—

Toon's Station, Tennessee, May 11, 1863[38]

Dear Jane,

I received a letter and two boxes of pills from you yesterday and was very glad to hear from you. Very glad that the money got through safe, also that you were well and the news that the church difficulties were being settled up. I came here last Wednesday; the Regiment is all along the road guarding. Two companies (C and G) here; we have a first-rate place. We occupy some houses to stay in and the water is the best we have found since we came south. We have to go on guard about every other day. I have been on picket guard twice and like it pretty well. I am on two hours and off six last night. I was on patrol guard. I stood there hours and then slept the rest of the night. We feel quite confident that the war is about over, although the report is that Hooker's army is on the wrong side of the Rappahannock to hurt the rebs much.[39] There is a great deal of activity in this department. I will send you a paper that will tell about Grierson's raid the whole length of Mississippi.[40] I got a letter from George today. He is at Vicksburg and is well. James has been some sick, but is quite well now. The 9th Regiment has gone below Vicksburg and George is left in charge of the Adjt. quarters. George thinks that the war has come to its last days.[41] When I get to writing, I can't think of anything so I have to lay by a spell. I saw Fred the day I came here. He is about the same. He has got his pay. Tell Susan to write cheerful letters to him.

May 12, 1863

I am on patrol guard tonight and as the rest of the boys have gone to bed, I thought it would be a good time to write to you as I don't come on till 11 o'clock and don't want to sleep before I come off guard (at 2). I am sorry to hear that Kitty has a sore eye. I wish I could send you a bottle of eye salve I have got. I think it would cure it. I hope I can get home time enough to eat some of your garden sauce. I think that if I could be at home a few days, I could fix the garden fence so as to keep the cattle out. My faith is as bright, yes, brighter than when I enlisted that we shall meet again, and I try to live and do my duty so as to please my heavenly Father, and my trust is in him and I can cast all my cares on him and he gives me strength in everything, and I feel that he has answered my prayers in a wonderful manner. My prayer to him is that your faith may be as read the slip to finish.

Toon's Station, Tennessee, May 14, 1863

Dear Jane,

I thought as I did not have anything to do today I would write to you. We don't have much going on that is interesting and don't have much to do, so sometimes the time hangs heavy. The boys feel pretty well the most of the time. Last night they got to making a noise and our first lieutenant told them if they did not stop, he would put them in the guardhouse.[42] They thought they would as lives go there as not. So for about a half an hour they made all the noise they could and then as they had let off the surplus steam, they quit of their own accord and after a while, about a dozen got to singing sacred music and kept it up for nearly an hour. It sounded first rate. They try most all means to pass the time away. There was a Negress with 3 children came in here yesterday that belonged to a man in Mississippi. The woman she had been to work for sent word to her master to come after her and she said she would die before she would go back, so they sent her to Bolivar to see the powers that be. I guess she will not go back. Co. G got to shooting rats today and made a mistake and shot into our barrack. They killed the rat, though, but we asked them to point their guns the other way, as we don't have any particular wish to be shot.

May 16

I hear from Fred most every day, and he keeps about the same. They are going to send him to the hospital in Iowa and I now am looking for him every day to come down in the cares. I would like to see you all and hope I shall soon. I shall try and send Emmett a brass trumpet or eagle. They are such as we wear on our hats. Try and get suitable books for the children to study, and read to them and have them read the Book of Books so that they may learn the way to eternal life. Tell Ella and Emmett to write and tell Kitty that I hope that the war's head is about chopped off so I guess that she will not have to come down here. With love and kisses to you all, I remain your affectionate husband, Silas W. Haven.

Toon's Station, Tennessee, May 16, 1863

To the Baptist of Rockford, Iowa[43]
Brethren and Sisters,

It is some time since I have been able to meet with you and I thought I would try to meet with you by letter; although I have been absent, I have not forgotten you. My prayers have been for your welfare and that you might always keep your lights trimmed and burning. My prayers for myself has been that God would help me resist the temptations that beset me on every hand, and to always prove faithful to my profession and to do each duty in his fear and I feel that he has answered me in a wonderful manner. My faith is brighter and I have been strengthened so that I have felt no inclination to join in any of the various camp vices, so many which abound in the army, and I feel to thank God that he has been so wonderful [to] me and that I ever set out to serve the Lord. With God's help, it is as easy to serve him in the army as in the peaceful scenes of domestic life and it is my determination to still follow on and try God helping me to live as near to Christ as I can and to run the Christian race with real hoping to win the prize at the end. We have very few chances to have public worship, but a few of us have met at an appointed place and have had prayer meetings, and I think that they have done a great deal of good. Some have announced their determination to serve the Lord and I hope that when the regiment gets together again, that more will join us. War is a terrible thing and is inflicted upon a nation for the punishment of sins. The sins of this nation has been great, both North and South, and God in his mercy has born long with us. We are now and have for the last two years under chastisement and it is time that we as a nation repent of our sins and acknowledge that God is the Lord, and implore him to accept the sacrifice of blood and treasure already offered up as a sufficient atonement of our sins, and that he will stay the tide of war and cause the olive branch of peace to wave once more over this land, and that he will make it a nation where liberty, both civil and religious, can be enjoyed by all. Pray for me that I may always prove faithful.

Toon's Station, Tennessee, May 19, 1863

Dear Jane,

I received a letter from you informing me of your health, how you get along. I am sorry that Kitty's eyes still keep sore, but glad that the money has all got through safe, as you must not be surprised if you find twenty dollars more in this. As it happens I don't want one at present as it would cost too much, and I am getting along pretty well now and my health is improving, so I shall trust the rest to letters. I am glad that you have got along as well as you have through the winter and spring so far, and that you have confidence in me that I will not blame you for the amount you spend. I have talked with Fred a number of times about how you would get along and I don't think that he will blame her, but the amount might surprise him at first. Tell her she had better note down the articles that she buys and the price, and then he would understand it better. I think that you will get along as far as money matters are concerned if I get my pay once in four months. There is nearly three months' due me now, and I am in hopes that I shall get my two months' pay soon. Pay all your debts as fast as you can (I have no more for you to pay) and then you can use your money to a better advantage. We heard the news of the battle on the Rappahannock, but our disaster did not weaken my hopes of an early termination of the war. We had some pretty good news from Vicksburg today, if it proves true, which will more than counterbalance the eastern news.[44] I suppose you would like to know how we get along down here. I will give you a little description of camp life. There are two companies here to guard the railroad. Each company sends 9 men to some stockades (places built to protect men from cavalry). They are from three to five miles from there and they stay five days at a time. Each company every other day does the guard duty here. It takes eighteen men and six non-commission officers for picket and three for patrol. Our picket posts are from forty rods to a half mile off, and all we have to do is to have a man on the lookout. Each man takes his turn, two hours at a time. I was on yesterday and read the most of the time. We only have patrol at night and three stands that, one at a time. I will close by sending love and kisses to you all. From your affectionate husband, Silas W. Haven.

Toon's Station, May 22, 1863

Dear Jane,

I thought as I was on picket today I would commence a letter to you and if I could find anything interesting, I would finish it. My health keeps about the same, not sick enough to take medicine, not well enough to do hard duty. I have to keep watch two hours so you see we have a pretty easy time of it every other day. We don't have anything to do, only to drill about an hour just at night. Once in a while a gun is fired on picket, but if only one gun is fired, no attention is paid to it, but if two or more is fired, the whole garrison gets out into line and an officer with a dozen or more men go to the post where the firing was to find out what is up. Last night about nine o'clock, three guns were fired on the same post that it was a few nights ago (Company I was on guard). We got into line in a hurry and a few of us marched up to the post and found out that they fired at what they thought was a horse, but did not know whether a man was on him or not. This morning then they come to examine the place where they heard the noise. They found a dead- COW.[45] So the idea of guerrillas vanished from them, not to be revived till they come on guard again, which will be tomorrow. There may be guerrillas here, but I don't believe that they have fired on our pickets yet, nor do I believe they will, as they would lose more than they would gain. There are all kinds of insects here. The flies are thick everywhere. There are lots of lizards in the woods and old fences, and rats by the wholesale. One come onto my bed last night, but he left quite sudden, probably thought he was not wanted. I sent you twenty dollars last Wednesday.

May 23, 1863

I will try to finish this letter so as to send it off this morning. I could not think of anything to write last night so I wrote that song that I promised to Ella when I was in Memphis. I suppose you would like to know how I get along for clothes. Well, I have got the same that I drawed in Dubuque. The pants I have mended once and will last me quite a spell. My shirts will last me this year out. I am going to draw the next time (in about two weeks) a rubber blanket, a pair of pants and a pair of shoes.[46] I am now wearing my shoes and pants that I had on when I left home. I do my own washing and mending, and cook my own coffee. I don't buy much to eat as Uncle Sam furnishes me with good provisions. I have bought some milk and eggs. We have mostly ham to eat. We get potatoes once in a while and they sent us a lot of sauerkraut last week, which was real good. The freight reported a lot (eight or ten) guerrillas out about a mile, and a lot of our boys have gone out to ask them how they get along. They took their guns along with them as they did not know but what the gents might be saucy. I don't know as I can think of anymore this time, so I will close by sending my love and kisses to you all. Hoping to meet you all soon. I remain your affectionate husband, Silas W. Haven.

I am in a measure alone in the company, although if I was taken very sick, I have a few I think (Crowell, Decker, Dean from Flood Creek and Daniels) and some two or three others that I could depend upon for care.[47] I don't feel any concerned but what I should get along us for as comfort and care was concerned, you write that you never have anything good to eat but what you want me there to help you eat it. I would like to be there first rate, although I don't have a craving appetite for good things. I guess I could eat them if they were set before me. I have twice picked my tin cup full of berries (black) when I was on guard and mashed them up with sugar to eat on my bread (biscuit). We had some fresh mutton a few days ago and have got some sheep and cattle herded for our use, but I don't fancy the beef down here as it is lean and tough and my teeth are poor. I thank the children for their letters and will try to write to you, Ella, Emmett and Kitty next time. With love and kisses to you all, I remain your affectionate husband, Silas W. Haven.

Toon's Station, May 26, 1863

Dear Jane,

There is some talk that we shall stay here another month as the citizens want us to stay, but I don't know whether we shall or not. We must be patient and hope for the best. My faith is still bright that this war will soon close. You up there are looking for the decisive battles to be fought in the east, we down here think different. The reverse of the eastern army don't affect us much for we think that when Vicksburg falls (which is ours now, I expect) that it will hurt the rebels more than the fall of Richmond. I think that Rosecrans will have a big battle and then the way will be open for the whole south and our armies down here are not idle, as the Rebs have found out to their cost and will still keep finding out, and some bright morning they may possibly find out that Jeff Davis has taken French leave, which they appear to be afraid of. Things now look pretty bright to us down here and all the soldiers feel pretty well. I am glad the old cow has come in. You had better get a bell to put on her and then you can tell when she is around. I got a letter from Julia today, all well there. She had had a letter from Jacob.[48] He was well.

May 27th

I did not finish this yesterday so I will try to get it done before the mail goes out. I was on patrol guard last night from 8 to 11. There is a lot of contrabands come in this morning going to Jackson. With love and kisses to you, Ella, Emmett and Kitty, I will close for this time. From your affectionate husband, Silas W. Haven.

Toon's Station, Tennessee, May 29, 1863[49]

Dear Jane,

As I have not got but a short time before the mail goes out, I will try to fill this half sheet. I believe I wrote that there were lots of blackberries here. I have not been out to get any yet. The darkies are getting rather scarce. Those that are Union men are willing that slavery shall be abolished if the Union can be preserved. The secesh want to hold on to the Negro, but will find out that they can't. When you hear anyone talk about the constitutional rights of the South, you may set him down as a Copperhead for the secesh have repudiated the Constitution, and the southern unionists don't thank them for their sympathy. Tell Ella and Emmett that I would like to have them write. Tell Kitty that I am sorry she has got sore eyes, and I hope that they will soon get well. Give them all kisses for me. With love and kisses to you all, I close by signing myself your affectionate husband, Silas W. Haven.

Toon's Station, Tennessee, May 30, 1863

Dear Jane,

I am again on picket and I improve the time to write a few lines to you, but it will be a pretty dry letter as there is no news stirring of any account. I expect that we shall leave here in a few days. The talk is that the government is going to throw up this road as they have got the road nearly repaired from Grand Junction to Corinth. Where we shall go will be hard to tell. We may possibly go somewhere on the road between Memphis and Corinth, and we may (and I hope) go to Helena.[50] There was two trains went to Jackson last night after the 1st Brigade. They are just coming back as I hear the whistle sound. Well, I have just been to the depot and saw the trains pass. There is a good deal of speculation where the troops are all going to. Some think Vicksburg, some Rosecrans, some Helena and some think down through Mississippi by the way of Holly Springs, but it is all speculation. I think that all the troops will have their part to do. Those that are not needed to guard railroad will be after the rebs pretty sharp and will keep them busy, and I don't think that the North will have cause to grumble about the inaction of the army. It tried pretty hard to rain last night and this morning, but only made out to lay the dust and now the sun shine hotter than ever, but we have a nice cool breeze. We get along pretty well by staying in the shade.

June 2nd

I take my pen today to try to finish this. I was in hopes to have got letters from you but the mail did not come down on the train this morning, but I am in hopes that it will be tonight. They are going to throw up this road in a few days so I don't expect that we shall stay here much longer. The Negroes are leaving too. They say they won't stay if the soldiers go away, a lot went today. The planter here tells the Negroes all sorts of stories to keep them from leaving and going into the army. One is that there was about 7,000 Negro troops killed at Vicksburg, which don't look very likely as we did not have any Negro troops in the field or fight.[51] We don't get much news from Vicksburg, but we feel pretty sure that it will soon fall without the sacrifice of many more lives unless the rebs attack Grant in the rear. If they do, they will be sorry as Grant has received large reinforcements on purpose for just such an emergency. 23 divisions have gone from Memphis and he is getting some by the way of New Orleans, so if Joe Johnston comes in Grant's rear, he may possibly find that they are not asleep and may possibly get bagged himself. My health, through the blessing of providence, is still improving and I am able to do all duty required of me, and the way things go on, I feel that the war will soon end. I don't know as I shall send any money this week; if I do, I shall write another letter. It costs me most, if not quite as much, for papers as it does for tobacco, but I have only spent since April 17th about $6.00 for everything I have bought. Love and kissed to you and the children, I close by subscribing myself your affectionate husband, Silas W. Haven.[52]

—

CONFEDERATE GEN. JOSEPH E. JOHNSTON, in charge of the Confederate forces in the West, had wanted Pemberton to join him outside of Jackson, Mississippi, rather than end up trapped inside Vicksburg. Johnston, in Jackson, Mississippi, gathered a force of about 30,000 men with plans to attack the Union soldiers that had laid siege to Vicksburg. Union commander Grant had been concerned about an attack on his rear, but he outnumbered Johnston and believed that if Johnston broke the line, Grant would seal it and then Johnston would be trapped inside Vicksburg. Johnston remained indecisive, inactive, and had problems communicating with Pemberton inside Vicksburg. He never attacked Grant.

CHAPTER 3

# Everything Is Quiet in Camp Today

## *June–August 1863*

In the summer of 1863, as Union armies triumphed across the country, Pvt. Haven and his regiment remained in Tennessee, guarding the Memphis & Charleston Railroad. Col. James Gilbert received special orders in June 1863 to guard bridges over Wolf and Grissom Creek at Moscow, Tennessee.[1] Throughout his stay in Moscow, Tennessee, Haven commented on the victories at Gettysburg, Vicksburg, Tullahoma, and Port Hudson. He also used the time to again explore his thoughts on religion, camp life, and the political climate in the United States.

—

Moscow, Tennessee, June 9, 1863

Dear Jane,

I was very much disappointed in not getting a letter from you this week, as I have got them pretty regular so far every Monday or Tuesday. It is about a week since I have had a chance to write to you as we have been on the move most ever since. We were relieved last Tuesday night and waited till after noon the next day for a train to go to Jackson. When we got there, we got on another train and at night came back to La Grange, and Friday we came to this place. We marched from La Grange (12 miles) and the most of the company went five miles further, but I stayed here rather than to ride horseback and was going down the next day, but our company was ordered back and so I did not have to go. There is 7 company in our regiment here; one is 5 miles below and two have not joined us yet, but are at La Grange. We are guarding the railroad and we are 39 miles east of Memphis, and it looks as if we should make quite a long stop of it here. The country is quite pretty around here, but the place has been mostly destroyed. There have been quite a number of troops stationed here, and when they left, they left quite a lot of stuff behind such as coats, pants, caps, camp dishes. Some of our men got them good overcoats, boots, but as I had enough and could not send it home, I did not pick up much. I got a lot of buttons, which I shall try to send to you. I suppose you would like to know how I get along. I have been first rate in coming from Jackson to La Grange. We had to ride on the top of the cars and as we came slow, it was 3 o'clock in the morning before we got in and it rained some besides, and then I rolled up in my blanket and laid down on the depot platform and slept till 7 and we did not go in to camp till in the afternoon, and the next morning we struck our tents and marched here. I stood the march pretty well as I was in the rear guard. We did not have to carry our knapsacks as they come on the cars. I have only been on guard but one night for over a week, but shall have to be on now every other day, I expect. I was on Saturday night and am on today. I was pretty lucky as usual in getting on camp guard as it rains today and we have horses to stay in and guard Q. M. stores, but I have to go on guard and shall have to lay this by for two hours.

Well, I have just come in from guard and I suppose you would like to know what I have had to do. Well, I had to keep watch that no one carried off any quartermaster stores and I did that by reading nearly all the time. There was three trains passed going to Memphis while I was out; one of them had a battery on board, which it is disturbing on the road. It left two pieces of cannon (brass) here. I expect it came from Jackson as they have left that place and throwed up the road from Grand Junction to there and now run straight to Corinth from Memphis. The probability is that we shall have to stay here to watch the road all summer and see to the guerrillas, which we are able to do. We have about two hundred horses and mules here to do the scouting in with, so I guess that the rebs will have to keep quiet. There has been quite a lot of families come in and going north so I don't think it will strengthen the secesh much by sending Copperheads to them as there is [a] lot of Union men down south that will go north as fast as they can. There is lots of Negroes coming in every day. Two come to our regiment while we were coming from La Grange. They bred horses. I hardly know what to fill up this page with as it seems so long since I got a letter from you. I was in hopes to hear of the safe arrival of the one that I sent twenty dollars in today. I don't expect that I shall hear from Fred, only by the way of home, so you must write where he is. Write often as I don't depend on any letters, only those that I get from you, and I look for them every Monday, but I will close this to get my supper. From your affectionate husband, Silas W. Haven.

Moscow, Tennessee, June 11, 1863

Dear Jane,

I received a letter from you yesterday afternoon (part of our mail went to La Grange and came back) and was very glad to hear from you, but sorry that you did not get a letter from me that had had $20.00 in it, which you had ought to have had on Saturday, May 30; probably it got detained and you, I hope, have got it before this time. You wanted to know how I liked Sophronia Daniels's man. I like him very well. He is steady, although full of fun and is one officer that don't curse and swear.[2] You think the war is not going to close very soon. We think different down this way as we don't depend on the papers that have to print news whether they have any or not, and they can't print anything about the movements of the army. We are here where we can judge for ourselves. I don't suppose you up there could give any estimate of the number of troops that is now at Vicksburg.[3] We can by our own observation. I saw, when in Memphis, over 40,000 go down besides what went from Helena, and there has gone from this vicinity as much as 12 or 15,000 so that Grant must have as much as 150,000 men under him now and he will capture Vicksburg and whip out all the forces that can be sent against him if he is unsuccessful there. I shall begin to think that the war will last a year or two longer, but I don't see anything to make me change my opinion yet, not even the scare at Washington.

I mended my pants yesterday and put a watch pocket in my new ones and took off my drawers and throwed them away so as not to lug them around. I have worn my woolen shirts all the time till Monday [when] I put on my blue one that I had last summer so as to wash both my others, so you see, we are not afraid of frost here, although the nights are quite cool, but not so cool but what I have slept outdoors sometimes. I generally get under cover as we have very heavy dews here and I would get my face pretty wet if I did not keep it covered up. I hope you will have good success with your garden for I am in hopes to help you eat some of it. We don't get any garden sauce here as the folks did not plant much, for the soldiers have got all they raised here to fore; they (soldiers) help themselves to milk when they can coax the cows with salt to stand still. There is lots of apples and peaches here and the soldiers are stewing the apples now. Tell Ella and Emmett I expect a letter from them soon so they must write so that I shall not be disappointed. Kiss them for me and don't forget Kitty and tell them I think of them (and you) every day and am careful of my health. I have a nice little hatchet I wish I could send home. Another company (E) has joined us today and I guess after a while the whole regiment will get together again.[4]

Read to yourself first

I got my other sheet full and as I don't come on guard yet awhile, I thought I would try to fill a half sheet more. I don't want to make too large a letter as I am going to put ten dollars in this. Write as soon as you get a letter with money in it. I sent a paper yesterday with a spoon in it and shall send another tomorrow. Tell Kitty I will send her another bill to replace the one that she lent you, and to be a good girl and be patient, and pa will come to her before long. If there is anything you want to ask me or to have me tell you, write and I will try to answer the best I can. I don't show my letters to anyone and I am going to burn them up as often as they get to bulky so that no one will be apt to get hold of them to read. I read one that was left by the other regiment that told things that I would not like anyone to read, even if they were strangers. I thought I would send you a list of my expenses so you can see what I buy and how I keep my accounts. Write how much you have left after paying all your debts.

Table 1 Money Spent, Spring 1863

| | | |
|---|---|---|
| 18-Apr | Tobacco sent home | 10.15 |
| 21 | Postage Stamps | 0.25 |
| 22 | Portfolio, ink, matches, tobacco | 1.15 |
| 25 | Newspaper | 0.10 |
| 24 | milk sent home | 0.70 |
| 27 | newspaper, paper, envelopes and stamps | 10.60 |
| 29 | tobacco and gingerbread | 0.50 |
| 4-May | Sugar | 0.10 |
| 5 | Newspaper | 0.10 |
| 8 | baking bread | 0.05 |
| 10 | Pie | 0.05 |
| 11 | tobacco | 0.20 |
| 13 | newspaper, baking bread | 0.20 |
| 15 | eggs and tobacco | 0.40 |
| 17 | Sugar | 0.05 |
| 19 | newspaper, paper | 0.15 |
| 20 | sent home | 20.00 |
| 22 | smoking tobacco | 0.10 |
| 26 | Newspaper | 0.10 |
| 27 | postage stamps | 0.25 |
| 28 | Newspaper | 0.10 |
| 29 | tobacco, paper | 0.30 |

| | | |
|---|---|---|
| 31 | milk, watch crystal | 0.20 |
| 2-Jun | tobacco, newspaper | 0.20 |
| 4 | Tobacco | 0.10 |
| 5 | tobacco, matches | 0.20 |
| 6 | Beer | 0.15 |
| 9 | Tobacco | 0.10 |
| 10 | newspaper and tobacco | 0.20 |
| 11 | Newspaper | 0.10 |
| Total | 46.85 | |
| Sent Home | 40.50 | |
| Spent | 6.35 | |

You see that the most of my expenses is for tobacco. The beer I got that night that I got here, but I must close with love and kisses to you all. I subscribe myself your affectionate husband,
Silas W. Haven.

Moscow, Tennessee, June 14, 1863

Dear Jane,

I don't see what has got into the mail for it don't fetch me any letters or papers. I guess it is because there don't anyone write to me, only you, and I have not had but one from you this month. I am on guard today and as I don't have anything to do, I thought I would spend my time in writing, but don't know whether I can find enough that will be interesting to fill out this. I have been on guard pretty regular every other day, but as our regiment is all getting together, I only come on once in three days, and when the other two companies get here, I guess I shall not have to be on guard only one day in four. When we are on picket, we don't have to stand on watch only about two hours, and as I am on the reserve today, I may not have to stand at all so you see that guard duty is not very hard. Some little nigs come in day before yesterday and told about a nest of guerrillas out about three or four miles, so a lot of the boys mounted horses and went out to shore them up.[5] They found them, but could not catch them. It appears that they had been there some time. They stayed in the woods daytimes and come to a house after their meals. Our boys get to the house rather too quick, and the guerrillas discovered them first and fired on them and run for thick timber. Our boys fired back and chased them a piece, but the colonel would not let them go far as there want but a few of them out and they might get separated and gobbled up. Well, I am out under a tree setting on a block and have got a small box on another for a desk and it is a pretty good place. There is quite a nice cool breeze and I set my ink stand on my paper to keep it from blowing away and there come a gust and turned the ink over, which accounts of this black spot on the paper. There is a nice peach orchard here and quite a lot of oak trees, which make it real cool and shady. The peaches are not quite ripe but are full grown, unless they are going to be very large. The secesh around these diggings have suffered some. The town mostly destroyed, farms laid waster, cattle, horses, mules carried off, and if this war lasts much longer, it will be left a howling wilderness or have to be repeopled by a better set of inhabitants. God grant that this war will soon close and this nation be a land of peace, where all both black and white can enjoy the freedom that was intended that they should enjoy. I have just received a letter from Jacob, written June 9th.[6] He had just got letters from you and Julia. He was well. Soldier's life is pretty hard when he is sick, but when he is well, it comes easy. My health keeps pretty good and I feel pretty well the most of the time. I worked all day, day before yesterday, fixing my tent and have got it in pretty good shape for summer quarters. There is three of us in together and only one (Howdeshell that you saw at St. Charles) helped me any.[7] There is a good many that are spiritualists, but they are generally as bad, if not worse than those that don't belong to any church. I try to live the best I can and keep aloof from all their vices and wicked plays, but I enjoy myself as well, if not better, than them sot of them. Hoping these few lines will find you enjoying good health. I close by sending lots of love and kisses to you all. Remember me in your prayers, from your affectionate husband, Silas W. Haven.

Moscow, Tennessee, June 17, 1863

Dear Jane,

I was on guard yesterday and did intend to write, but they did not have corporals enough and as I had a watch, they had me to act as one, and I had to see that the guard was relieved every hour, so it did not let me have much time either to write or sleep as I set up till one o'clock and got up again at half past four, and it is so hot and the flies bother so that I can't sleep any today, but I guess that I shall make up lost time tonight, as the nights are real cool and nice and have been quite pleasant. You write that they have formed a sewing society there, and want to know what the soldiers need the most.[8] I shall answer I don't know; we have more clothing than we can carry and I could have picked up a cart load here that was throwed away. If you could send any eatable, some butter would come very nice, although it would be more like oil before it got here as it is some warm about this time. It would suit the soldiers the most to have the proceeds go towards making their families comfortable than to have it sent here. I know they would feel much better and feel better contented with hard fare if they knew that their families are comfortable and are well provided for. The most that I have heard say anything say that the folks never have done what they promised to, and if they do anything for or sell anything to, they will charge more than they do to anyone else or rather above what they can get anywhere else. I hope they don't serve you so I am sorry you have not got the money I sent, but I am in hopes that you will get it after a while as I rather think it is missent as they were changing the distributing office about that time, and it may have to go to the dead letter office and back before you get it. I sent you ten dollars last week and sent one yesterday with five cents in it for Kitty. With love and kisses to you, Ella, Emmett and Kitty, I close by subscribing myself your affectionate husband, Silas W. Haven.

Moscow, Tennessee, June 19, 1863

Dear Jane

I am again out on picket and I am pretty lucky as I have always got on the same post and also on the reserve and by the way that they are putting the guard on. I don't think I shall have to stand at all. There is no news here to speak of. All is quiet down here, only the boys began to talk some about furloughs again. I hope some of them will get them as soon as I get my pay again, so that I can send it home safe. I don't know as I can get one on the account of the expense, for if that twenty dollars is lost, you will need all that you can get to get along with and I am in hopes that the war will close before fall. There have been a number of men here that come from Vicksburg. They say that Grant can take the place any day, but think that he is holding off so as to either save life or to whip out Joe Johnston's force at the same time. The fall of Vicksburg, I think, will be the death blow to the Southern Confederacy, as it will let loose about two hundred thousand men to go to other points.[9]

June 21

I forgot to tell you that day before yesterday I went a short distance to get some water where there was an orchard turned out loose, and got all the plums that I could eat and got some apples and stewed. Yesterday morning, just before we were relieved, we heard some firing. The long roll sounded and in less than no time, the battery boys started out with their guns and it want but a few minutes before they were talking in approved style. They shelled the woods a spell and then went back to their quarters and all was quiet before we got to camp. It appeared that a body of guerrillas was trying to burn some culverts, and some of our men saw them on the railroad and thought they were citizens, and went out on the track to find out what they wanted, and they fired on our men (from Company G) and then skedaddled. Our men fired back, but they were too far off to either of them do any hurt. I am on guard again today. I will try and finish this so as to send it out tomorrow. I will quit writing for today as I am out in the sun and my conveniences are not very good. One of our men from Company H shot himself yesterday morning and had to have his big took off close up to his body. I was acquainted with him. He went to Vicksburg with me. My health is pretty good. I am trying to build me a shebang to live in while we stay here. I don't expect to get it done today as I have all my boards to fetch, about forty rods. The whistle has just sounded for the mail train so I am too late to send this today. John Book, the man that shot himself, died today. It seems that all the men that got shot in the 27th shoot themselves. It takes a great while for men to learn how to handle a gun.

Moscow, June 22

I must try to fill out another half sheet and I guess it won't be a very hard matter, as a body of cavalry went through here today going to La Grange with prisoners, mules, plunder. They have been down in Mississippi and was sent up with the extra baggage they had taken. They have taken a lot of mules and brought away all the Negroes, and destroyed the crops, burnt the wheat in the field and all the fences and towns wherever they have been laid. They had quite a lot of Negroes and they were all mounted on mules and horses that they had captured. They had also a number of prisoners, some caissons too and a printing press. The rebs (Forrest's force) went into Jackson and went to conscripting, and our force (7th Kansas Jayhawkers) and 7th Iowa and some others went there and liberated the men and wiped out the rebels and burned the town. I guess they will be quiet for a spell, but it is getting nearly time for taps (9 o'clock) and I will close by sending love and kisses to you all from your affectionate husband, Silas W. Haven.

---

Confederate cavalry commander Gen. Nathan Bedford Forrest raided several Union locations throughout Tennessee throughout the month of June 1863, beginning at Triune, Tennessee, west of Murfreesboro, on June 11, 1863. Forrest moved on to Jackson, Tennessee, but Union forces followed him in and kept control of the town.

---

Moscow, Tennessee, June 25, 1863

Dear Jane,

I was very glad today to receive a letter from you stating that you were all well, also that you had received the letter containing $20.00. I have been very anxious to hear and I did not get any letter at the regular time. I was afraid that something had happened. I rather expected that the letter with money in it would come around after a whole as they was changing the distributing offices about that time. My health keeps about the same, although I got wet yesterday and caught a little cold. All the able-bodied men that was in camp went on a forced march to La Grange at two o'clock yesterday morning, expecting that that place was going to have an attack, but when they got there, they could not hear of any force and so came back. They heard that there was six thousand rebel troops had taken Grand Junction and before our boys got there, it had dwindled down to two thousand, and when [they] got there, it dwindled down to twenty guerrillas seen, so they took the cars and come back. The cavalry (3rd Michigan) went through here yesterday morning on their return from the raid down into Mississippi. They were pretty jovial, although they were as wet as drowned rats. They had tried their best to catch Chalmers, but could not get nary fight out of them.[10] They left the country desolate, burnt towns, cotton gins, cotton, wheat both in the shock and standing, all the fences, and confiscated all the Negroes, horses, mules and cattle. They brought about 500 Negroes, and 200 head of cattle through here, and more went to Germantown with the 2nd Iowa (they were out together). The boys see lots of guerrillas every day or two. The ones that was with me on guard day before yesterday [thought] they saw some in the road, about a mile and a half off. I saw the same, but I guess it must be that my eyesight is growing poor, for I made out them to be cattle, that is in my own mind, and before I came off guard, they crossed the track twice and come up within half a mile and the boys had a notion of going to get some milk, but still they stick to it that they saw guerrillas. I don't believe that they saw guerrillas. I don't believe that there is a dozen within ten miles of here. We should find out pretty quick if there was as the Negroes will let us know.

June 26

They are forming Negro regiments pretty fast and they make good soldiers and learn the drill pretty quick, in fact quicker than most of the whites as their mind is entirely on learning and they have nothing else to think of.[11] All the officers from colonel down to orderly sergeant are white, and they are chosen from the old regiments and have to pass examination so that they will be well officered. There has been a rumor that our brigade is under marching orders, but I don't believe it as we are guarding the road from La Grange to Germantown and if we leave here, other troops will have to come in and there is no more at Corinth than they need there, but still, it don't make much odds to me where I am as I am the same kind care wherever I am, and my faith is bright that I shall be protected and preserved to return home and meet you all again.[12] I know it must cost you a considerable to live and am sorry that I did not send my money by express so you could have got it all together. I hope you have got the last I sent before this time, which will make fifty dollars that I have sent in large bills. I want you should use it as you see fit, as I shall feel better if I know that you are well provided for and comfortable. At the end of this month, there will be four months' due us, but I don't expect to get more than two at the next pay day. As soon as I get it, I shall send you at the rate of ten dollars a month; that is, if I get two months' pay, I will send twenty dollars. I would like to be there at your celebration, but business down here will prevent. Tell Kitty I will send her some more sassafras if I can find any here, but don't think I can. Also I would like to see her little birdies, but more than all, I would like to see you all, which I hope to before long. With love and kisses to you, Ella, Emmett and Kitty, will close for this time by subscribing myself your affectionate husband, Silas W. Haven.

You write that I must not be afraid to take medicine. I am not provided I can have some that will do me any good, but they don't have a very full supply or of many kinds. Their principal medicines are opium, quinine, blue mass and Spanish flies for blisters.[13] I am taking for cough ipecac, tincture of opium and niter, and have had one blister on my side and expect to put another on tomorrow. I don't intend to doctor much here in camp. With love and kisses to you all and hoping that we shall meet again, I remain your affectionate husband, Silas W. Haven.

Moscow, Tennessee, June 30, 1863

Dear Jane,

I received your letter of June 21 today and read it with much pleasure and I thought as I had a little time, I would improve it. I am on picket guard. The place where I stand is at a block house and I have stood one hour, and shall have to stand two more from eight to ten tonight, and then I can lay down and go to sleep. My health still keeps about the same. We were mustered for our pay today. When we shall get it is another question. You make a little mistake when you think that we go farther off, as I am 60 miles nearer Memphis than when I was at Jackson. Moscow is only 40 miles from Memphis. I am glad that you have got the $20.00 safe and was in hopes that you had got ten more before you wrote. I guess that you have got all the papers that I have sent and will send some more soon. I sent one with eleven buttons in it. I wish you would write how many letters you have got since I went to Corinth. I have not eaten many blackberries, yet when I do, I shall not need a teaspoon, as I have got a larger spoon that I think will go better. There is plenty of berries, but they are mostly outside of the lines and I have been busy building me a shanty to live in and I wanted they should get a little riper before I went after any, but I will leave the rest till I get to quarters and write with ink.

Moscow, Tennessee, July 1, 1863

Dear Jane,

I will give you a little description of my house that I live in. I went to work and built an addition to a shanty 5 feet wide, 7 long and 7 high at one end and 10 at the other. I have a door in one end and my bunk along one side, with a window (hole) at the head of my bunk on the side and a large window place opposite of the door, and a shelf about 2½ long by 1 wide to write on. I have a stool to set on and have got a box to put my haversack and bread rations in so that I have all things in nice order and don't have anything laying around to fetch the flies in. So you see that I can keep pretty comfortable. My bed is an old battened door, with a board 4 inches wide on one side. I spread my overcoat on it and roll in my blanket and have my knapsack for a pillow and sleep very well. It is not quite as soft as feathers, but it suits me better. There were a number of secesh soldiers crossed the railroad track about a mile and a half below where I was on guard, but they did not trouble us. Also, there were six guerrillas seen this morning. They will have to look out now as there is two companies of the 6th Illinois cavalry here come today. They will not stir them up some, I reckon. The water in the creek rose three or four feet last night, and the block house where we stood on guard was surrounded with water so that we only had one guard out at a time, so I only had to stand one hour, but I did not get to sleep till after twelve o'clock as the gnats bit my face, hands and feet so that I had to cover all up, and it was rather too warm for me to sleep so till late. I put my stockings on and covered my face with a newspaper and so got the start of them and got to sleep and slept till ½ past six. Tell Kitty that she can have the earrings if she has her ears pierced if I could get them here. I would send them to her, but I shall have to send the money and have you buy them. I will try to send paper with some eye salve in it tomorrow if I can. If you get it, rub a little on the eyelids occasionally. I have got quite a lot of buttons yet and could get more, but don't want to carry them around. I can't get anything here suitable to send to Ella so you must divide what I send as well as you can, but I shall have to lay that by for tonight as tattoo has just beat and taps will come before I get my bed fixed if I don't look out.

July 2

I wish you would write more about the church, how they get along and whether they are going to settle a minister or not, also whether they turn out to meetings well, for I take a great deal of interest in the church matters there. We don't have many church privileges here, but we intend to have prayer meetings. Our chaplain is not much a hand to go ahead, but generally waits till the boys start prayer meetings themselves. I don't come on guard only once in three or four days now, which makes it rather lazy work soldiering. I wish you would get your miniatures taken and send to me. Get them in a case if you can't get them all on two plates; have one a plate and put it on the case loose. Write all the news and write often. With love and kisses to you all, I remain your affectionate husband, Silas W. Haven.

Moscow, Tennessee, July 7, 1863

Dear Jane,

As I had a little time before taps, I thought I would commence a letter to you. I somehow feel pretty well and by the actions of the boys in the regiment, I guess they all do. Yesterday afternoon, a dispatch came in that Vicksburg surrendered on the 4th.[14] It was just what we were looking for, but still it elevated our ideas some and some of the boys made the bar suffer. The colonel excused us from all but necessary guard duty and dress parade. Jacob wrote that he would like to be up there to help celebrate the fourth, but as he could not, he did not know but what he should have full as good time. It appears that they celebrate the fourth at Helena in earnest, as the ubiquitous Price thought he wanted the place, but it appears that there was a few obstructions in his path and so he made up his mind that he would advance backward, but you will hear about it before this gets to you. Jake said that they had got some butter from Rockford and wished that Fred and I were there to help them eat it up, but as we could not be there to help them, he thought that they would try to worry it down, but there goes taps. Lights must be put out so I must stop for this time.

—

MAJ. GEN. STERLING PRICE commanded some Confederate infantry at the battle of Helena on July 4, 1863. Largely overshadowed by Vicksburg and Gettysburg, Helena emerged as a defining battle that secured eastern Arkansas for the Union army, commanded by Gen. Benjamin Prentiss. The Confederates lost over fifteen hundred casualties, compared to two hundred Union dead and wounded. Confederate Gen. Robert E. Lee received his "thrashing," as Haven refers to it below, at the Battle of Gettysburg, Pennsylvania, fought July 1–3, 1863. Confederate Gen. Braxton Bragg had retreated across the Tennessee River on June 30, 1863. Gen. Rosecrans now controlled central Tennessee, and Bragg fled to Chattanooga, Tennessee, by July 7.

—

July 9

I was on guard yesterday and I will try to finish this before the mail goes out. I had a pretty good place to stand yesterday. I suppose you have seen it in the papers before this time that Lee had got what he did not want—a good thrashing and I expect that Bragg will get the next one, which will leave the Confederates in a rather precarious situation. It seems to me that the beginning of the end of this war is in sight. We all feel pretty well down this way and want peace. We want to give the rebs their constitutional rights first, which is a good thrashing, the only rights they can claim at our hands. We don't want any hatched-up peace and by the looks of things now, I think that when we have peace, it will be permanent, but I will close this sheet. Respects to all, Silas W. Haven.

Moscow, Tennessee, July 12, 1863

My dear Daughter Ella,

As I got a letter from you the other day, I suppose you are looking for one from me, so I will try to write one to you as plain as I can with a poor pen. I was very much pleased with your letter. I see that you improve in writing very much, and I hope that you will improve your school hours in study so that you can make a better show than the most of the ladies do down here. I was in the provost marshal's office yesterday and three women came to take the oath and neither of them could write their names. Their ages were 36, 23, and 22. They did not appear to care about it at all. The women down here most all use snuff and tobacco.[15] The way they use snuff is to have a pine stick and wet it and put it in the snuff and chew or suck the stick. A very disgusting habit, worse than using tobacco.[16] The flies are not quite so thick as they were, but there is any quantity of gnats, fleas, mosquitoes and lice (we call them grey backs), besides other kinds too numerous to mention. Dogs, cats, rats, mice and goats are quite plenty, and Negroes are also a southern institution take them all together. I had rather be excused from living where they are as numerous as they are here. Apples and peaches will soon be ripe and then I am going to try to get my share of them. I suppose you would like to know what I had for supper. Well, I had some warm biscuit and molasses and coffee, and I bought a blackberry pie today noon and eat a piece of that and have got a piece for breakfast. We had built some brick ovens and our cooks bake biscuits and buy blackberries and sugar and make pies and sell to the company at about the cost for materials to make, which is 10 cents apiece.

July 15

I will try to finish this this morning so as to have it go out today. The cavalry are playing bob with the guerrillas. They brought in a number yesterday. We are not going to leave here at present as our brigade will have to stay here, probably till the war is over. You must write again as I like to hear from home after this. From your Father, SWH

Moscow, Tennessee, July 12, 1863

Dear Jane,

As everything is quiet in camp today, I thought I would write a few lines to you. My health keeps about the same, although I have had the headache and my bowels have been out of order for a few days back, but I have not had to lay by any yet. I was on camp guard yesterday and had quite a battle with fleas and grey backs, and as usual came of conqueror such battles are of frequent occurrences and I guess are about the only battles that the 27th will have. No men are lost on our side, but pretty heavy slaughter on the rebs (i.e., flies and grey backs). I did not have anything to do in the daytime yesterday, as I was a patrol, but one of the men got sick and I had to stand or set four hours last night (from 10 to 12 and 4 to 6). I set in a chair on the tavern stoop, guarding a woman that won't take the oath. They have had her here for nearly two weeks. I have not seen her yet. They say she is quite bitter against the North.[17] The cavalry brought in two men yesterday that professed to have come here to get rid of the conscription, but just at night they (the cavalry) found a lot of papers, which told another story, so that the colonel put them under strict guard and today send them to La Grange as spies. It appears they were up in there parts conscripting and getting all the information they could of the numbers and position of our forces. Two hundred and fifty of our regiment and the cavalry have gone out today on a scout and if there is any rebs near, they had better look out. One of our men yesterday carelessly threw his gun under his tent (the tents are most of a foot or so from the ground) and hit the hammer of a loaded gun, and it went off and a buckshot hit a man in Company E in the leg, but did not happen to be more than a flesh wound. The war news is cheering and it looks as if the South would soon be compelled to give up. There is a rumor that we are going to move from here in a few days, but we can't tell how true it is. The talk is that our brigade is going to Columbus, Kentucky.[18] If so, we shall be still nearer home. The fighting in this western division is pretty near closed. I think when Port Hudson is taken, the Mississippi will be clear. Bragg's force has left Tennessee, with Rosecrans close behind to keep him moving, and Grant's army is stirring up Johnson, and Lee's force [is] trying to get out of Meade's track. Give my respects to all. This from your affectionate husband, Silas W. Haven.

—

AFTER THE FALL of Vicksburg, on July 6, 1863, Union Gen. William T. Sherman led soldiers toward Jackson, Mississippi, where Joseph Johnston had remained for the entire Vicksburg campaign. Gen. Franklin Gardner, commanding Confederate forces at Port Hudson, surrendered his army to Union Cdr. Nathaniel Banks on July 9, 1863. Port Hudson, the last Confederate position on the Mississippi River, opened up the entire river to Union control for the duration of the war.

—

Helena, Arkansas, July 16, 1863

To: S. W. Haven

Dear Brother,

We had a pretty good fight on the fourth, [commencing] at 4 o'clock in the morning and lasted till noon. In fact it was pretty hard fight. Their loss in killed, wounded and prisoners was 25 hundred or more, about 800 killed and wounded. We celebrated the fourth on the eighth and fired salutes in honor of the taking of Vicksburg. Had a good speech from General Prentiss, Gen. Solomon and several others.[19] We have had two or three scares since. They are talking that they think there is a force near here now, but I guess that it is only a camp story, for our lines was opened for trade with loyal citizens yesterday.

Port Hudson is ours. Secesh must be pretty near played out. Hope so at least. The prisoners that we took on the fourth was on a steamboat and started for Memphis in half an hour after we took them. We had some as finer shot at them on open ground as we could wish and we improved them. We fired 200 rounds from our gun. We had a very bad accident the other morning. We was ordered to fire a salute of thirty-six guns; the last shot was fired by No. 6 gun. When William Davis was ramming it down, the gun went off and killed him. He was terribly burnt, both hands torn to pieces and one shoulder. It throwed him about 10 feet. He did not come to his senses at all, lived 2 hours, did not move, only to breathe hard; the first occurred we have had in our battery. Can't stop to write any more, so good bye. J. R. Knapp[20]

Moscow, Tennessee, July 21, 1863

Dear Jane,

I received a letter from Susan Sunday and one from Jake yesterday, and was in hopes of getting one from you today, but as I did not, I thought I would commence one to you. I have not been very well for a few days back. I caught cold and had the neuralgia pretty bad, but a couple of Ayers pills cured that and I guess I shall be so as to go on guard the next time my turn comes. I don't see why Fred don't get letters from Susan as it was directed right. I wrote the same day to him and I guess he has got it before this time. He was up past here a few days ago, but I did not get to see him. I will send Jake's letter in this so you can read it for yourself. We don't have any news here, only war news, and the most of that you get about as soon as I do. We don't have anything to do, only guard railroad and the guerrillas don't trouble our section much. They tore up the track between here and Corinth yesterday, but they had it repaired before night. A lot of our boys went outside of the line yesterday after apples and berries and found three guns (double barrel) and a number of horses with U.S. marked on them, and brought them in with some other troops. Our cook made the apples into pies and we eat here tonight. Col. Hatch gave Forrest a drubbing up to Jackson the other day, and I guess that it will not be a great while before the guerrillas will be scarce in this neighborhood.

---

HERE, HAVEN REFERRED to another attempted raid by Confederate cavalry under the command of Gen. Nathan Bedford Forrest. Col. Edward Hatch, born in Maine, lived in Iowa when the Civil War began and commanded the 2nd

Iowa Cavalry early in the war before receiving a promotion and command of the 9th Iowa Cavalry. He spent much of the war fighting Confederate raiders in Tennessee and Mississippi.

—

July 23

I will try to send you a paper this week. A lot of us have put in and buy a paper every day to read and keep in the company, but I must hurry so as to get this in before the mail goes out. Write often for I am very anxious to hear from you. Write all the news. I will write again when I get a letter from you. With love and kisses to you all, I remain your affectionate husband, Silas W. Haven.

Moscow, Tennessee, July 27, 1863

Dear Jane,

I received a letter from you today, dated July 19, the only one I have got for two weeks from you. I was sorry that your eyes are sore and I am in hopes that that eye salve will cure it. I have not been very well for the last two weeks or so, but am getting so that I feel pretty well now and able to do my regular duty. I don't have much appetite, but that don't bother me, as I don't eat so often. The war news keeps coming in, cheering for the Union. Even if Lee's army gets back to Richmond, the fate of the Southern Confederacy appears to be sealed and hence will soon dawn upon us, and the vocation of those who are now battling for freedom will be gone. The way things now look, I think I shall be at home to spend Christmas with you, if not before. Things down here remain about the same. We are going to have some new guns (Enfield rifles) distributed to us sometime this week.[21] They were brought in on the cars Saturday. They will be some lighter and a great deal better than our old muskets, but our old muskets have been a benefit to us in some respects; if it had not been that we were armed with them, this regiment would probably have been in a number of battles, and instead of being here, we should long ago have been to Vicksburg, as far as I am concerned. I don't know as it makes any odds for I have faith to believe that I shall never be killed in battle but shall return home again. Well, I have just come back from helping move our new guns from the cars to the Q.M. There is five hundred guns and 50 boxes (one thousand cartridges in a box) of cartridges. I expect they will be distributed tomorrow. There has been some talk that a recruiting officer for the regular service (cavalry) was coming here to see how many he could get out of the 27th to enlist. If he does come it will play smash with the regiment, for over half of the effective men will enlist and have us to go somewhere to recruit. Our forces down here are not going to keep quiet because they have got the Mississippi River open, but are determined to fetch this war to a close if fighting will do it, and we believe that is the only way to close it. Well, I have just eat my supper consisting of warm biscuit and butter, cold, baked mutton, a baked apple, a piece of apple pie and coffee and now I will try and finish this, for I come on guard tomorrow. I hope you will raise some garden this year. The boys are just beginning to fetch in new corn and potatoes. Write about the children and have Ella and Emmett help you fill out your letters, and try and take good care of your eyes; that salve cured mine. Just rub some on the lids once or twice a day and wash them out with cold water. But goodbye for this time, love and kisses to you, from your affectionate husband, Silas W. Haven.

Moscow, Tennessee, July 30, 1863

Dear Jane,

I got a letter day before yesterday. It was the one that I had ought to have got a week ago. It had one in it that was written in March. They was very interesting to me; it pleased me to think that Kitty was bound to have one of my pictures. I believe I would let her keep one if she has got a good box to keep in it. I would send you another if I could get it taken. The war news keeps coming in good for the Union. Last night a dispatch came that Morgan was gobbled, which was just what we have been expecting, and soon I expect you will hear from Grant's army, for they are not idle.[22] We are quite anxious for the fall of Charleston, and it seems that when that falls that the secesh leaders would have to hunt their holes pretty soon or they would run the risk of getting a hempen cravat.[23] The talk is that the government is going to put the draft in force, and the rumor is that this regiment is going to Davenport, but I don't put any faith in such rumors. Everything is quiet down here. A lot of our boys went and ambushed a road for a lot of guerrillas last night, but did not see any. They went out a few days ago and got four into the trap, but they smell a large mice, and skedaddled. They fired on them, and the report is that the 50th Indiana boys found one dead and buried him. I don't know as it is so if it is. It is the first rebel blood the 27th has drawn. It is getting nearly dress parade and I expect I shall have to go on guard tomorrow, so I must finish this tonight. My health is keeps about the same. I don't have any appetite, but our boys go out foraging every day and bring in apples, corn, so I get a piece of pie and I guess I shall get along. With my respects to all and love and kisses to you and the children, I remain your affectionate husband, Silas W. Haven.

Moscow, Tennessee, August 4, 1863

Dear Jane,

When I came in from picket guard this morning, I found a letter from you, which I read with much pleasure. I was glad to hear that you were all well and enjoying yourselves. I found five two cent stamps, just the kind [I] have to use now to send off papers, and two pens and I thought I would try them, and I believe they write rather better than my fold pen on this paper. I guess that Ella won't. You must take good care of them and write how they are every time you write. I have just come in from shooting my gun, the first time I ever shot it. The guards have to shoot their guns every morning, but I have been on camp guard and did not load and got a good while I drew the load. I believe that I wrote that our regiment was going to stay here for the present, although we have rumors that it is going to Dubuque to help enforce the draft, but I guess that we shall stay here till the war is over. It would please the regiment to help enforce the draft if there was any resistance made to it. The Copperheads would not get much mercy if they hold back as the whole regiment is down on the captain. When I am well, it is no harder to go on picket guard than stay in camp. I think it would have been better for Fred and I if we had gone into the battery in the first place, and if I was well and there was any chance, I would go into it now, but as it is, I shall stay here as long probably as I stay in the service, and I think I can get along and do my duty if I can have a fair chance. I think that I could get into the Invalid Corps at any time and if our regiment is ordered on a march from here, I don't know but what I shall have to go any way.[24] If I should, I should probably be stationed at Memphis. I had rather stay with the regiment as I think that the war is about closed up, but I will write more on another sheet.

August 5th

There is a rumor that this division is going out further east to guard railroad.[25] Also, that all that are not able to march and carry their accoutrements are going to be put into the invalid corps. I amongst the rest, but it is only camp rumors, not to be depended on. Our boys go out most every day and get apples and corn. They go with a six mule team and about ten or fifteen with a team; they take their guns with them for the benefit of the guerrillas if they see them. I don't go out as I don't care about being out in the hot sun any more than I can help. Well, I must try to get this side covered as it is most time for the cars to come in and I want to send this out today. I am in hopes that I shall get a letter from someone; if I do, I will let you know. I shall try to send you a paper today or tomorrow, although I don't know as they are much account, for I expect you get all the news before you get them. I wish you would write the date of the letter you get so that I can tell how long it takes for them to go from here to you. Write how the church gets along, whether they have any talk of settling a minister there or not. I think that your Union leagues are good things up there, but the Union Leagues that I belong to are the most effective down in this section, and some of them might do some good up there, but with love and kisses to you all.[26] I subscribe myself your affectionate husband, Silas W. Haven.

I got a letter from Jake. I will send it in my next, but I must hurry to get this to the office. If you have money enough to send me a box of pills, you may send them as I have only half a box left, although I have a lot lent out, but I don't want to get out if I can help it.[27]

Millville, August 6, 1863[28]

Dear Silas,

I have kept you looking a great while for this, but I have not forgotten you. Your father is hauling logs. I am cowboy, mill maid, chamber maid, wash woman and kitchen maid. In fact, you may say I am chief cook and bottle washer; at least I have handled a good many bottles and steeped lots of herbs for two weeks past. But God has been merciful to me. He has granted me good health and caused me to feel cheerful since the mercies of God endureth forever. Well, Silas, we have met the Copperheads in Millville and beat them a week ago last Sunday. The Methodist minister was met at the church door and requested to preach or he could not enter the church. We told them he should preach as he pleased and that too in the house, and pushed himself through the crowd and did preach a telling sermon. Last Sunday, the Presbyterian minister preached there and they tried to rout him but failed, so now we know the Copperhead in this township and outsiders will not come to intrude. It takes a Copperhead to threaten a good Union man [who] can look them out of countenance. I suppose you have heard of the great riot in New York. A few more such will save our army in the field many battles. It works wonders for the Union cause. The draft will be carried out, riot or no riot. I am looking for something to turn up now every day that will before the shooting of the days of our tribulation, perhaps as the first gun was fired in South Carolina, so will be the last, but I must hasten for I want to send this off and promise you to write more next time. I don't think of anything more now. You must be as careful of your health as you can. By all accounts the whole army is in motion and something will be done, but we fear the hot weather will tell hard on our poor soldiers. May Almighty God protect them, and may the day soon come when we will have wars no more forever. I hope you will excuse this haste. Your father is about ready to start so I have you to correct all mistakes and write soon. I will send you a paper soon. I got a Memphis, I suppose from you. May the best of heaven's blessings rest on you is the earnest prayer and desire of your mother. C. Haven[29]

I drew a shirt day before yesterday. It was a first-rate one if I had thought they had been so good.

Moscow, Tennessee, August 10, 1863[30]

Dear Jane,

I got a letter from you today containing ten postage stamps and I thought I would commence tonight. My health keeps about the same, neither sick nor well. It just come to my name yesterday and it was the first time I had been off duty for three days in succession since I commenced doing duty, unless I was excused off for sickness, but last night there was ten men detailed to go out on a scout and so I went and came in this morning, so I shall not have to go on guard for three days. It seems that our officers got word that there was a lot of guerrillas was going to cross Wolf River, about five miles below here, and about 90 out of the regiment went to catch them. We started after dark and went on the railroad track, and then struck off for the ford through the woods. It was very dark and the road was nothing more than a path, and it bothered us some time to get there. Although they have ambushed that place four or five times, they got lost two or three times and had to stop and hunt for the road. We got there and got fixed in ambush and waited about an hour, and then we heard them on the other side of the river and one came across and they were preparing to swim their horses. When our men made a little noise, one (a Dutch man, I believe) dropt his gun and then they smelt a large mice and skedaddled. We thought we had them once and made ready to pay them our compliments, but it proved a false alarm. I suppose you would like to know how I felt waiting for an enemy. Well, I felt just as cool as I do on dress parade. I thought it was rather too bad to shoot at men when they was not thinking of any danger, but I thought they would be somewhat surprised. I think that if our officers had not sent only twenty men, they would have made a pretty good herd of horses and probably some prisoners. I stood the journey pretty well. I only slept about an hour and that was on the soft ground with my cartridge box for a pillow. I feel some lame today, but guess it will work off by morning. It is pretty hot, but the nights are some cool. I got along first rate. I am glad that Ella and Emmett (don't Kitty have a share) have bought some birds. I expect they will be a great deal of trouble, but they will pay for themselves, even if they don't raise any birds to sell. I forgot to say that I got some papers today. I thank them very much, although I had read the *Harper's Weekly.* I don't very often see a Leslie here.[31]

August 11

I suppose you would like to know what kind of clothing I wear [in] this hot weather. Well, my pants and my shirt are woolen, a black wool hat and a when I go on dress parade, I wear a blouse (knit) the rest of the time, except when I am on guard at night. I go in my shirtsleeves. It seems rather hard that you have to cut your own wood, and I am afraid that if you stay there alone this winter that you will suffer with the cold. The prospects of the war are pretty favorable for it now. I think that there will not be much more fighting done, especially down this way. Charleston and Mobile have got to fall and then if the Rebs don't knock under, we will get them all into Richmond and starve them to terms of unconditional surrender. I don't get any news from any of our folks yet, but I am in hopes that I shall today. With love and kisses to you, Ella, Emmett and Kitty, I subscribe myself your affectionate husband, Silas W. Haven.

Moscow, Tennessee, August 18, 1863

Dear Jane,

I received a letter from you yesterday and was very glad to hear from you. I got one from mother, which I will send to you in this as I shall not have time to write a very long letter before this goes out. I sent you a paper with some flower seeds in it. I sent you a flower a short time ago and I put another in it with the seeds, also a rose. It is a vine some, like a morning glory. I don't know as the seeds will grow and I am going to try to get some more like it. I will try and get you all the different seeds I can, but flowers are pretty scarce about here. There is no news here at present. Some of the regiment go out foraging every day. Some of our company went out yesterday and got a lot of peaches and apples. I wish I could send you some. The guerrillas are pretty quiet around here. I believe that a lot from the regiment are going out today on a scout to try to hunt up some. I don't think I shall go as it is too hot to go rambling around the country on bootlegs errands. Three guerrillas fired on the Negro pickets up to La Grange a few days ago after firing two or three rounds a piece. The darkies threw down their guns and run, but they run right toward the guerrillas and fairly tired out their horses and took all three prisoners. One of them (the guerrillas) was wounded. The folks up north need not say that Negroes won't fight, for they will and they make first-rate soldiers. But I must hurry. I will send you another paper and some for the children, and will write again if I can find anything to write about. You must favor your eyes as much as you can and take good care of your health. With love and kisses to you all, I will close. From your affectionate husband, Silas W. Haven.

In camp at Memphis, August 22, 1863

Dear Jane,

You will probably be surprised to see where this is dated. Last Tuesday night, the order was read on dress parade for us to be ready at an hour's notice to leave and Wednesday (I was on guard, but I had my things packed, ready to start) the order came for us to be ready to start on a march at 2 o'clock in the morning.[32] I was not relieved till three o'clock so I did not have time to pack up anything to send home and I started with them all, but I could not stand it to carry them and so I throwed away my overcoat, a pair of drawers and a shirt and some other things. The drawers and shirt was not of much consequences. I stood the march pretty well as after we had gone four or five miles, I got my knapsack on the wagon. We marched 15 miles a day the first two days and today we have marched ten or twelve. We are about three miles north of Memphis and I don't know whether Fred is in town or not as I heard that he was going home on a furlough this week. If he is here, I shall try to see him and send home my coat and blanket, as I don't want to carry but very little with me on a march. We saw some nice country that we passed through, but it looks somewhat desolate, especially in some places. I suppose you are wondering where we are going, that is what we all are doing. The whole brigade is here. It consists of the 62nd Illinois, 50 Indiana, 27 Iowa, 49 Illinois and an Illinois battery (6th, I believe). We got here about 9 o'clock and the talk is that [we] are going to be paid today, but I hardly think that our pay rolls will be ready or that they will get to us even if they were, but we shall get it as soon as they can get it ready and then we shall start off. I suppose you would like to know how I stand marching in hot weather. Well, I stand it better than I expected and I guess that it will be better for me than laying in camp as it give me an appetite, and we don't march more than fifteen or twenty miles a day. The first day I come pretty near giving out three or four times, but the doctor came around and give me some whiskey with some kind of medicine in it and it helped me. There was quite a number gave out and had to be sent on the cars. The second day our Lieutenant bought a canteen of whiskey and gave some to the men, and I guess that our company came in to camp in the best condition of any in the regiment.[33] I just saw one of the boys that has been with Fred in the hospital and he says Fred is expecting his furlough every day. I am going to try to see him today if I can. There is so much noise I can't hardly think nor concentrate my thoughts to write.

August 23

I got a chance to see Fred a little while last night and I left my blanket, dress coat, mittens and a few trinkets with him. He will probably get his furlough in a few days and fetch them home. There is three little hymn books; give one to each of the children. Save my account book as I have kept a journal of every Sunday since I left Dubuque and a daily account of the chapters I have read and other things that I wanted to keep track of. I also sent my portfolio home as it would get jammed in my knapsack. You must not worry about me if you don't get letters regular as I don't expect that we can get a chance to send them very often. When you get your money, you had better send for a paper (*Evening Post* or any that you like better) so that you can have something to read. With love and kisses to you all, I will close. From your affectionate husband, Silas W. Haven. Our regiment is in the 3rd brigade, 3rd division, the 16th army corps.

On Board Boat *Grisbeck,* August 24, 1863

I send this by the chaplain to Dubuque.

Dear Jane,

I have only got time to write a line to inform you that I am well and we got our pay today on board of the boat, and when I went to express it, they said it was too late and as the chaplain is going to Dubuque, I guess it will go safe and I will send it by letter, but it is getting dark and we are most to Helena. I will close this and try to send you a letter from Helena. I will send you all the money I can share, which will be 35 or 38 dollars. With love and kisses to you all, I will close. Write often. From your affectionate husband, Silas W. Haven.[34]

A messenger has just come in and says that Old Price has left Little Rock, and there is some doubt about our leaving here very soon, but still we may as all things are very uncertain in war, and it is all guess work with the privates where they are going, even after they get started on a march.[35] The officers know how to keep secrets pretty well. SWH

CHAPTER 4

# The Arkansas Expedition

## *August–December, 1863*

In the fall of 1863, the 27th Iowa traveled throughout Arkansas on an expedition to secure portions of the state firmly into Union hands. After Gen. Steele captured Little Rock, Arkansas, in September, the regiment remained in the city on guard duty for a few weeks. The regiment returned to Memphis at the end of the year for an additional round of guard duty in the region. Haven offered extensive military details on the campaign throughout the remainder of his letters in 1863. The autumn of 1863 saw quite a bit of action in the western theater, as Confederate forces won a convincing victory at Chickamauga, in northern Georgia, only to be later ejected from Chattanooga, Tennessee, by the end of November. The fall of Chattanooga opened the door for Union commander Gen. William T. Sherman to march toward Atlanta the following spring.

—

Helena, Arkansas, August 26, 1863

Dear Jane,

I improve this opportunity of writing a few lines to you. We got here night before last, but did not leave the boat till yesterday morning. We had a pretty good time coming down, but at night the wind blew up cold and we were quite cold sleeping. There were two regiments on our boat, which made it pretty crowded. Our boat run against the gunboat as we were coming into the harbor and broke her guards some, but no other damage done. I don't know how long we shall stay here, but not long. There was some talk that we were going to stay here, but we had orders to start this morning, but the boat that the 49th IL was on was run into night before last and sunk. Five men jumped overboard and was drowned. The regiment lost all their mules, guns, ammunition and camp baggage. The ammunition of the battery was also on board and lost, so I expect that we shall have to stay a few days till they can get ready to go along. I expect that we shall go to Little Rock to guard a provision train through, and then we may possibly come back here and stay. The troops are about all gone from here. I saw Fred the day we started, but was in such a hurry that I could not think of anything to say to him to have him tell you. They paid three companies of our regiment Sunday and then was going to pay the rest in the morning, but at twelve o'clock we was ordered to get ready to go on board the boat (we did not leave camp till sunrise) and I give up hopes of getting any pay, but they paid us after we got started late in the afternoon, and about dark I went to have my money expressed, but was too late so I wrote a little with a pencil and put $38.00 dollars in a letter and gave it to the Chaplain and he will get it mailed at Dubuque, so I guess it will go safe. I think that I shall have my likeness taken if I can get a chance today and send [it] to you. If you get yours taken, run the risk and send it to me. My health is pretty good. I think it will be a benefit for me to go on a march. With love and kisses to you, Ella, Emmett and Kitty, I close for this time from your affectionate husband, Silas W. Haven.

Helena, Arkansas, August 27, 1863

Dear Jane,

As we are yet in camp I thought I would write you a few lines to let you know how I get along. I did not get a chance to get my picture taken yesterday, and I don't know as I shall get a chance before we leave here. We changed our camp yesterday, marched about two miles south west of town. I suppose it was done to keep the boys from running to town at nine o'clock today. We had orders to be ready to move immediately and after we got packed up, the Colonel said we should not move today. We expect to move in the morning, but it is uncertain. We are camped in a pretty place in front of a large house. I drove two stakes and put a pole on them and set up shakes around, so I have quite a shelter. The 49th IL came in today. They did not lose any men but all their wagons, part of their mules, some guns and a lot of baggage. There are some Negro troops here; a regiment came in day before yesterday, which made a pretty good appearance. I am sorry that you have so much trouble with your garden. I should think that Mitchell would know enough to know that you were not obliged to fence against unruly cattle, nor did I think that he was of that kind of persons that would not take care of his cattle if they were troubling his neighbors, especially if that neighbor was a soldier's wife. If I was at home, he would not want to talk insulting to me more then and he would take care of his cattle too or I would for him. I expect that Fred will be at home before you get this and maybe he may say a few words to him: that a man that has unruly cattle and will not yard them nights is no man at all. Tell Ella I am glad she has got her birds, and I hope she will take good care of them till I come home, and I will try to make her a cage. I hope that in your next I shall get a letter from Emmett. Tell Kitty that I would like to come and see the pigs and birds, and I am glad she is learning to spell. I want to see you all very much and hope I shall soon. With love and kisses to you all, I will close for this time. From your affectionate husband, Silas W. Haven.

Clarendon, Arkansas, August 30, 1863[1]

Dear Jane,

I have just got my bedroom built and I thought I would commence a letter to you to let you know how I get along, but I don't know when I shall get a chance to send it to you. We left Helena at 3 o'clock on the morning of the 28 and marched 13 miles. The first eight in the rain and I carried my knapsack, and then put it on the wagon and I have not had to carry it since we got into camp, about three in the afternoon. We started the 29th, about 4 o'clock in the morning. Our regiment was in the rear and Company G was rear guard. The bushwhackers followed us all day just before we stopped for dinner. We halted a spell and three came up pretty close, and our Lieutenant sent 5 or 6 men to give them our compliments, but the bugle sounded for a march so they came into the road too quick, and the rebs saw them and began to move off, but they went to cross the road and our boys fired on them. They made their horses travel some, you had better believe. When we slept at noon, they came up on us before they were aware of it. They whirled their horses just in time to save their bacon as three of us would have fired in five seconds more if one of our men had not got in the way. I should have fired as it was half of the company went out to skirmish with them and was shot at twice and shot at them three or four times, but without effect. The rebs were very poor marksmen as they were in the woods and our men were in the road not more than fifteen rods off. I don't know but what it was wicked, but I felt just as if I wanted to shoot at them myself, and was in hopes that the Lieutenant would detail me as one of the skirmishers, but would not volunteer because I had told you I would not go into any danger of my own accord. I felt just as safe as I have at anytime. We marched 23 miles and did not get into camp till nearly 9 o'clock. We started at six o'clock this morning and got here about one without any incident worthy of note, except some of the men set a cotton gin afire. It is getting so dark. I shall have to put this off till next time. With love and kisses to you and the children, I will close for this time. From your affectionate husband, Silas W. Haven.

Brownsville, Arkansas, September 4, 1863

Dear Jane,

I seat myself under a black walnut tree, which has been my sleeping place for two nights back, to write you a few lines to let you know how I get along. We crossed White River the 31st and marched twenty-three miles, all but seven on prairie and a very pretty prairie too, with timber in sight all the time, but the houses were not close together and water was very scarce. We suffered some. I get along pretty well, but got pretty dry the last two miles before I came to water. We camped at night near some pond holes, where we got plenty of water and killed some beef. We started at 4 o'clock the second of September and came to this place. We get along very well before dinner for water and marched eleven miles in the afternoon. It was very hot and we marched very slow, but quite a number gave out. I got along very well till we just before we stopped and when we stopped, I found that I was pretty well bushed out. We stopped in the woods close to the village to rest and then we came two miles west to camp. We marched 20 miles, which made pretty tall marching for a brigade yesterday. I came back to camp and found Jake and John Mahoney waiting to see me. So I went down to their camp and stayed two or three hours and had quite a visit with them all. The boys all looked natural and hearty, only Jake has the diarrhea some. I was down there again today and stayed about four hours. The boys are all pretty lively as usual. Jake showed me his last letters that he got from Rockford, and among the rest one from Ella, which I read with much pleasure. Jake was pleased to get a letter from her and thought it was a very good one with lots of news in it. Jake showed me the guns that was in the Pea Ridge fight.[2] One had the mark where a ball hit it on the muzzle and dented it. We are about twenty-five miles from Little Rock, and we may possibly have a little brush with the rebs before we get there, but if the report is true that has just come in, we probably will not have anything to do, only to take charge of the deserters that came in and guard prisoners. Two of our company went out yesterday and brought in the hind quarters of a hog that was pretty fat, and the whole company had all that they wanted to eat, and this morning a lot went out and killed one that would weigh 150 pounds. So you see, we don't suffer for something to eat if we can find it. I want to see you very much. I think about your days and dream of you nights. I hope the time will soon come when I shall. I hope that the war is about closed up, so that we all can return home again. I hope that Fred will get his discharge so as to be at home, for I think that then you will get along better, not that I expect that he will do much, but he will see that things are done. My prayers to God are for your welfare. With love and kisses to you all, I remain your affectionate husband, Silas W. Haven.

Brownsville, Arkansas, September 6, 1863

Dear Daughter Ella,

I thought as I had a little time today I would commence a letter to you, although I have no news to write and I don't know when I can send it away. I have not had any letters since I left Helena, but am in hopes to get one tonight by the supply train, which is coming through from DeVall's Bluff. I was down to the battery yesterday and saw Jake and the rest of the boys. They were all well, only Jake and Charles Knapp, they are having the dysentery some.[3] I saw Jake this morning. The whole army started for Little Rock and when the battery was going by, Jake stopped a few minutes. We started with the rest, but after marching about three miles (one mile west of town), our brigade camped. Why we did not go on I don't know, but expect that we are kind of a reserve force and will have to guard the supply train through the rest of the army. I think very likely that we shall start tomorrow. The water that we get is pretty poor and a good ways off, but the hogs and cattle hold out pretty well and we live on fresh meat the most of the time. The boys take them whenever they want them. I did think that the fleas and lice (grey backs) were bad enough, but the jiggers are worse than both put together. They are a small insect about as big as the head of a pin and red. When they bite it, itches and swells up a large blotch. They eat into the flesh, just like a wood tick. They keep me scratching nearly all the time. I saw Gleason and Tim Folger today. Gleason was getting better and Tim had a shake of the ague today.[4]

September 7

I did not have a chance to occupy my nice sleeping place last night as I had to go on patrol guard to guard the supply train, but I guess I shall have a chance tonight as I don't see any signs of moving today, but still we may. I only had to be up till ten o'clock. You must write often, write how your birds get along and how you get along. What books you have studied and about the neighbors and everything that will interest me that you can think of. Write whether you have a Sabbath school and all about the meetings. I have not been to a meeting since we left Moscow. Our chaplain has gone home on furlough. I expect you are getting to be quite a young lady so that you help your mother a great deal. You must try to serve your Heavenly father and always try to do that that is pleasing in his sight. With love and kisses to you, I bid you a goodbye for this time. From your father, Silas W. Haven[5]

In camp at Brownsville, Arkansas, September 7, 1863

Dear Jane,

As I have a little time and have got the children's letter finished, I thought I would try to send them off from this place so I will write you a few lines, although I can't think of any news to write, and it is pretty hard writing on a march as there is a great deal of noise—a continual humming, which distracts one's mind so that it is hard to think. The rest of the army went forward yesterday and I think that by tomorrow, we shall start. The general opinion is that we won't fight. There was a brigade of infantry went out last Thursday on a reconnaissance and the cavalry went within six miles of Little Rock, but saw nary a reb. We are drawing clothing today. I have drawed a pair of sock and am going to have a woolen blanket as I find a rubber blanket is not of much account to sleep under as it gathers all the steam from the boys and gets quite wet before morning.[6] The regiment postmaster says that no mail came through on this train for our brigade, which is quite a disappointment for us. The climate agrees with me first rate down here, but I don't like the insects and vermin that breeds here, such as body lice, flees, jiggers and flies by swarms and other things too numerous to mention. I have not seen but a few snakes, but any quantity of lizards. The water is rather bad on the whole. I don't think that I want to live down here, especially among the Negroes. The women through here are bitterer secesh than the men. I want to see you very bad. I think about you all the time and very often dream of you nights. It seems sometimes that I cannot stand it to not see you, but God gives me strength to go forward in the path of duty that I believe that he has marked out for me, and I feel that he has protected me and has given me patience to bear all trial without repining, and I feel that I shall live to return home to you again soon. Let us put our trust in him without doubting and look to him for help in times of need, and try to so live that when I am permitted to return to you, we can enjoy the smiles of divine providence and be better prepared to enjoy life here on earth that is accorded to those that prove faithful in heaven. With love and kisses to you all, I close by subscribing myself your affectionate husband, Silas W. Haven.

Millville, September 7, 1863[7]

Dear Silas,

I take my pen to answer your letter of August 18, which we received some two weeks since was, I think, but five days coming from Memphis. I thought I had answered it, but you say I have not, so now here it is whether or not I have had considerable on my hands for a month past visiting the sick and have been sick myself. Just getting able to sit up a little. Have been sick going on two weeks.

The rest of our family and friends are well. Hope this may find you the same. It is very sickly yet, but the disease is not so obstinate as at first. Thought it held me pretty hard for four days and reduced my flesh and strength. But I think I will get along now. We have good news on news every day from the army. The whole rate massacre at Lawrence, Kansas, by Quantrill's band of guerrillas is awful to think of.[8] Copperheads say that will be the warfare if the Union army is successful. Well, I don't know but it will be so. If it comes to that in Iowa, there will be a slaughter of snakes. Guerrillas fight without government organization and ought to be executed without trial. The only way to stop warfare is to shoot them once wherever found. The men mean enough here to shoot his neighbor for if they thought they would not be found out. It is hard saying, but it is even so. The Northern Copperheads are far beneath the Southern traitors. Our election is to come off now soon and we have two army officers racing for governor. Stone rides the Union horse and Tuttle the Democrat with a copper snake's tail.[9] Tuttle must want office awful bad to bow and creep and beg of the crawling reptiles for votes. My opinion is Tuttle, if he gets the election, will turn out a real Copperhead, so I hope the soldiers will not help in the deception. A man ought not to be trusted that will lead a Copperhead ticket. I tell you the last struggle is on the party, and as the soldiers are aware that the rebels have received them with Union banners and soldier's uniform. I hope they will because of this last trap that is set for them in the state of Iowa and not have the bloody scenes enacted here as were in New York City. We have heard of the fall of Fort Sumter and we anticipate the fall of Charleston now soon. Then we may anticipate further that rebellion has got a mortal stab. You know how I feel on the war question. But as a kind providence has favored our army thus far, we will trust him to the end. For I seriously believe God has had the ordering of all things pertaining to this war. So also I believe we shall, through him, be victorious in the end and our nation become as in times past the admiration of all nations of the world. I have not said anything about our domestic affairs and I don't now as there is anything that would interest you. Everything goes on as usual. We have a good crop of corn and potatoes. Your father hauls logs for a lively hood. I don't know what he would do if he could not find a log to move. I think he would go to war. Please tell Dan Walker that Sam Smith's youngest child was buried yesterday.[10] I expect he hears from home of the other family deaths, and give my respects to all that may inquire for me. For sure I have a peculiar regard for the soldiers, especially those from this vicinity. I don't know of anything more to write. I hope you will be careful of your health, and may Almighty God guide and protect you in all things both temporal and spiritual as the great desire of your mother, C. Haven.

Little Rock, Arkansas, September 12, 1863

Dear Jane,

I once more take my pen to let you know how we get along. We left Brownsville the 8th and marched twelve miles. The next day we marched two miles into camp. The 10th we started for this place with two days' rations in our haversacks with the expectation of having a little fight. After marching seven miles, part of the force crossed the river on the pontoon bridge and our Brigade came up the east side of the river. We had not marched before the Rebs opened fire on the force the other side of the river, but we had to leave pretty sudden and after going about a half a mile, they undertook to form a line in an open field opposite to us and the battery in our brigade opened fire, and you would have laughed to have heard the boys laugh and halloo as the rebs scattered and skedaddled when our shells burst among them. They skirmished all the way to Little Rock.[11] We could see them occasionally on the run and see the shells burst, but could take no part in it. They had got all prepared to fight us on this side, but our General Steele was rather too much for them and when he crossed the river, he outflanked them so that Price thought he might as well run when he had a chance. Our men put the pontoon bridge across in the night and the rebs planted some cannon to rake it, but the river is low and the cavalry forded and got on to them before they were aware of it. It was a pretty dear day for Price. I don't know yet how many he had killed and wounded, but it is said that there is 700 killed; the wounded they carried away. It is said we lost thirty or forty killed and wounded, but nothing definite yet.[12] We have taken quite a lot of prisoners and more coming in all the time and giving themselves up. They burnt five boats, a gunboat that was plated with railroad iron was laying up high and dry; [it] has not got through burning, yet they also burnt some cars (eight, I believe) and a few buildings on this side of the river, but they had to leave too quick to destroy much. Our boys was very much disappointed because they could not have a hand in, but we were rather too far off (about a mile and a half with a river between). Also the Dubuque battery thought it was rather too bad that they could not burn any powder they were behind us, but I did not know it till night. I went to the river to wash and fill my canteen and came across John Mahoney, so I went to their camp and took supper with them.[13] The cavalry chased the rebs 8 or ten miles that night and are still after them. They will be very apt to disperse Price's force. The report came in yesterday that Gen. Blunt had taken Fort Smith and was heading Price off.[14] I don't know how long we will stay here, but I expect that we shall go to a different camping place today. It may be that we shall be left to guard this place, and we may go from here to Arkadelphia about sixty miles from here. It is my impression [that] if the cavalry and Blunt succeeded in dispersing Price's force (they have burnt and taken some of his wagon train already), that when we leave this place, we shall take the back track to the Mississippi River. The fighting is, [I] think, all done in the southwest, at least it looks very much like it now. I want to see you all very bad and it looks more every day that I should soon. You must write often so that I can get a letter whenever a train comes through. With love and kisses to you all, I will close for this time. From your affectionate husband, Silas W. Haven.

Little Rock, September 15, 1863

Dear Jane,

I received a letter from you Sunday and was very glad to hear from you. I got a letter from Julia, also the box of pills you sent. I wrote you all the news about our march here and as everything is quiet, I have no war news to tell at present. Our loss in the skirmish was forty killed and wounded. I did intend to write yesterday, but a lot of the boys got outside of my tent night before last gambling and with the noise they made, kept me awake till about one o'clock. I give them to understand that it was the last time that they would keep me awake. We also moved our camp about a mile up the river and have got a very nice place to camp on the bank. I don't know how long we shall stay here. I expect that we are waiting for orders from Grant. My health is good at present and I have a good appetite. We are on half rations, but we have plenty to eat as the boys fetch in a part of a beef about every day. The hard eat to get along without is our sugar and coffee. I am going to buy me some tea, so I guess I shall get along, especially if we have beef soup three times a day, as we have for a spell back. I got a pumpkin today and am stewing it. The butternuts keep coming in all the time, glad enough to give themselves up. I have not been to town yet, but have the promise of going tomorrow, and I will try to find out something interesting to write about that the rebs sent after corn down the river, returned yesterday and got up to our batteries before they found out that Little Rock was in our possession so they had to surrender. The Dubuque battery has gone across the river today so I expect that I can see the boys very often. I saw them day before yesterday. They were all well, except Charles Knapp.[15] He had a little fever, but nothing serious.

On picket, Little Rock, Arkansas, September 20, 1863

Dear Jane,

As I am hopes that I can send this off tomorrow, I will try to finish this so as to have it ready. Our captain got back Friday and as usual did not see any of the boys that was left at Memphis, but two came through with the supply train yesterday and said that Fred had got his furlough, so I suppose that he is at home by this time and he will tell you all the news.[16] I am well and have a first-rate appetite, can eat about as much beef soup, beef steak, sweet potatoes, hard tack as any one. We don't have much to do. This is the first time that I have been on guard since I got here and have only been on fatigue duty twice, two hours each time. I expect that we shall have brigade drill occasionally. We had one last week. There was some rumors that we should go to the Gulf, but as Grant has transferred the 14th Army corps to the gulf and our division commander (Gen. Kimball) is here and they have arranged the forces, I think that the whole army will stay here to guard this place and the railroad till the state has time to come back into the Union.[17] I think that probably that we shall stay in this state for some time. There appears to be more Union sentiment here than there was in Tennessee. The citizens appear to be glad to see the old flag and surprised at the treatment that they get at our hands. A man (citizen) went to an old log hut close to where we are camped and dug up ten thousand dollars in hard money that he had buried to keep away from the secesh. We are in the first Division, first brigade, and 4th Regiment in the brigade.[18] Some of the boys have just brought word that part of the army is under marching orders with ten days' ration, probably to go to Arkadelphia to occupy it. If so, our brigade are in for a "heap of rest" at this place. This is a good place to stay and as healthy as any we have been in and fewer guerrillas about, so I guess that we can stand it as our boys say we are good for tall marching and can stand a heap of rest. The 50th Indiana and 62nd Illinois are building log huts for winter quarters, and I expect that we shall soon. We are in for stopping here for quite a spell.

September 21

I heard church bells yesterday the first time for a long while, and it seemed that I was near civilization. With love and kisses to you all, I close for this time. From your affectionate husband, Silas W. Haven.

Little Rock, September 26, 1863[19]

Dear Jane,

I once more take my pen to write you a few lines to let you know that I am well and getting along first rate, and enjoying myself as well as I ever expect to while absent from you and the children. We have been pretty busy for a few days back building barracks to stay in. I am on guard today or I should not have got time to write. I was out six miles northeast of here to the rebel fortifications to get some lumber. They built fortifications at every spot where they thought we would come in, but we did not care about giving them the advantage of breastworks and fallen timber when we could get some other way. The country is quite hilly and rocky after getting out two miles, and it is not but a little ways out to the mountains and timbered all the way. Our brigade are all building winter quarters and we shall probably stay here till spring, I think. There is more real Union feeling here than at any other place I have been in the South. The soldiers of Price's army are coming in every day and some are not satisfied to go home and stay, but want to have a hand in putting down the rebellion, so they enlist in our army. We have a number in our regiment. The most we stand guard for is to keep the boys from roaming about the country and pillaging. Our brigade was searched yesterday to found out some stolen good money. There was not anything found in our regiment except a few blankets in our company. The orders now are very strict and I guess that we will have no more trouble. It seems that the rebs are coming to grief all around. You ought to have heard the cheers that we give. It is the general impression of both officers and men that the war will close before spring. Secesh is completely played out in this state, and I think that before the first of January that there will be no need of any troops on the west side of Mississippi. This state will be back in the Union as soon as it can get back. There is a number of thinks that I think of writing to you, but when I begin to write, I can't think of them. I saw a St. Charles paper the other day that had the delinquent tax advertised and lots four, five, six, seven, eight, twelve and ten of block twenty-six were delinquent. If they are sold, get someone to bid them of for you in your name if you can. I think that if we could get them or three (six, seven, eight the ones that we live on), they would make as pretty a place as there is in Rockford. It is about time for me to go on guard, so I shall have to let this rest a day or two.

September 29

I did not get to send this off yesterday so I have a little time. I will try to write some more. We have got our barracks nearly finished. We built a log house and covered with shakes and took our lumber to fix our bunks. My bunk is a top one in the end and I have lots of room. We are going to draw some more clothing in a few days. I am going to get a blanket, dress coat, shirt, pair of drawers, pair of socks and a haversack. We draw for three months. I don't think that I shall ever throw away any more clothes; if they can't carry them, I will stay and guard them. Everything is quiet here, no guerrillas to keep us busy, but we have plenty of grumblers and they keep rumors of moving flying through camp pretty much all the time. I think if we move from here before spring, we shall go back to Tennessee, but I guess that we shall stop here a spell. I want to see you all very much. I think of you all the time and try to live in such a manner that when I do come home, I shall be as free from vice as I was when I left. Tell Ella and Emmett to write and Kitty must tell you something to write for her. Goodbye for this time. From your affectionate husband, Silas W. Haven.

Little Rock, Arkansas, October 4, 1863

Dear Jane,

I was very glad to hear from you that you were well and getting along as well as you are. I was afraid that you would be bothered to get your hay as it was so scarce. You must try to get your wood so as not to freeze and get somebody to chop it for [you]. I think that it is rather too hard to work for you to chop your own wood and do your other work. I was in hopes that Fred would get his discharge so as to be at home this winter. I think that if he only goes to Keokuk or Davenport, . . . he will get it at Memphis, as some have got it there. Our company has got a first-rate oven and place to cook, all in one. We had roast beef, warm biscuits and cake for dinner. So, you see, we live well. We have coffee three times a day and I drink not much less than a quart. They don't allow the boys to go out and forage on their own hook any more, but furnish them full rations. The boys do get some meat occasionally in spite of the officers. Two of our company and the 1st Lieutenant got here last night. One, Joe Rich, went home on a sick furlough from Moscow and got it extended 30 days when he started from home.[20] He could hardly set up. He come back as fat as a pig and as tough as a pine knot. The health of the company is good. We have only two on the sick list. I was on guard last Wednesday and expected to be on tomorrow, but guess I shall be one to go out foraging picking corn. I will bid you goodbye for this time. From your affectionate husband, Silas W. Haven.

Little Rock, Arkansas, October 9, 1863

Dear Jane,

I received a letter from you last Monday. I had been out foraging that day. I had to go about fifteen miles from here down the river. We had a pretty good time. We went after hay. The team that I went with got loaded first and come back about half a mile opposite a potato patch, and we all got a few potatoes. I got my haversack and haversack pocket full for my share. Some of the boys got hogs, but I did not know in time that the officer with us would let us fetch them in till it was too late. The plantations are mostly put into corn and our boys are gathering from those plantations that are deserted or the owners are in the secesh army. They are getting forage for three months, so we shall probably stay that length of time.

October 10

I will try to write a little more, although I expect it will be hard work. Some of the boys are reading, some talking, and some playing cards and they make a considerable noise. I was in hopes that you would get letters as often as once a week, but I guess that the trains did not match with the boat. You need not be afraid that bushwhackers will get hold of me as there is none around here. There is too many loyal citizens about here for them to flourish, and we have so many cavalry scouting the country. They might possibly get caught and some of our men don't believe in fetching in guerrillas, so they keep shady. The health of our army is good. Some of the boys have the Arkansas quick step, but it don't amount to much.[21]

Little Rock, Arkansas, October 15, 1863

Dear Jane,

I thought that I would write you a few lines to let you know how I get along. My health is very good with the exception of a little cold. We had an election day before yesterday and got two months' pay. Our regiment went 371 for Stone and 78 for Tuttle. I was over to the battery yesterday. They had 74 for Stone and 27 for Tuttle.[22] So you see that we have a few Copperheads in the army. I have not had any mail this week, and as there is no news, time hangs rather heavy. I am in hopes that we shall get our mail oftener than once a week. I bought a Little Rock paper, which I will send to you; also I will send you some locust seed and three Muscatine seed and more if I can get them. We don't draw our clothing yet, but the weather is quite pleasant so we don't mind it much, only nights. I get pretty cold before morning. I was on guard Monday and expect to be on again tomorrow or next day. The 27th had to stand all the guard one day, which makes my turn comes quicker. We don't have much to do, not near as much as we had at Moscow. The troops over the river are preparing to build a barracks. I don't much think that we shall move from here this winter unless we go down to Washington in the southwestern part of this state to drive the rebs from here. It looks now as if we let Holmes alone a short time, his troops would all desert as they are quite dissatisfied with Holmes on account of the Helena battle, and he has just superseded Price.[23] They are getting up some regiments of Arkansas troops. Will probably have one or two regiments in the field in the course of two weeks. They will be a great help to us as they know the country and know who are Union men. Col. True has gone away and our colonel is commander of the brigade. There is none of the boys like Colonel True and we hope he will get a place in a Negro brigade.[24] Everybody likes our colonel. The other day when I was on guard, a deer ran through camp. A lot of the officers followed him and killed him a short distance from the reserve where I was on. I shall send you ten dollars in this. I bought some postage stamps and I guess I can get them now when I want, so you need not send any unless you send a few two-cent ones. Write how your money holds out and all the news about the Rockford folks. With love and kisses to you all, I close for this time. From your affectionate husband, Silas W. Haven.

Little Rock, October 23, 1863

Dear Jane,

I guess tonight I told the boys that they must dry up their noise after taps for I would take measure to have it dried up. They don't like it much, and I expect they will try it. If they do, they will find that I am a man of my word, for I don't intend that three or four shall make a noise to keep us awake. If our own officers won't stop it, the colonel will and it might not be very pleasant for a private to report them to the colonel, which we shall do if they don't. One of our men (Charles Wood) was arrested for threats made. One of our men (B. Parker) joined the company today and the captain says that Mahoney is ordered to the regiment to do duty.[25] Write all about your money matters. I sent you ten dollars last week and should have written before, but have waited for a mail and when it did come in, I did not have time before the boat would leave the bluff. I will send you ten more in this and I expect that we shall get our pay the forepart of November for two months. I was quite pleased to get another letter from Ella and hope she will write often. I will answer her better pretty soon. I wish Fred was well enough to join the regiment. If he overstays his furlough, they will take his pay from him. I think that after a while, they will give him his discharge. I am so sleepy I can't think of anything more to write, so I will put this by for tonight.

October 24

I can't think of anything new to write this morning, so with love and kisses to you all, I will close. From your affectionate husband, Silas W. Haven.

Little Rock, October 30, 1863

Dear Jane,

The weather has been quite cold and rainy for a few days back, and I have kept pretty close to the fire. I have not been on picket for most two weeks, which was very lucky, as I have not drawed any clothes yet. They don't get their clothes very fast, only four blankets, two overcoats and some dress coats have been drawed yet. I expect to get some soon. We are going to be mustered for pay tomorrow, and I expect that we shall get our pay next week. We shall settle up our clothing bill the next pay up to this time. I expect that I shall have a little coming to me and I shall buy me some extra clothing, such as a pair suspenders, handkerchief. I have sent you twenty dollars, ten in a letter, which I expect you have got before this time, and if we get our pay next week, I think that you will get along pretty well this winter, as I shall send all I can spare to you. I don't know as there is much news to write. They had a little bit of a fight with Marmaduke's force the forepart of this week; three or four thousand attacked five hundred of our men at Pine Bluff and after a sharp fight of four or five hours, they got finely licked out and as usual skedaddled.[26] A company of men came in here from Lewisburg, and are have been sworn in to the service, and have drawed part of their clothes and are waiting for the rest. They expect another company in, in a day or two. When they get their army they will raise havoc among the guerrillas if they show their heads. There are meetings about every night out to town, but I have only been to meetings only Sunday as my clothes are hardly warm enough to be out nights. Some of the boys go out hunting, but have not made out much yet, only to get one turkey. Deer and turkeys are quite plenty, and I am going to give them a try myself one of these days. I think I can fetch in a deer if anyone can. The pigeons are quite plenty here, but as shot is scarce, not many are killed. I am glad that you have got a lot of potatoes, and I hope you will have good success in keeping them this winter. I don't have many to eat as they cost too much from $1.25 to 2.00 a bushel. I make Uncle Sam board me. I bought a half pound butter and don't know but what I shall buy some more and a few potatoes. Butter is fifty cents a pound, tobacco from sixty cents for smoking to $2.00 for chewing, cheese fifty cents, onions fifteen to twenty cents a pound. One of our men McConnell has just got back and the boys are telling him about our coming in and make so much noise that I shall have to stop writing as I can't think of anything to write.

November 1

I was out foraging yesterday and did not get a chance to finish this. We are still gathering corn. We have to go now twelve miles for it. I was quite amused last night to see men in the company, our captain and his sergeant George Smith got a commission to go to Iowa and recruit for the regiment and did not tell us that they were going till last night.[27] I don't think that is the right place for them. They had ought to recruit down here instead of in Iowa for if they are going to hold command over men in the army, it should be over blacks as usual. They have a nice little whiskey spree last night, but none of them got very drunk. I don't think of anything more to write, but will try to write again this week. I think you done pretty well getting your hay. You got it cheaper than I expected. Write all the news. Write whether you are getting anything from the company this year. With love and kisses to you, I will close this time from your affectionate husband, Silas W. Haven.

Little Rock, November 7, 1863

Dear Jane,

I received a letter today from you and I improve this opportunity of answering it. I am well and the weather is quite warm so I get along pretty well. I have been on guard once this week and expect to either come on again either to forage or guard in a day or two. We had a rumor that we were going back to Memphis, but as we have had such rumors every week, I don't believe any of them till I get started.[28] I got three pens in the letter today, and they came very acceptable. We are pretty well situated as far as wet weather is concerned. Our barracks are good and they have got ours built out on the picket posts. So that we can keep pretty comfortable. Hoping to soon meet you all. I close by sending my love and kisses to you all. I will close for this time, from your affectionate husband, Silas W. Haven.

Little Rock, Arkansas, November 11, 1863

Dear Father and Mother,

I had just got ready to write, but had not made up my mind who to as I heard that the mail had come in and I found that I was one of the lucky ones. One letter bore my direction so I took it and on opening it, I was much pleased to see that it was from you. I was glad to hear that you were well and hope you will continue so. My health is pretty good and I take as good care of it as I can. When we started out here, I throwed out some of my clothes for fear that I would give out and we have not drawed any yet and it is very cold so that I suffer some when I am on guard. The last time I was out I borrowed an overcoat so I got along pretty well. I don't think that when we got here that there was but one overcoat in the company, but some of the boys that was on furlough brought theirs so we have 6 or 8 in the company now. I expect that we shall draw some today. The weather is about as hard on men here as it is in Iowa. We have not had much rainy weather yet, but we have had enough to know that there will be some mud when it does come. Our troops had a little brush with some of Marmaduke's foragers at Pine Bluff a few weeks ago and give them a nice little thrashing.[29] There was 600 of our cavalry and five or six pieces of cannon against twenty five hundred and twelve pieces of cannon and after fighting five hours, they thought that Pine Bluff was sour grapes and they did not want it so they left it be, but our force would not let them be but followed them and give them more grapes than they wanted. Our general sent a force to head them off, but the rain delayed the artillery, so that they was a little too late. Our forces drove them through Arkadelphia and come back. I rather think that they will see another scouting party of about five or six thousand down there soon. We don't have much to do here. We have to stand guard or forage once in five or six days; the most that we have to do on guard is to keep our own troops in and that don't amount to anything as all go out that want to. We generally at night build a good fire out of rails. By the way, if Uncle Abe replaces the rails that we burn, it would take him one while even if he is a first rail splitter and make ourselves as comfortable as we can. We should be first-rate mark to shoot at if there were any guerrillas disposed to try us, but we are not afraid and if you had any doubts about there being a lot of Union men here, I believe Gen. Steele reports 1,600 enlistments since we come here and more a coming every day. The health of the troops is pretty good. You need not feel any alarmed about Little Rock being attacked for if they could hold it with force that they had here. They can't raise enough to wrest if from our possession. Things look rather dubious for the born feds. They are getting into rather close corners and poor Val from Canada can't help any, and I guess that the Copperheads will see the necessity of keeping quiet.[30] They probably [could] if they could hear the curses of the soldiers from all regiments that is launched at them. The elections cheered the hearts of the soldiers and I guess that there will be but few regiments that gave Tuttle a majority. With love and respects to you all and hoping that through the mercy of God, we shall meet again here on earth and that soon I will close for this time. From your son, Silas W. Haven.

On Board Steamer *Rose Hamilton* going down White River
November 17, 1863

Dear Jane,

We got orders last Saturday at 4 o'clock PM to be ready to leave on the cars in the morning for Memphis and after we got ready, as there was not cars enough to take two regiments at a time, we were going to wait another day so I got a pass and went over to see the battery and immediately after I had gone, they had orders to leave at five o'clock and I did not get quite back to camp till they started. We went to the depot and it was nine o'clock before we got started. The cars did not get in till seven. The boys all feel pretty well and have great times. There was three or four sutlers on the train that come in. They crowded around one of them and he throwed out a bundle of papers, but they could not eat that so they watched their opportunity and rolled out a barrel of apples and some other things. They got three bags of apples and two butter, I believe, and they were quick to dispose of what they started then and went to another sutler that had unloaded below, but he was too smart for them and rolled a barrel of apples out to them and told them to help themselves. So they did not try to steal from him. The boats are rather small and don't carry only part of a regiment. There is four boats in our fleet besides the gunboat. Our boat is pretty well crowded, but still we get along first rate. So we live pretty well on beef, hard tack and coffee. This is a pretty river but is very crooked, and there is some guerrillas along the banks. Today the gunboat had notice that there was a lot at a point that was going to attack us, so we get all ready to give them a warm reception, but they did not show themselves. They don't fancy attacking boats when the gunboat is close by as they are very apt to get the worst of the bargain. There has been quite a number of towns on the river but are hardly destroyed and nearly all deserted. I suppose that you are wondering what we are going to Memphis for and General Hurlburt has sent all the troops away from there and want us to provost guard at Memphis and to guard the railroad to Corinth. I expect that our regiment will be provost guard. There is only two regiments (the 27th Iowa and 49th IL) of our brigade going. Now I don't know when or whether the rest of the brigade will come. I did not believe that we should leave Little Rock till spring for I rather thought they needed us there the most of any place, and were it not for getting the news, I believe I should rather stay there than to go to Memphis.[31]

November 20

I was sleeping on the hurricane deck and laid quiet about an hour, but as it did not hold up blowing, I went below and found a place in the cabin to set down and I kept my chair till morning. The boat had to lay by till six o'clock and I am afraid they won't get to Memphis till night, which will make it very disagreeable about unloading, especially if it continues cold and wet. I expect that you are having snow about this time. I hope you are well prepared for winter weather, with plenty of wood and warm clothing. I got a dress coat of one of our men that did not want it. I am going to have it charged over to me, so I am dressed quite comfortable. One of our men got left at Helena. He went to get a dram of whiskey and I guess that by this time he is tight in jail. We have had quite good times so far and everything gone off quite pleasantly. I like riding on a steamboat first rate and I hope that sometime that we can all take a ride together, for I know that you and the children will like it. I hope the time will soon come when we can all be together again. I think of you every day and often dream of seeing you nights. You must give lots of [love] and kisses to the children and tell them I want to see them very much and they must write to me. With love and kisses to you all, I remain your affectionate husband, Silas W. Haven.

Memphis, November 25, 1863

Dear Jane,

We got here safe last Friday night and came into camp Saturday. We did not have any tents and did not get any till late Sunday night so we had to lay out to the weather, which was clear but pretty cold. We are camped on a ridge among the timber and the boys are building places to set their tents on about four feet high. Our tents are the wedge tents, the same kind we had first. We have only four men to a tent and as soon as my comrades can get [one] to use, we are going to build up a house so that we can fix conveniences for writing. We have had no duty to do yet, but I expect that we shall have to go on provost guard tomorrow as we are going to draw clothes this afternoon. We drew our pay yesterday. I got thirty-three dollars and fifteen cents. Seven dollars and fifteen cents was for clothing due me for last year. I am going to buy me some things that I can't draw with it as soon as I can get to town. We shall have to dress pretty well and keep our things slick if we go on provost guard. There is plenty of peddlers in camp and they sell lots of apples, cakes. In fact, you can buy most anything you want and the most of the boys put in pretty well for something to eat. I have bought some apples and butter. My appetite not being very craving, I let the cakes and chicken pot pie pass. Write all the news and send me a St. Charles paper that has got the proceeding of the institute in it if you can. With love and kisses to you, Ella, Emmett and Kitty, I close for this time. From your affectionate husband, Silas W. Haven.

In camp at Memphis, Tennessee, December 1, 1863

Dear Jane,

I received a letter from you tonight at roll call, dated November 22nd, and was very glad to hear from you. I am glad that Fred (as long as he can't get his furlough extended) has reported back to Davenport as I am in hopes that they will do justice by him here. I received a letter from you last Friday and have written you one, but was in a hurry so I will read it over and try to answer both in regular order. I should not think the folks would like the idea of having a whiskey saloon opened in town. I guess that the man must be a Copperhead as it is the men of that stamp that generally like to be in the whiskey business. I think that I shall try to come home next spring or summer. The way things look now, I think, we shall stay here this winter and by next spring, I hope that the war will be over, as our armies are now and have been ever since July gaining advantages and we keep all we get, and Grant has the command at Chattanooga and he is slow but sure, as you can see by the last battle there he gained great advantages with but small loss. I don't think there is much show for the 27th regiment to get into a fight. In reading the letter over for the I don't know what time, I found a line informing me that the money I had send had all gone through safe, so I feel a little better. I have not got the minutes of the association; get if you have not sent them. I wish you would, but I must close as I expect that I shall be on guard tomorrow. There is lots that I want to write but can't think of now, but will try another time. With love and kisses to you all, I bid you good night. From your affectionate husband, Silas W. Haven.

Fred would have been pretty near right if we had not been under orders to leave. I probably should have been on picket the 15th of November. We left at night and rode most all night.[32]

Memphis, Tennessee, December 6, 1863

Dear Father and Mother,

I received a letter from you last Friday, but have been so busy fixing up that I have not had any time nor conveniences to answer it. I am on picket guard today and as that is rather lazy business, I brought a sheet of paper along and try and write some. My conveniences for writing are of the poorest kind so I don't think that I shall make out much. We got fixed up very well at Little Rock for winter and are now fixing up here as well as we can. I don't know what our brigade and division numbers are before we went to Little Rock. We were the 3rd brigade of the 3rd division of the 16th army corps at Little Rock. We were the 1st brigade, Kimball's provisional Division, 16th army corps to of the regiments of the brigade (the 62nd IL and 50th IN) are at Little Rock, yet also our battery (3rd IL) the two that are here (the 27th Iowa and 49th IL) are commanded by Col. Gilbert (our Col.). The brigade was commanded by Col. True of the 62nd IL and known as True's Brigade till he went home, and we all hope that he will find a command somewhere else. Our brigade was under orders night before last and yesterday to be ready to take the cars at a moment's notice to go to Collierville to thrash out a force of rebs that were marching.[33] They had their fight yesterday and as they did not need us, we did not go. I have not heard the particulars, but will write them when I get to camp.

December 9

I have not got any particulars about the fight out east, only that the rebs got a nice thrashing out to Moscow. The war news has been very good ever since last July. Our armies have been dealing telling blows on the rebs till they have scarcely got a foothold only at Richmond and if they don't look sharp, it will turn out as I said when I left home i.e., that the army of the west would conquer the rebs out here and then go and take Richmond in the rear. It looks a great deal like it now. Chattanooga is ours and Grant is at the head of affairs there, and he is of the kind that keeps doing something, and he about always makes it win. Banks is cleaning out Texas and if he needs any help, Steele will extend it to him from Little Rock.[34] I imagine that we shall soon hear that Jeff Davis and company has run the blockade for safer quarters, and the Confederacy is without a head and will therefore fall through. I hardly think that there will be any more pitched battles for I don't think that the rebs will stand. We have got pretty near fixed up for winter. My health keeps pretty good for me, although I have now got a bite on my neck, which troubles me some. So I guess that now my mail will come regular, but I will close this for my neck aches so that I can't think of what I want to write. Hoping soon to meet you all again on earth, and that the blessings of Divine Providence follow us and guide us in the path of duty so that we may so live that when we are called hence, we may be prepared to enter into that and rest that is prepared for all those that prove faithful to the end. From your son, Silas W. Haven.

---

FOR THE REST OF 1863, Haven remained encamped in Memphis, Tennessee. With a large amount of downtime around the holidays, Haven wrote several letters over the course of a month that covered the weather, his health, guard duty, and his wishes for the holiday season to his family. Many of the details are repetitive and do not shed any new light on his experience as a soldier during the war. Haven did write that the regiment expected to stay in Memphis through the winter, that the armies made tremendous progress "cleaning out the rebs," and that the war should be over soon, with the seceded states back in the union by July 4. His eyes bothered him throughout the month, and he got out of some guard duty due to his eye ailment. Haven commented on Christmas, asking his wife to inform him what Santa brought the children. He also commented on seeing a black holiday festival, stating, "It is holiday time among the darkies and they are flocking into town dressed to the highest notch to have a nice little time."[35]

CHAPTER 5

# The Meridian and Red River Expeditions

## *January–May, 1864*

After returning to Memphis, 1864 emerged as a pivotal year for Pvt. Haven as he saw more military action and awaited the presidential election. However, despite the excitement of both endeavors, Pvt. Haven remained plagued by disease, boredom with picket duty, and a constant longing to return to his family. The Meridian expedition in February 1864 forced Haven to march several miles a day, and he held up well during the march. During the Red River campaign in March and April 1864, Haven participated in battle and left a wealth of details about his experience in the following letters. The spring also ushered in more optimism for the conclusion of the Civil War as Gen. Ulysses S. Grant, now in command of all Union forces, launched an ambitious Overland campaign to eliminate multiple Confederate armies across the landscape.

—

Memphis, January 6, 1864

Dear Jane,

Just as I got this letter started, the mail came in and brought me a good long letter from you, which I read with much pleasure. We have been having some pretty cold weather here. The last day of December, it rained till most night and then snowed and sleeted till most morning, and New Year's day it was pretty cold all day. I was on picket and had as much as I could do to keep warm as the smoke would get in my eyes and made them ache. I have not been on picket since as I caught cold, and my eyes and throat bothered me some, and the weather was so bad that I thought I had better stay in camp and [see the] doctor. I expect to be on [picket] tomorrow. It rained just enough three days ago to turn our snow into ice so that the ground is covered with ice and it is rather slippery traveling; quite a number in town got their limbs broke by falling down. One broke his back, so the papers say. I was in town today after hay for the regiment and I saw one nice lady set down on the ice. The river is filled with anchor ice and looks quite cold, but as cold as our weather is, I don't expect it can match yours up there. There is quite a number of our company out on detached service so that we come on guard, some oftener. Some have got furlough from Cairo, I hear.[1] One (Dan Dean) you may possibly see.[2] I don't hear anything said about pay yet, but I think that we shall get it soon as some of the other regiment are signing their pay rolls. I have only got a dollar left now. I suppose you would like to know what I had to eat Christmas and New Year's. Well, I had bread, coffee and meat. New Year's I took my meals out on the picket post. I think that I will make up lost time when I get home. I have not slept inside of a dwelling house since I left Dubuque. When we were at Moscow, we had a church for guard house. I stayed in that two or three times, so you see I have had some experience of [a] soldier's life. I hope it is most over; by the way that the rebs are placed now, it looks as if the Confederacy would collapse soon. I suppose that before this gets there, that the scare about the draft will be over. I was some in hopes that some few would get drafted there. I wrote to Fred a short time ago, but have not heard from him yet, but I must close for it is getting late and my bunk man is rather unwell. With love and kisses to you all, I remain your affectionate husband, Silas W. Haven.

—

IN JANUARY, Col. James Gilbert investigated a complaint filed by Mrs. Julia Baker. She claimed men of the brigade took items from her residence in Memphis. Gilbert appointed an investigative board and wrote, "They will ascertain as near as possible the kind, quantity, and quality of the goods taken, with their value, by whom taken and how disposed of, identifying, if possible, the men. If not able to identify the men, ascertain the company or companies. If the companies cannot be ascertained, ascertain the regiment, reporting the facts as early as practicable to these headquarters." No specific records mention if the culprits had been located.[3]

—

Millville, Iowa, January 10, 1864[4]

Dear Silas,

I once more take my pen to write to you to let you know we are yet in good health. Hoping this may find you enjoying some great blessing. We received yours of the 6th and 9th a day or two before Christmas. Well, we went and got blockaded in with snow and did not get home till the 5th of January. But we had a good time visiting and got home safe in two days after we left. Well, all is well that ends well, and I think I will be satisfied to stay at home the rest of the winter. I hope you don't have such big snow storms down south. It is quite healthy now in our vicinity. We have had the coldest weather that has been known in this country for many years, though we have not heard of any casualties yet, only frozen toes and fingers; perhaps we may hear of many, read once when the recruits become neglected. The mail from the East has not come in to Colesburg since December 29th and the same at Dyersville.[5] Well, you see I have commenced on the wrong page of my sheet. I have just found it out, but I guess you will read it just as well. Your father and Inez have gone to meeting today. It is quite pleasant but rather cold; snow is about two feet deep in the woods, on the prairie from two inches to ten feet, so you may guess what times we are having. But we don't mind the snow or cold weather as long as we have cheering war news. We feel that before the next Fourth of July, we will have rebellion among the things that were, and that the Southern Confederacy will [be] a reproach to all those that have sustained it thus far, which will include many that will wish they had been sustaining a better cause. I do believe that if the Southern leaders want only [to] save their necks even through his grace, we shall have peace at once. But the thing is done and we are bound to have justice, let the cost be what it may, that all future generations may see and take refuge that the way of the transgressors is hard. We have every reason [for] full confidence in the way our government has been administered, for there have been a heavy tide against every move, but the deaf have been made to hear and the blind to see, and all through the maneuvers of the Copperhead wing of the Democratic Party. Through great tribulations we are brought in the error of our ways, [and] so it is with nations. The Egyptians worshiped slavery, not to the laws of God, and would not be satisfied on promises until the king with his were drowned in the Red Sea, so perhaps maybe with Jeff Davis and company and that is fast approaching, as I read from reports in Congress, that [a] resolution has been brought forward to have the president appoint commissioners to meet for peace with the authorities at Richmond. A Copperhead resolution, but tabled by the Union, and I hope and pray it may never be found again that the credit of our national constitution may be strong enough to annihilate all treason for the future.[6] Our nation is growing stronger every day and will continue so as long as this rebellion lasts. Our country is becoming more and more united, and God is prospering us in our deeds of national consanguinity. Therefore let us be of good cheer and hope for a better state of news in future, for we have been tried as with fire, and what God has meant for our good, may it prove a blessing to all Republican governments throughout the whole world. God grant that our sacrifice may be acceptable as a peace offering and our homes once more made glad that domestic war has ceased. I don't know as there is any particular news to write. The last we heard from George, he was at Paducah, Kentucky, as James says, to work in kitchen of a hospital. James was at Bridgeport, Tennessee. We have not heard from Ed Thayer since he left New York for Morris Island. I had a letter from Jane the same day I got yours. She wrote very cheerful. I sent you a paper while I was to Laura waiting to run the blockade. We send our *Watchman* and *Reflector* to George every week without taking it from the office. Inez is at home this winter. Our family numbers only four. Mark goes to school. Finally everything passes off like a dream without any material change. Copperheads are still as mice and Union has it all one way. The draft has ceased to be a terror, and the voice of music is heard in our streets, sending forth praise to God, and the reign of witchcraft and treason is hushed in all our social gatherings. So you see that we feel that the dawn of better days are fast approaching and now as my paper is about used up, I will close. May the God of all grace be your guide, is the prayer of your mother, E. Haven.

Memphis, Tennessee, January 13, 1863

Dear Jane,

The Mississippi River is blockaded with ice so that there has not been any mail lately, and I don't know as this will reach you very quick but as the boats are whistling pretty smart today. There is not much news down here. It has been so cold that there was not much stirring about. There is rumors pretty often that we are going to move a few days ago. We were going to relieve the 12th Iowa at Pocahontas near Corinth. It is now the rumor that we are going down the river and in east of Vicksburg.[7] I don't know but what we shall, but still I don't believe that we shall leave this place before April. I was down to town the other day and there were sights of cotton laying on the levee, waiting for shipment, and more coming in every day. A couple of Jews went out to buy some cotton the other day, and they got out about 30 miles east and a guerrilla come up to them and presented his revolver and made them give up theirs and their money, and told them that he would have them in the ranks, but as he was putting the money up, they caught him and throwed him down and beat his brains out with the revolver (they did not dare to shoot as there was a lot of guerrillas a little way off), and got one on to the horse and one on a mule, and left for this place as they could. They lost their teams, but got their money and about $300 dollars more back, besides a lot of secesh money.

I guess they won't venture quite so far out of the lines very quick. I and my partner are building us a nice shanty, ten by twelve, if the weather is favorable; can finish it in a couple of days. We had a little goat stay with us a few days. It was very nice pet, but as we did not like to make our parlor kitchen and bedroom a stable, we put him out and some of the rest of the boys have took him. I am very anxious to hear how you get along through the cold weather. I am afraid that you will suffer some of the cold days for the want of wood. Write all the news and write often. With love and kisses to you all, I will close for this time. From your affectionate husband, Silas W. Haven.

Memphis, Tennessee, January 19, 1864

Dear Jane,

I was very glad to hear that you had got through that cold snap without freezing. I was afraid that you would run out of wood and suffer. We had it very cold for this climate the first of the month. I was on picket Sunday and it rained nearly all day, and about two o'clock it turned around and snowed a little and froze today. It is a nice sunshiny day, and I guess that before night that there will be plenty of mud. One year ago today I was examined here in Memphis and marched for discharge. I don't think that the government has made as much as I have by keeping me for the first four months. I did no duty and had we been called on to go into the field, I should have been of no use, but as [it] is, I have been as to do some duty and recovered my health so that I am able to do all that is required of a soldier, except to march and carry my knapsack, which I don't expect we will be required to do. The talk is pretty strong that the 16th army corps is going to move. It is the general impression that we shall go to Jackson, Mississippi. I expect that they are going to open a line from Vicksburg to Jackson and so on out to Atlanta as soon as Grant gets possession of that place if we have here, it will [be] between this and the 10th of next month.[8] I expect that we shall get our pay this week. It looks to me as if the war was about over. I think that if the rebs will fight any more, that there will be the largest battle of the war near Chattanooga. It looks as if they were preparing for it on both sides, and I guess that Grant will have enough men to meet all that the Confederates can send against them. I expect that our business will be to guard the line of supplies while others do the fighting. I wish I had the one hundred and fifty dollars to buy Weeks' place for I think that it would be worth that to us for a home. We had a new recruit join us yesterday and are expecting more every day. Tell Kitty that I would like to see her doll and am very sorry that she lost her earring, and I hope she will find

The Haven Family Grave site, Rockford, Iowa (image taken by author)

Left: The grave site of Sarah Jane Haven, Rockford, Iowa (image taken by author) Right: The grave site of Laura Olive Haven, Rockford, Iowa (image taken by author)

The 27th Iowa Infantry Reunion, Independence, Iowa, September 9-10, 1885 (courtesy of Larry Morphew)

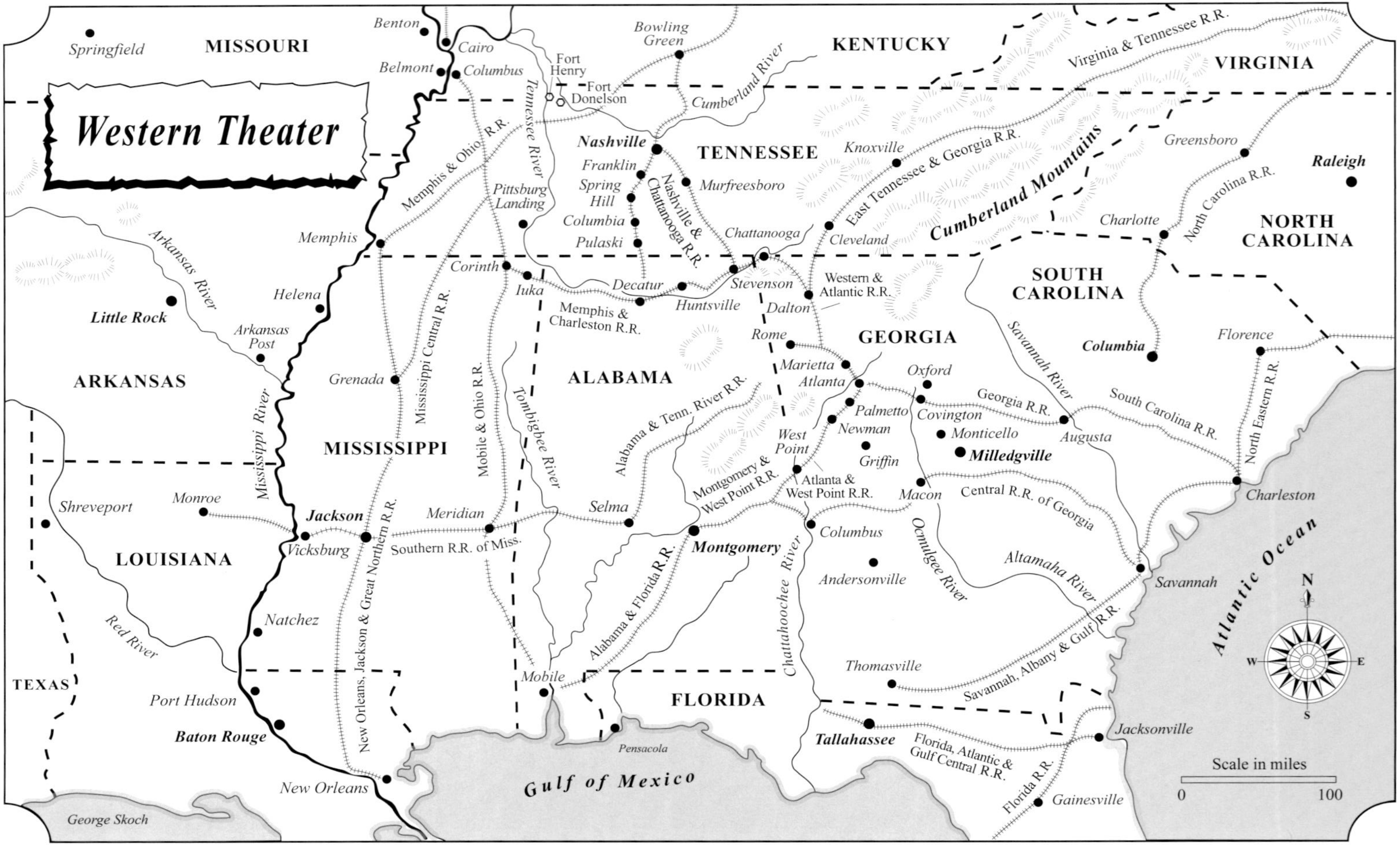


From *Victors in Blue: How Union Generals Fought the Confederates, Battled Each Other, and Won the Civil War* by Albert Castel. Used with the permisit again; if she don't, let me know. Does Ella wear any earrings yet, and does Emmett play on his drum? This cold weather I expect that we shall have some more mail today. I will try and send you some papers today. I can't think of any more to write at this time, so with love and kisses to you all, I remain your affectionate husband, Silas W. Haven.

Don't spare the trees if they will keep you warm.

Memphis, Tennessee, January 22, 1864

Dear Jane,

When I came in from picket this morning, I found a letter from mother (which I will send you in this) and I thought I would commence one to you. I expect that this is the last [time] that I shall date from this place, at least for some time, as I expect that we shall leave here the first of the week. I don't know where we shall go yet, but think it will be to Jackson, Mississippi, east of Vicksburg. My health is pretty good at present, and we are having some fine weather just now, and I hope it will keep so while we are moving. I am in hopes that we shall get our pay before we leave, and I guess that we shall after we get our next pay. I don't expect that we shall get any more for four or six months.

Jan. 23, 2 o'clock PM

We have just got our regular greenbacks, which came very acceptable.[9] I passed ten cents off for apples before I got to my shebang, and I have disposed of them and thought I would finish this and send it along. I think it is very certain when or whether we leave here as they had orders not to turn over anything. We never had have orders to march, only to be ready to march tomorrow, and the major says we shall not go tomorrow if we don't leave before Tuesday or Wednesday.[10] I will write again. Write whether you get any money from me. I suppose you need some by this time. Write whether you have got any county orders this year. With love and kisses to you all, I will close for this time. I remain your affectionate husband, Silas W. Haven.

Memphis, Tennessee, January 22, 1864

Dear Father and Mother,

When I came in from picket this morning, I found your very interesting letter, date of the tenth, and I hasten to answer it as I expect to be quite busy for the next few days. My health is middling good at present. We had an extra cold spell for this climate. The first of the month, New Year's Day, I was on picket and caught a very hard cold, which bothered me some so that I did not go on guard till the 11th. I am well enough now to stand my guard when my turn comes, which is about every fourth day, but I expect I have stood picket for the last time in Tennessee, at least for some little time, for the tide of war is moving south and the 16th army corps is going to change its base, where to I can't tell at present, but I rather think that it is [to] open a line from Vicksburg east to Jackson, Mississippi, and so on to Atlanta, when Grant gets that place. I think that our brigade will be stationed at Jackson or some point on the Ohio and Mobile RR so as to be ready to cut off troops from Atlanta or Mobile. It is thought by some that we shall go direct to Shipp Island so as to operate on Mobile.[11] The way things look now, there is going to be either a big battle in Georgia in the spring or the Confederacy will collapse, and if Grant is successful, it will end the war, at least it is my impression. I expect that we shall leave here the first of next week. We have got pretty good winter quarters (the second we have this season, and if we have to build again, I think Uncle Sam ought to pay us extra wages) so we get along pretty well through the cold snap, rather better than some of the citizens did. Wood is twelve dollars a cord. We help ourselves so we have plenty. We were pretty well blockaded for a week, or the boats did not run on account of the ice. The army feels pretty well and is in pretty good spirits. We all feel pretty confident that the spring campaign will close Jeff Davis and company out, and the sooner the concern is closed out, the sooner we shall get home, and if there is left any Copperhead concerns, we will close them out in short meter. I have got one last page and I don't see as I have written anything interesting or can think of anything that will be. We have not got our pay yet and I don't know when we shall, and I have run short of funds and paper and don't want to visit the sutler. We have had nice weather for a few days back, and last night was the best night I have had on picket for this winter. I was in hopes that we should stay here but till the rainy season was over, but I presume we are better prepared to leave now than at any other time. We soldiers, when we get fixed up, hate to move, but after we get started, we want to keep moving. I still hope that before another winter, we shall all be at home. I want to get once more where I can enjoy religious privileges, and I think the time is not far distant. My prayer to God is that this war may cease and this land may become a land of promise to all God-loving and God-fearing people. With my respects to all and love to yourselves, I remain your son, Silas W. Haven.

Memphis, January 25, 1864

Dear Jane,

I did not intend to write to you yesterday, but just as I got ready to write, I had to go on fatigue duty, which was leading teams with the household goods of the first Alabama cavalry. The government is evacuating the road to Corinth.[12] The families of the Union men, especially soldiers, have got to come out of the way of the guerrillas. It was the hardest-looking sight I have seen to see over a hundred families, both whites and Negroes, compelled to leave their homes and all laying at the depot, waiting to find a place to go to, and that too at short notice as the place had to be cleared before the cars came in at night as there was four trains expected with refugees on. There were children of all ages, from a week [old and] up, and a lot of them at that. We worked till night and then did not get them all moved. I went to town today and bought me a supply of paper envelopes and stamps. The talk is very strong that we move tomorrow, but still I think that I shall have to go out on picket as I think it is an even chance whether we stay. The talk is that we are now brigaded [but] how true it is I don't know till after dress parade, then I expect we will know whether we leave tomorrow or not. It is rumored that we are brigaded with the 14th Iowa, 32nd Iowa and 118th Illinois. I will finish this after I found out and if we start tomorrow, I shall send it off. The weather is very pleasant now and if we move, I hope it will continue so till we get settled down again. We have stayed here about as long as at Little Rock, about as long as we stay in one place at a time. Some of our men (Noble and Fletcher) got here last night and one (Fletcher) had seen Fred.[13] He said that they were making out his papers to send him home. I hope they will.

January 27th

I was not relieved till noon today and I found the regiment gone, and it is now most night, and I have just got your letter and hasten to get this in to the office. I expect that we shall stand either tonight or in the morning for down the river. With love and kisses to you all, I remain your affectionate husband, Silas W. Haven.

Our band is playing, so I guess the boats will start soon.

Private

It is quite a while since I have written you a private slip, so I will start one and fill it out if I can. I sent you twenty dollars and forty cents to spend. I did think that I would send you five more if you thought that you would need it if we go away. I may want it before I draw again if we stay here. It may be that I will not need it. My health is pretty good, although bowels are a little out of order, but I get along with that pretty well with Ayers pills. My liver troubles me some when I catch cold, but I have got along pretty well so far and have done duty, except a little while, about New Year's. Ever since I left Moscow, I feel that this war is about over if Grant is successful in the spring campaign. I think that it will be brought to a close. If we move from here, it will be to Jackson, Mississippi, so I guess that we have been as near a battle as we shall get. The most I hate leaving here for is on account of the mail. You must not be surprised if you don't get letters from me for some time, at least till we get settled. Write often. I shall try to write as often as once a week. Tell Kitty that pa loves her and also that he loves you all. Write more particulars about Kitty's throat. Goodbye for this time. From your affectionate husband, Silas W. Haven.

I sent you a twenty-dollar greenback. Write whether you get it.

On board Steamer *Des Moines,* going down the river, January 29, 1864
Dear Jane,

We left Memphis yesterday and are steaming down the river. I expect that we shall stop at Vicksburg and go from there to Jackson, Mississippi.[14] It may be that we shall be located at Vicksburg. The whole division is going and I don't know but what more. We are in the 3rd Division, 2nd Brigade, 16th army corps. We are brigaded with the 12, 14 and 32nd Iowa Regiments so ours is an Iowa brigade, except the battery, which is the 14 Indiana Battery. We have had a very nice time so far, only we had to lay by a spell this forenoon on account of the regiment. We had got a few miles below Napoleon. You can judge something about the weather as there was a lot of little boys and girls selling apples in Memphis yesterday, barefooted. I guess that if they had been in Iowa, their toes would have been some cold. The troops are in pretty good spirits. They all think that the war will be about closed up with the spring campaign. There is seven boats in our fleet, and there is a band on two of them, which makes [it] quite pleasant. Our band has got so that they play pretty well. I would like to have you to take a steamboat ride as I know that you and the children would like it. I am in the cabin writing, but there is so much bugging about that I can't think of what I want to say, so I can't send this out till I get to Vicksburg.

January 31st

We got here yesterday noon and are fixing to march out last of here, how far I don't know, but where it is 140 miles. It rained last night and I slept on the ground with my rubber blanket over me and my woolen one wrapped around me, and waked up this morning as dry as a duck. I have not seen much of the place yet; it stands on a bluff and is quite a nice place. I don't expect that I can send any more mail for sometime, so you must not be disappointed if you don't get any letter for three or four weeks. With love and kisses to you all, I close for this time, from your affectionate husband, Silas W. Haven.

Camp of the 27th, three miles east of Vicksburg, February 2, 1864

Dear Jane,

We moved out here yesterday, and I thought I would commence a letter and perhaps I should have time to finish it before we left here. I have seen pretty rough country, but around here is ahead of anything I ever saw before. We are camped just outside of the line of fortifications, where the hardest fighting was done, of which are scattered all over the ground in the shape of balls of all descriptions, shells, pieces of shells and graves of the fallen soldiers; scattered among one is within two rods of where I slept. I saw the bones of a man on the bank of the river where we landed. I was over to Fort Hill today where Gen. Logan undermined and blowed up.[15] I saw the arm bones of a man lying on the top of the ground. I got a piece of the root of the tree that Grant and Pemberton met under.[16] I have made a ring and cut out a heart, which I shall send home if I can for keepsakes. Night before last it rained pretty hard and I got my woolen blanket pretty wet. I slept with two others and they built the tent while I was gone, and it rained. The water [was] up on to my feet. I had to get up and dream it away before I could sleep. I fixed my rubber blanket over me last night and slept alone. It was a little frosty last night. There is some talk that we shall go tomorrow, but how true it is we may go and we may not. It is hard telling. We are ready to go at any time. I expect that we (our regiment or brigade) will be a guard for the ammunition train. I understand that our 1st Lieutenant (Rupe) is appointed quartermaster. I hope he is as I had rather have Reiniger to command the company than him.[17]

---

SHERMAN'S ARMY skirmished some in Jackson and Baker Creek, near Clinton, Mississippi, before moving onward to Meridian. The soldiers lived off the land, captured Confederate supplies, and destroyed railroad lines and cars along the way. The successful expedition, with relatively no casualties, lasted about a month before the regiment returned to Vicksburg on March 4, 1864. Of note, the soldiers took a limited number of rations with them, ten days' worth, and lived off the land, which emerged as the same strategy Sherman would utilize in the march to the sea later in the war.

—

Camp of the 27th Iowa, 52 miles east of Jackson, February 10, 1864

I will try and finish this, although I don't know as General Sherman will let any mail go from here till the object of the expedition is accomplished. We are making a grand raid and have a force enough to carry everything before it. We are making now for Meridian and may go to Montgomery. We shall have another force join us at Meridian. I stand it pretty well and have carried my knapsack every day, and yesterday, we marched 25 miles. Our front has had some skirmishing, but of that I will write on another sheet. I saw a dead rebel soldier and a Union soldier that was killed skirmishing just before we got to Jackson, and we passed a dead rebel today that was killed just this side of Hillsboro. I expect that you will get the account of our movements in the papers before this reaches you, but don't worry about me as I am in the hands of a kind providence who will, I believe, protect and preserve me from all danger. With love and kisses to all, I close for this time. From your affectionate husband, Silas W. Haven.[18]

Camp at Canton, Mississippi, February 28, 1864

I have just got in from picket and find if I am in a hurry, I can send off a letter, so I will try to get it in. We have to be on a grand raid and have some tall marching, as we have marched every day till yesterday, except one. My health has been good and I have carried my knapsack all but two half days, but shall try to have it carried on the wagon the rest of the way. We are going to stay here a day or two and then I expect that we shall go to Yazoo City. I will write again from there. With love to all, SWH

Millville, Iowa, February 28, 1864[19]

Dear Silas,

I once more take my pen to address you to let you know we are all well. Hope you are enjoying the same blessing. I wrote to you the 10th of January and have not heard from you since, but that makes no difference. I know you would be glad to hear from us, and we can write when you can't. We know you are now in some of the Gulf States and feel anxious for your welfare. James is home now on furlough. The 9th Iowa have re-enlisted. George is at Paducah, Kentucky, nursing the sick and wounded. It is quite probably he will stay there until his term of service expires. He was well the last we heard from him. I don't know as there is any news of importance to write. The war news is encouraging and if the reports from rebel sources are correct, we feel quite confident that our armies will be disbanded before another winter. There has [been] a great many regiments re-enlisted and will be back in the field again soon so that the spring Campaign will have veteran troops to force the rebel conscripts, which causes tumult and consternation in the Copperhead rank at home Arkansas and homes in and in have become almost naturalized. The noose is tightening and rebels tremble while Copperheads took on again at the ruin they have done both to themselves and the country. Surely the day of retribution is near at hand. There is nothing that holds the Confederacy together now but the obstinacy of the leaders that one not benefited by the proclamation reports says that some of the prominent commanders of the rebel army are advising all that can to desert and let the commanders take care of themselves, and reports say also that many have been executed for entertaining such sentiments. Well, I should not be surprised if within three months, there was a meeting in the rebel army and, like the Jews of old, [they will] destroy themselves. We hear that the rebel army in front of Chattanooga [are] fighting among themselves and deserting every day. I was told the other day by one of our neighboring women that she and I would not like to see this never end. I told her I did not know as we should, but that was no sign that the rebellion would not be put down. She said the president was calling all the time for more troops. I told her I knew that and we were raising an army every year and if the rebellion lasted twenty years. There was a generation now born this year that would be ready for the field by that time, and a crop coming in every year. She said it was almost blasphemy to talk in that [way], but I still persisted in the belief and gained the best end of the argument. We have a great many chicken-hearted Union bubbles here at home, and I delight in blowing them. I don't know as I have heard a discouraging thought yet. I have felt impatient sometimes at the tardiness of our government, but I have got over that now and [am] full willing to wait government-appointed time. So good bye from another. I shall write more if I don't send this off tomorrow. E. Haven

Camp of the 27th, 3 miles east of Vicksburg, March 5, 1864

Dear Jane,

We got here yesterday all safe, and I got two letters from you, dated January 24 and 31, and a letter from Sam and a paper from Jack. I was some disappointed in not getting better news, but am in hopes that we shall have some more mail before we leave here. I expect you will like to know how we got along with our raid so I will commence and write up my journal. We left our camp a short distance from where we now are on the 3rd of February and marched 15 miles on the 4th; we crossed Big Black and in a short time, our advance commenced skirmishing with the rebs. We marched twelve miles and camped on Jeff Davis plantation.[20] The 5th, our advance, was skirmishing nearly all day. There was a division ahead of our brigade, but we could hear the cannon and saw some of the effects as we passed along. Three of our men wounded and one dead and a dead rebel, besides a number of dead horses, and just before we camped, some cannon shot passed near us and ours that was shot at the 17th army corps. We marched fifteen miles on the 6th. Our Company went out a foraging about two miles and we moved our camp two miles in the afternoon, and I was on picket at night. On the 7th, we passed through Jackson and marched 11 miles, camped near Brandon. On the 8th, we only went 7 miles. On the 9th, we marched 25 miles, about 10 of it after dark. On the 10th, we only went 8 miles. Our cavalry had a skirmish with the rebs at Hillsboro and left a dead reb [on the] side of the road. On the 11th, we went 13 miles besides part of our regiment; went two miles on the wrong road and had to turn back. On the 12th, we left our train and marched 14 miles. On the 13th, we marched 13 miles and just before sundown, the cavalry and infantry pushed ahead as the rebs had blockaded up the road so as to delay our batteries and teams. We marched at quick and double quick time for about 4 miles over the hills, and routed the rebs out of their camp and camped on the same ground. On the 14th, we marched 12 miles and got to Meridian about 5 o'clock on the 15, it rained in the forenoon [and] in the afternoon. We went 4 miles on the 16th. We went to Marion (6 miles) and tore up track. On the 17, we went 3 miles out and tore up RR track and come back to Marion. On the 18, we stayed in camp. On the 19, we went out 10 miles foraging and came back to camp. On the 20, we started back, marched 23 miles. On the 21st, we marched 20 miles. On the 22nd, we marched 16 miles. On the 23rd, we marched 15 miles and put back to Hillsboro. On the 24th, we marched 17 miles. On the 25th, we marched 7 miles. The bridge on Pearl River broke down so we stayed in the woods on the east bank. On the 26th, we marched 15 miles, two miles west of Canton.

We expected that we were going to Yazoo City, but did not. On the 27th, we stayed in camp and at night, I was on picket. On the 28th, stayed in camp and on the 29th we were mustered for pay and went out 4 miles and tore up R.R. Track. March 1st, we started for this place in a rain storm, mud ankle-deep, marched 18 miles. March 2, marched 11 miles. March 3 (my birthday) marched 20 miles and crossed Big Black. March 4th, marched 14 miles. We have had good weather the most of the time; some nights were pretty cold with the exception of two or three nights. I have slept on my rubber with my woolen blanket over. One night four of us built a shelter with pine boughs, and when it looked likely to rain, we fixed our blankets for a shelter. I have stood the march first rate, and in a few days' time would be ready for another march. I did not change my clothes while I was gone. When I got to Canton, I took my shirt off and washed it in cold water and put it on wet. I don't know how long we shall stay here, not more than two or three days. I expect that we shall go up the river, and there is some talk that we shall go from Memphis to Florence, Alabama, by the way of Corinth, but I must close for this time.[21] With love and kisses to all, I remain your affectionate husband, Silas W. Haven.

Camp of the 27th, near Vicksburg, March 7, 1864

Dear Jane,

I thought I would start a letter today and if there is any prospect of our moving tomorrow, I would try and finish it. We took turns in marching; the brigade that was in advance one day went to the rear, the division the next; the same also with the regiments in the brigade, and the object of the expedition was to cut off the railroad communications and damage the rebs generally, which was done pretty effectually. You will probably get a better account of it in the papers than I could give you as I don't know anything, only what [the] commander [says and] my own observation, and that was but a small part of what was accomplished. Most every house on or near the road was pretty effectually cleaned of provisions, and every horse and mule was taken, and cattle and hogs had to suffer some, and the soldiers have a particular way of getting honey out of the hives, which is to tear them to pieces and pick out the honey and let the bees sting if they want to. The day we got to Marion we got a hive for our company and I had all I could eat; also the day we went a foraging, I went into a yard, where ten or a dozen hives were broken open and picked out some. I have had some at other time. There was quite a lot of cotton burnt and nearly all the cotton gins and fences made first-rate firewood. There was a great many houses burn on the way out, but not so many backs. The towns of Clinton,

Brandon, Hillsboro, Decatur, Meridian, Marion, New Marion and some others were burnt. I don't know what the boys of the army is; our regiment has one wounded and six missing. One of them is supposed to be killed as they were attacked while out foraging as we were coming back. The most of our loss is those that straggled and got taken prisoners. I expect then we shall start in a day or two on another expedition. The talk is that we are going up Red River to be gone a month to open communication with Texas. I shall leave all behind but my blankets. I shall not even take a change of clothes as it will be useless weight, and when the three brigades in the Division had taken their turn in the advance, the division went to the rear and another took its place in front. Our regiment did not come in the advance but once, and that was the day that we left Canton and it rained all day. Our regiment had the praise from Gen. Sherman of keeping in files and not straggling of anyone. One regiment (178 NY) was strung all along the road and we had a considerable fun with them. We also had a regiment (17 NY) with red caps that straggled some. We called them red-headed woodpeckers. We had good weather, with the exception of two days to march and the most of the way. The roads were pretty good. The country from here to Jackson was pretty hilly from Jackson to Meridian. It was through pine woods. We started from here with twenty days' rations, and the second night out found that about a third of the crackers were spoilt, so we only had half rations to Meridian and quarter part of the way back. We got the rest by foraging. We would get plenty of meat, but had to stop and grind meal on our way back. There was plenty of mills so that we did not actually suffer for something to eat, although some of the boys will say (I expect that they had to live on parched corn). I did not have my haversack empty but once, and there I did not get any meal at night and eat all my crackers for breakfast and dinner. I have got a lot of secesh paper and I will try to send you a sheet. I will also try to send you a paper. There will be no use to take writing materials as we can't send any letters till we get back. I stood this march first rate and know how to prepare to get along with another more comfortable. You must not feel uneasy if you don't get any letters for some time as it will probably be a month before we get back, and we are going with force enough so that there is no likelihood of our getting into any fight and as I keep my place in the ranks. There is no danger of my getting gobbled. I want you to write regular so if there should happen to be any mail sent through, I should have some. I would like it if you could to send your miniatures. With love and kisses to you all, I subscribe myself your affectionate husband, Silas W. Haven.[22]

On board steamer *Draden,* March 9, 1864

Dear Jane,

We marched from our camp three miles yesterday [with] all our things packed in our knapsack, and although our loads were pretty heavy and it was a hot day, we found that we could take them quite easy compared with a month ago. It rained all day and we had to march a mile up the river to where the boat lay in the mud, which was no easy job as the mud is rather sticky. I expect we are going up Red River on a kind of a raid, to be gone thirty days, and after that I expect that we shall go to Memphis or Columbus to stay awhile.[23] We are going in force that there is not probability of our getting into any fight with the rebs. I don't expect that we shall get any pay till we get back so you must get along the best you can. Our sergeant that is at Floyd recruiting wrote to some of the boys that the supervisors were not going to pay the dollar a week any more, which I think is a perfect shame as the men that join now get bounty enough now without the company paying them two hundred more and taking the small pittance that they have been paying to the families of those that volunteered eighteen months ago and have stood the brunt of the hardships. I hope it is not so, but if it is, they will hear from the soldiers in a voice that they will not like. I thank Ella and Emmett for their kind letters and will answer them when I can get time. They must be patient for I don't expect that I can send any letters out for a month or six weeks to come. I was sorry that Olive had been sick. I know pretty well what the earache is and know how to pity her. I hope she will not have it anymore. I have no fears of the rebs shooting me as they are rather poor shooters and are afraid of getting too close to us, and most of all, I have faith in God that he will protect me from all harm, and that eventually he will restore me to you and the children, and my prayer is that you may have that faith and to put your trust wholly in him and then your fears for my safety would vanish away. With love and kisses to you all, I remain your affectionate husband, Silas W. Haven.

Up the Red River, March 18, 1864

Dear Jane,

I heard some of the boys say that a mail was going out in half an hour so I will try to write a few lines. Sunday we disembarked and marched out to a fort four miles out. When we got there, we found it evacuated; as usual we went back to the boats and made preparation for a five days' foot race and got ready to start at eight in the evening and marched till one at night, and got up at four in the morning and started at six, and marched about 20 miles and got here about 2 in the afternoon. Companies B and G was deployed as skirmishers about noon and beat up the brush, but could not get near nary reb in the afternoon; three companies, B, G and K, were but in the advance and we made quick time till we got to a town about 1 ½ miles from the fort, and then our regiment was stopped for guard duty till the soldiers had all passed. About the time that the column had all passed, we heard the artillery down to the fort, so we hurried along as fast as we could as it is quite natural for our regiment to do when there is rebs ahead and got to the fort in time to make the charge with our brigade, which was done in first-rate style and the works carried. Our regiment did not lose a man, although the shell and shot passed pretty near us. The rebs had a pretty strong fort, and in two weeks more would have had it pretty near impregnable. They had two splendid large cannon in the fort besides others mounting close to the river bank. I don't know how many guns, any prisoners we have taken (not far from 300 prisoners), nor do I know what the loss is. We had a sad accident happen in our company just before we was ordered to charge. We were all laying down, and a gun went off and shot one of our men through the breast, but we are in hopes he will recover. The mail is just going out, so with love and kisses to all, I close. S. W. Haven[24]

—

FOLLOWING THE MILITARY engagements at Fort DeRussy, Pleasant Hill, and Yellow Bayou during the Red River campaign, Col. James Gilbert reflected on the battles in his official report. He noted:

> When the column had moved by I assembled the guards and moved rapidly forward, keeping well closed up on the train just in my advance. When cannonading commenced the remainder of the brigade to which my regiment was attached were in the advance, having moved forward while we were on duty as provost guards in the town of Marksville. . . . We were ordered to relieve the Fourteenth Iowa Infantry, and moved up to do so, but at that moment a simultaneous charge was ordered. It was a long way to the fort (De Russy). The ground over which we must charge was well cleared of trees. Many logs lay on the ground, and several ditches were to be crossed. At the command, "Forward, double-quick, march!" the entire regiment sprang forward with a will, moving too rapidly at times for a long charge, but all the time under apparent good control. We sprang into the ditch on the east and south sides of the fort, and mounted the parapet in

all haste. When the fort was surrendered a part of my regiment, with others of other regiments, joined in a fire of musketry, and with them united in a wild, ringing, vociferous yell of joy. It was the first time we had ever charged upon an enemy's works, and it has not been reported to me that any officer or soldier failed to do his duty and to do it well.[25]

—

On Board of Steamer *Draden* near Alexandria, Louisiana, March 20, 1864

Dear Jane,

As I have a few minutes to write in before the mail goes out, I will try to write a few lines to you to let you know how we get along. My health has been good, except I had a diarrhea last week, which most of the boys are subject to on this trip. I lay it to drinking the water and don't mean to drink anymore than I can help as I have plenty of coffee. This is the finest country we have been in down South. It is mostly settled with French. We have been here for the last three days and the troops are mostly camped on shore. I come on board last night as it was going to rain. The boys have been foraging a considerable. They get any quantity of sugar, molasses, lots of meat, chickens, beef, pork. I don't know how much longer we shall stay here, but not a great while, I guess, as Banks' force is close to here, ready to move. Our boys feel pretty well over the fight the other day and the colonel thinks there is no cowards in the 27th. We know that he is no coward and will not tell the regiment to go, but it is. Come on, boys. Our man that was shot accidentally [Jacob Beck] is getting well.[26] He was shot through the breast. It went in on the left of his backbone and come out near his throat. He was laying down at the time. The same ball cut another man [H. Perrin] a close call; they have blowed the fort and breastworks all to pieces.[27] There were about four thousand rebs here when we come, but they skedaddled for safer quarters and I guess will disperse, but I must close for this time. With love and kisses to you all, I close for this time from your affectionate husband, Silas W. Haven.

On board Steamer *Draden* at Alexandria, LA, March 22, 1864

Dear Jane,

A week ago last Sunday, we got off from the boats and marched four miles to take a fort, but the rebs left as usual so we marched back again and fixed up five days' rations, and started at nine o'clock at night and marched eight or ten miles and camped at one o'clock. We started again at five and marched about thirty miles, and had a fight of about two hours and took a strong fort and breastworks. The fort was named DeRussy.[28] I believe our regiment was in front and left in front at so that company G and B were the advance. We skirmished through the woods in one place, but did not find any rebs. We pass some of the finest country I have seen down South. The apples were all blowed out and corn was up three or four inches. The advance and foragers drove the rebs so fast that they could not burn the bridges, so we got to the Fort without any delay, and what was in the fort could not get away but had to fight or surrender. Our regiment was left back to a town two miles and a half as provost guard till the troops had all passed, and then we came up and took our place in the brigade after they had shelled them and they us a shell. Our brigade made a charge. The 27th was laying the furthest off, but got inside as quick as the rest. Our colonel was the first commanding officer in the fort, but the colors of the 24th Missouri were hoisted first. I don't know justly how many prisoners we took, but have heard it stated at three hundred and eighty. They were made enough because the rest deserted them and said that they would not fight anymore. One has enlisted in our regiment. They had some splendid large guns and they was just getting the range of our regiment as we charged. Quite a number of shot and shell passed and burst over us, but luckily did not hurt a man. One of the 14th Iowa killed the captain of the gun that was bearing on us. He had just got the gun loaded, but did not get the rammer out. I think if he had had time to have fired it, it would have been apt to have killed some. They had some strong breastworks on the river. One was covered with railroad iron. I suppose they thought that the gunboats could not do anything with it, but they give it a try when they went to destroy the breastworks and fort, and the third shot made a hole through the iron and threw half of a rail over a half a mile into the woods. I suppose you would like to know how I felt. I don't know as I can tell exactly as I was pretty well tired out, and when we were ordered to lay down, I generally would lay with my elbow on my knapsack as I usually do when resting on the road. I expected every minute to see some of the boys hit, but did not expect that I should [be]. The colonel rode around through the woods without fear. He sends three times for leave to charge; when he got it the dismounted and took the head of the regiment and when we come into line. He was forward of me the most of the time. We had a big log to get over and I went over it close to his heels. The boys kept up a continual yelling, but I did not [holler] as I wanted to save my breath to carry me into the fort. Just as we got orders to charge, a shell burst over our heads, and a man accidentally shot off his gun and the ball cut H. Perrin's cap and went clear through Jacob Beck.[29] It did not kill him and I guess he will get along. There is quite a number of men sick with the diarrhea caused by the water. I am in hopes that we shall soon proceed on the object of our expedition. I expect that they are waiting here for the water to rise, so that the boats can get over the bar, and when they do start, I expect they will soon clean the rebs out of this part of the country. Our destination, I expect, is Shreveport and as we have so large a force, I don't think that we will have any fighting to do. Banks' force is on the same errand, and part of them are here. There was about four thousand rebs here when we came, but they skedaddled as usual. Our boys have got great times foraging [for] sugar, and some are stewing down the new unrefined and eating the most of the time. The regiment had orders to be ready in five minutes' notice last night to go after some rebs about fifteen miles from here. I, being on the sick book, did not have to get ready. They got ready and stood until they were wet as it rained and hailed last night and then come on the boat to stay. I heard that some force took four hundred rebs, but don't know how true it is. The boys are doing pretty good business fishing. They catch them all the way from thirty up to near a hundred pounds. One of our men caught one that weighed fifty-three pounds and has just gone by that weighed eighty-three pounds, both caught by men of our company. I expect that a mail boat has just come up so I will lay this one side and see if I don't get some letters. With love and kisses to you all and an unwavering trust in God that we shall be permitted to meet again here on earth. I subscribe myself your affectionate husband, Silas W. Haven.

Camp of the 27th near Gratia, Louisiana, April 4, 1864

Dear Jane,

I thought I would write a few lines today to let you know how we get along and all the news I can think of, which will not be much, I guess. We stayed at Alexandria nine days. We went down the river about 20 miles to get rails and forage some one day. They got quite a lot of sugar at a sugar mill close to the river. We started on the 26 of March to march about 30 miles so that the boats could get up the rapids. We went 20 miles the first day and the second, we got to Blanchard's landing about noon, where we stayed five days and started day before yesterday and come to this place. How long we shall stay here, it is hard telling. Banks' men are ahead marching by land, which is the reason that we stop by the way, and if he don't have any trouble to take Shreveport, we shall probably be ordered back. We are a kind of a reserve for his force. I rather think that by the time we get to Shreveport that the rebs will be somewhere else. Their men are deserting in large numbers, and the men of this state and Arkansas will not fight any more. My health has not been very good since we took Fort DeRussy.

I had the diarrhea and a lame back. My diarrhea is well, but my back troubles me some so that I can't carry my knapsack on a march. I tried it the last march and give out and rode in the ambulance the first day. The second I told the doctor that if I did not have anything to carry, I thought I could get through so he had me put my gun cartridge box and knapsack in the ambulance so I get along very well. The boys all feel pretty well when they get out in camp. It is amusing to hear them last night they commenced about as soon as dark. It would first be one thing and then another. One initiating the squalling of a child, the braying of a mule, anything to keep a noise going. When they are on the boat, they are generally pretty quiet, trading watcher revolvers, melting over wet sugar (taffy they call it) into wet and candy is all the go now. I have only fixes over some once as I did not care about eating much while I had the diarrhea. I stirred mine into grained sugar. It tasted a good deal like maple sugar. I want to hear from you real bad, but shall have to wait till I get back and then I am in hopes that I shall get your miniatures. Write often and write all the news. With love to you, I remain your affectionate husband, Silas W. Haven.

—

IN THE FOLLOWING LETTER, Haven described the first major engagement that the 27th Iowa faced during the course of the war. Confederate Gen. Richard Taylor positioned his force at Mansfield, Louisiana, between Gen. Banks and Shreveport, Louisiana. After the battle at Sabine Crossroads, a federal defeat, Union soldiers fell back to Pleasant Hill. Taylor attacked the Union forces again the next day, April 9, 1864. Although the Confederates successfully advanced, the Union soldiers held, counterattacked, and won the battle. However, Banks, without any support from Gen. Steele, stuck in Arkansas, fell back to Grand Ecore, Louisiana.

—

Grand Ecore, Louisiana, April 14, 1864[30]

Dear Jane,

I expect that by this time to have dated this letter from Shreveport, but here I am, back at this place, safe. We started from here the 7th to go up the river and went slowly till the afternoon of the 10th, when a dispatch came from Banks to turn back, which we did not like very well as we were then within about 25 miles by land and about fifty by water from Shreveport. We got a dispatch that our army was falling back, had had a pretty severe fight and was pretty badly cut up, which made us pretty anxious to hear from the boys, but we found that we had business on our hands to get back, so we made our first preparation to fight our way with knapsacks and everything that could be made available. We made the return good. Yesterday, they made the balls fly some, but did not [do] damage to our company as our boys fired back so fast that they did not dare to show themselves, so they shot over us as three balls hit our boat, one went into the pilot house. The boats got under shelter of the bank so they did no particular damage, only we had to stay till nearly night before the gunboats could get off from the bar and keep the batteries busy so that the boats could run the blockade, which a few of them did. None got very serious by injured. Our boat did not start till after Sunday but for some cause, they did not shell us. Our army had a pretty severe fight at Pleasant Hill and met with a pretty severe loss. Banks' men fought the first day and got whipped out the second day. Our forces 16th and 17th army corps, about nine thousand men, fought twenty-seven thousand and whipped them. Banks then ordered them to fall back to this place (our Brigade the second); [we] lost 550 men in killed, wounded and missing. Our regiment lost 89, I believe, in killed, wounded and missing. Our company lost two killed [William C. Decker and March Olmstead] and five wounded. Two of the wounded was left in hospital on the field, severely wounded (viz. Sgt. Robert Beck and Stacy Purdy). The rest viz. John Wright wounded in the leg, James Noble in [the] shoulder, Sylvester Bennett in the knee. I have not seen all the boys yet as they have not got back from their expedition. The rebs took 18 or 20 guns from Banks the first day. Our men got nine from them the second. The rebs also got over a hundred baggage wagons from Banks so they have got provision, ammunition and clothing to last them some time as all of our boys lost their blankets as they took them off to fight and did not have time to go back after them. So I guess that the expedition is at an end for this time, as the water is falling fast, and I expect that we shall have to get the boats to Alexandria as soon as they can, which will suit us first rate as we don't have any wish to fight under Banks any longer, for it has been mismanaged all through. One thing [is] he was too slow and after he left, he ordered the transports to move up the river when we had not ought to have left here or, at most, more than two or three boats with rations and ammunition till after he had his battle, which he expected this side of Shreveport, and then in marching he had his baggage ahead of his infantry, which give the rebs a chance to cut it off, and after the battle, if he had pressed on to Shreveport, we should have got the place without any more fighting and our boats would not have been in any danger of being captured. The rebs did not know that there was any of the 16th army corps here till they made a charge on them, and then they found it out pretty quick. Those that were in the battle of Shiloh said that the freezing was worse and harder fighting than there. The 32nd met with pretty heavy loss. I got two letters from you this morning, which is the first that I have had since I started on this expedition. I was very glad to hear that you were all well, also that you had got your money from the county. Write whether you expect to get any this year. I am in hopes that I can get a furlough when I get back, but it is very doubtful whether I can so you must not be expecting me. I want to see you all very bad, but if I can't get a furlough, the time will soon roll around and I have faith in the divine providence that my life will be saved, that the same protective care that has shielded me for so many years will still be extended over me, and that we soon shall meet again. I dream about you often. I am in hopes that when I get back to the river or the next mail we get, that your pictures will come, for I expect you all have changed some and I see you in my dreams the same that you were when I left you. I still think that this war will close this season so that we all can spend our next winter at home. This expedition will be damage to us, but still it can be remedied. I have not shot my gun at a man yet, and I hope I shall not have to, but still, if it is necessary, I shall. Had I seen a man when they were firing on us, I should have tried pretty hard to have put him [down]. I had rather save a man's life than to take it. I was the means of saving one of our soldiers the night that we left here to go up the river. One of the 33rd Wisconsin fell from a boat just above ours and I was on guard. I thought where to find a rope in time to just throw it to him before we went under, but the boat he did not know how we got into the water and could not swim, but it is getting late and I will begin to close. Tell the children I think of them every day. I hope that the time will soon come when I can see them again. With love and kisses to you all, I will close for this time. From your affectionate husband, Silas W. Haven.

Alexandria, Louisiana, April 25, 1864

Dear Jane,

I seat myself to answer your letter of March 28th, which I got at Grand Ecore the 16th of this month. I have been on the boat ever since the 7th. My health has been pretty good, only my back and side will not allow me to march so I have been on duty part of the time on the boat. After we got to Grand Ecore, our boat took three or four hundred prisoners up the river to exchange. They were most all Texans. We had a pretty good time as they [were a] jovial set, and our boys traded notions with them for knapsacks. I traded my new gold pen off for two silver rings, which I want to send you as soon as I can. We had quite a time getting to this place. One boat snagged and sunk. They took most everything off from her and burnt it. I believe the army has not got here yet. They have had some fighting, and we heard that Smith's division (ours) had taken two thousand prisoners and nine pieces of cannon. I expect as they were nearly fifteen miles out this morning, and then I expect that we shall return back to the Mississippi. Our corps is going to Fort Pillow. I hope it is as I don't like the climate here, especially the water. We have just heard from the army. They have had a pretty hard time marching through as they have had to fight most all the way. I forgot to say that I got your miniatures all safe the same time I got your last letter. I think they look quite natural. The children have grown some. I take a great deal of pleasure looking at them. I like to hear how all the folks get along. There appears to be a lion in the path of the church there. I am afraid that they are too worldly minded to get along. I do hope that they will get a good energetic minister there soon to wake them up. I wish I could send you some of my surplus rations. I got a good deal more coffee than I can use; sometimes I sell it, but often give it away. The boys send some to other regiments on this trip. We get 40 cents a pound for it. Our rations that we draw are all good and we have plenty of them. The prisoners and Negroes that you heard that Sherman took on the other raid is a fact as I saw them or part of them with my own eyes and our regiment took some of the prisoners.[31] We are fetching away a large number of darkies on this trip. Our boat was nearly loaded down with them that we picked up on the banks of the river. There is some recruiting offices for darkie regiments on board. I guess they have got nearly a full company on our boat. I don't expect to write again till I get back to the Mississippi River. With love and kisses to you all, I close this time. From your affectionate husband, Silas W. Haven.

Alexandria, LA, May 4, 1864

Dear Jane,

I suppose you would like to know what the army is doing here, but I could not tell unless it is waiting for the gunboats to get below the rapids. They are damming the river now and I think that as soon as they can get the gunboats down, we shall leave here. The rebs are all around us, but I don't think that they will attack us for we have got a pretty heavy force here, and the gunboats can operate with the army and the rebs like to keep a proper distance from them. We had quite a scare a few days ago. The rebs made a dash on two divisions of the 13th army corps, and they burnt their tents and come into town. The troops all got out in line and just before night, our brigade went out about four miles where the dash was made and held the ground all night, but no rebs showed themselves. If Gen. Smith had the command of the army, the rebs would have been cleaned out this side of the Mississippi; as it is, the expedition is nearly a failure and Gen. Smith's troops (16th and 17th army corps) saved the army at Pleasant Hill and protected the eat [i.e., food] of the army to this place, and now Banks will not let us go back till he gets ready.[32] Although a great many reinforcements have come for his army, we think that he is afraid to have us leave till he gets ready to go. The rebs are at work on the river. They have fired into a number of boats below us and have captured two transports and burnt them (the *Emma* going down and the *City Belle,* I believe, is going up). I don't know whether it was destroyed or not.[33] I find you all looking at me every morning when I open my picture case.

Private
Dear Jane,

I expect you wonder why I don't go out with the regiment, so I will tell you my present situation. The day that we took Ft. DeRussy we marched so far and done so much double quicking that I overdone myself and I had the diarrhea and a pain in my side and back, and the Dr. marked me for a march from this place to Blanchard's landing. When we was going up with the regiment, they had to carry me, and when they started up to Shreveport, they also marked me to go along but not to carry any gun, but there came a detail for a guard on the boat and the orderly send me and when we started back, the doctor marked me as one to come on the boat. The other day when the regiment went to the front, I tried marching and made out by a great beat of exertion to keep up as they went slow, but I made up my mind that I should not try it again very soon, and I went to the doctor and told him just how I was, and showed him my breach, which I partly got in Memphis and which come out worse after overdoing, so I am excused from all marching or heavy duty. My health is middling good, only I have the diarrhea some and expect to have it more or less till we get out of this river. If I exercise much, my side and back troubles me some. I would like to know how Fred gets along, whether he is going to get his discharge and whether he has ever seen Captain Slocum at Davenport or not. Captain Slocum has not got back and we don't hear from him very often, and I don't care whether he ever joins the company or not as we get along very well without him.[34] Our colonel is as good an officer as there is in the service and the men all like him, and he takes some notice of me and will stop and talk with a sick man and ask them how they get along. From your affectionate husband, Silas W. Haven.[35]

CHAPTER 6

# Copperheads Are as Still as Mice

## *June–December, 1864*

THROUGHOUT THE second half of 1864, Pvt. Haven dealt with a host of health issues, including smallpox and constant diarrhea. As Haven recovered, his regiment participated in Gen. A. J. Smith's expedition to Tupelo, Mississippi (and its corresponding battle on July 14–15, 1864) and then on to Oxford, Mississippi, in August 1864. In September, the Iowans pursued Gen. Sterling Price, who raided large portions of Missouri and eastern Kansas. The 27th Iowa marched through Arkansas and Missouri, and then joined Gen. George Thomas and his army at Nashville, Tennessee, to protect the city from Confederate Gen. John Bell Hood's invasion. From June to October, Haven recovered from a mild case of smallpox in Vicksburg, spent some time in Memphis, and then returned to Iowa and spent time at Camp McClellan, in Davenport. Haven moved to St. Louis, the base of operations for his regiment, which was out fighting at Jefferson City, Missouri, in October. Although Haven was with the 27th Iowa for the Nashville campaign, he missed the battle due to nagging health issues. He used his correspondence with Jane to discuss the reelection efforts of Abraham Lincoln and the prospects of Union victory. As William T. Sherman captured Atlanta and marched to the sea, Philip Sheridan controlled the Shenandoah Valley, and Grant kept Lee in check at Petersburg, Virginia.

—

Smallpox Hospital at Vicksburg, June 2, 1864

Dear Jane,

I did not have anything to write to you after we got out of the Red River, but sent a letter that I had written before and as it is so long since you have heard from me, I expect that you begin to think that there is something the matter. Our boat was fired into two different days coming down from Alexandria, but nobody [was] hurt and the boat only hit three or four times. I was taken with a violent headache on the 17th of May and was quite unwell for two or three days. The doctor gave me some medicine, but did not find out what was the matter with me so I was transferred to the Hospital boat *Chouteau* and we got to this place the 24th, and I, with seven others, was sent to the smallpox hospital to get well, which I am ding quite fast. My scabs are most all dried up and picked off. I have only had to take two doses of oil, and now my bowels are regular, and I have a good appetite and plenty to eat. I am on half rations, which is beef soup and a slice of bread and fruit, either dried apples or grapes. I have tea and coffee with milk in it and sugar if I want, so you see I have plenty of that that is good to eat and am doing finely. I don't know how long I shall have to stay here, probably two or three weeks yet as they don't let them leave as soon as they got over the smallpox, but keep them till they get strong. I shall not have any scabs on me after a day or two longer, but am quite weak, although I set up and whack around the most of the time. The hospital is in quite a pleasant place, about three miles from town, and lots of apples and peaches growing all around. I expect that the regiment is paid or will be before I join it so that I shall not get any pay till July. So you will have to get along the best you can. I have not had any mail from you for some time. I expect that one mail was burnt on the *City Belle* below Alexandria and why I have not got any since I don't know. The last date was March 27th. I got the same time with the pictures. I don't expect to stay here long enough to get a letter from you so you must still direct to the regiment. With love and kisses to you all, I close for this time. From your affectionate husband, Silas W. Haven.

General Post Hospital, Vicksburg, June 10th 1864[1]

Dear Jane,

I suppose you by this time are anxious to hear how I get along so I will write you a few lines to let you know that I am getting along first rate. I have got along well ever since I come here, and today went to the convalescent table, where I had meat and beans to eat. I have taken but little medicine since I come here. The doctor gave me two or three sleeping powders and two doses of oil when I first come here, and then gave me whiskey punch till a day or two ago, and now I have a quart of ale a day to drink. I have also lived pretty well. I had beef soup, chick and oyster soup once in a while, and all the applesauce I could eat with once in a while blackberries and grapes. So you see that I have not starved and now I am put on [a] full meat diet so I guess that I shall get along. I don't know how much longer they will keep me here, probably two or three weeks as they don't want the patients to carry the smallpox to the regiment or send them away till they get strong as the smallpox is very weakening. I shall have to draw all new clothes as what I brought here were all burnt up. I don't know whether the government will furnish them or have them charged on my clothing bill. I have not got any mail yet and am very anxious to hear from home, but I suppose I shall have to be patient. I may not get any till I join the regiment, which has gone up the river, but to what place I don't know. You must not worry about me as I am foraging better than I should if I were with the regiment. They have excellent doctors here. They take great interest in the men, but I must close. With love and kisses to all. From your affectionate husband, Silas W. Haven.

I expect that Ella would like to comb my head now as I get a few lice in it, the first head lice I have had, but I am getting them killed off. There is a possibility that I may be detailed as nurse here as nurses are rather scarce.

Gen. Post Hospital, Vicksburg, MS, June 19, 1864

Dear Jane,

I thought I would commence a long letter to you today, although I don't know whether I shall send it from here as I am in hopes to get away from here in two or three days. I was reading today some of the letters I got from you, all of them speak about cold weather, ice, etc. It is not very cold down here. In fact, it is decidedly hot. Last night was about as hot a night as I have seen down south, and this forenoon has been a regular scorcher. The apples and blackberries are beginning to get ripe. I got a few apples yesterday and today I went to the blackberry patch (about ten rods off), and in a few minutes eat all I wanted, which was not a few. I am going to try to get the baker to bake me a blackberry pie tomorrow. I have got so that I can eat most anything. My bowels, with the exception of one day, have been regular. They fed us on potato soup three times a day without any fruit when I first went to the convalescent table, which brought on the diarrhea. I quit eating soup a couple of days and I was cursed with the diarrhea, but I did get some bread and butter, so I had plenty to eat that suited me. My health keeps good, although for the last three nights I have had no blanket to sleep on. I have lived the best here of any place since I came into the army. There is between twenty and thirty white patients here now, about all getting along first rate. One man has got the diarrhea with his smallpox, which renders his case rather doubtful. The most of the cases are light (called varioloid), although there is a few that are speckled enough. There is about one death a week in our camp. Some are fetched here in a dying condition. The camp for the darkies is about sixty rods off. They die off pretty fast for a spell, two a day was the average. The smallpox is decreasing. They don't come in as fast as they did, so I guess that they have got nurses enough, and I don't think there is any danger of their keeping me for one. We had some stewed fresh beef, stewed dried apples, a can of tomatoes boiled in the can and bread (there is only three that goes to the convalescent table now; seven was sent away yesterday), not much of a bill of fare, but we had plenty of it. Tomorrow is our ration day. Last week, some of the darkies stole some of our rations so that we did not have so much of a variety. The darkies are great on stealing. I believe I wrote all my share of the letters from you at Memphis as I hear that the head goes of the regiment is there at present of the Red River expedition, and before this time you have read the full particulars of it, so you can judge whether a cotton and nigger pays or not. Had Banks pushed ahead and let the cotton alone, the expedition would have been successful without the loss of so much life and property. Although he got quite a lot of cotton, sugar, it is no offset for the useless waste of life. Had they held the battlefield one day and buried the dead, which our Gen. Smith wanted to, we could have claimed the victory for the rebs were fairly whipped. They call it a drawn battle, although by Banks' course, they reaped all the advantages. I have written one letter for a man in my tent that first had the smallpox and then syphilis and has lost the sight of an eye. The refugees are nearly all sick and the children are lousy enough to run a sawmill. One little girl, about as big as Ella, fell down a hatchway yesterday. She fell about eight feet and struck on her back and head. It did not break any bones, only gnarred her some. She is around this morning, as well as ever. While I was writing the other day, a refugee woman died. She left four or five children; one is a babe not two months old. They buried her in about two hours after she died.

June 23

I have been here a month and shall probably leave tomorrow. The doctor was going to send in three names today, but the quartermaster was absent. I could have got away two or three days ago, I expect, but I thought if I stayed a day or two, I could hear where the regiment was. I have not heard from them, nor have had any mail sent to me since I have been here. I think you will find this letter long enough if there is nothing in it. I expect to find some. I have lived pretty well since I have been here, especially since I have got well enough to eat blackberries and apples. I sold the coffee that I brought here (nearly 2 pounds) to some darkies for 25 cents, which is better than leaving it here. I have got to leave everything I brought here, and all I expect to get will be a suit of clothes to wear away. I shall try to get vouchers for what I leave so as to get pay for them when I get to the regiment. The weather has been quite rainy, cool and comfortable for a few days back, but it is a hot one today.

On board of steamer *Madison,* June 30, 1864

I did not get away from the hospital as soon as I expected as they had made new regulations to only discharge Mondays of each week. After I got my discharge from hospital, I came to the soldier's home at Vicksburg and stayed there till yesterday. When I got aboard of this boat (which, by the way, is a slow one) and we got started about midnight and have got as far as Milliken's Bend, where they have been taking on wood ever since about 3 this morning, and probably will be till noon before we get started. The soldier's home is a first-rate place to stay. We had good fare and beds. The soldier's homes are carried on by the Sanitary Commission. My health is pretty good at present. I did not get any clothes except what I had on, only I managed to wear away one of my shirts and brought my cap. I expect I shall have to lose my knapsack, two blankets, a dress and an overcoat and a shirt as that is what I had to leave there. There is quite a lot of soldiers from the hospital, paroled prisoners on this boat, besides a lot of white refugees who are going north. It is a pretty hard-looking group of people. I have got this long letter pretty near full, and I will mail it as soon as I get to Memphis and write again when I get to the regiment. I don't know yet where the regiment is, but expect that they are somewhere on the Montgomery Charleston Railroad. I want to get with them before they are paid off. If I don't have to wait two months more for my pay, which will be pretty hard on us, for you need some pretty bad by this time. I know I do as I am most out. I have only two envelopes, paper most out and also my stamps.

Helena, Arkansas, July 2[2]

Well, we have got to this place all safe, although we expected to get fired into yesterday. We saw some guerrillas, but we outwitted them, I expect, by going around an island. I expect that we shall get to Memphis tonight and I won't be sorry as we are pretty well mixed up, soldiers, refugees, and darkies, and this is a regular hay pen of a boat, and a regular slow concern too. I want you should write all the news you can think of as I am very anxious to hear how you all get along, and tell Ella and Emmett to write as I want to see how much they have improved. With love and kisses to you all, I will close for this time. From your husband, Silas W. Haven.

Memphis, Tennessee, July 4, 1864

Dear Jane,

I got here night before last, all safe, and yesterday morning I went to the soldier's home and after I got my breakfast, I commenced to hunt the whereabouts of the regiment out; did not make out much till afternoon, when I got into the hospital and found a lot of the boys there. The regiment is at La Grange, and they have sent all the boys that are not able to march to the hospital and Ft. Pickering. While I was at the hospital, Capt. Slocum came in and so he got my mail for me this morning. I was glad to hear that you were all well and that Fred had at last got home. It appears that death has been at work in Rockford and vicinity. The Red River expedition was a pretty hard one on our regiment. Our company lost eight dead, besides quite a number that will not be fit for marching, myself among the number. The boys are keeping up a continual cracking with their fireworks. The militia has been parading around here and I believe that they are going to have quite a time the afternoon and evening. My head is so confused with the noise that I will close for now. With love and kisses to all, I close for this time. From your affectionate husband, Silas W. Haven.

Private

It is sometime since I wrote anything private, but I thought I would write a few lines in this. I expect that if I had my pay, I could get a furlough I would take one with, but I should have to get transportation and it would delay me so that I would not have more than four or five days to stay at home. The regiment is at La Grange and I think that I shall go out there tomorrow.[3] I would like to be with the regiment when it is paid as then I would get my pay and if they are not paid this month, it will be two months before we can get any. The captain thinks that it is useless for me to go to the regiment as I am not fit for duty such as they have to do as my rupture won't let me march or do any hard work, and I don't know as I have written about it, but I have partly lost my voice. It will wear off after a while, but it may be a year first. You see that they can't do anything with me at the regiment. If I was at home, I could help around a considerable, but that I expect will be an impossibility. Good bye, SWH.

Fort Pickering, Tennessee, July 5, 1864

Dear Jane,

If you get all the letters I send this week, you will have a pile of reading. I drew off some verses while at the Hospital at Vicksburg, and I thought I would send them to you and write a few lines to let you know where I am. I came to the fort last night and they told me that it was not necessary for me to report to the regiment first, but if I was not able for duty to stay here. I wanted to see the colonel and see if I could not get some pay for the clothes that I had to leave at the Hospital, but Lieutenant Colonel Lake is on duty here in town, and as soon as I can get a pass, I shall go and see him and if there is any chance to get pay, he will tell me how, and if I had my descriptive roll here, I would be all right for then I could draw me some clothes.[4] I need a blanket very bad as I have not got anything to sleep under. I am sorry that the old cow is furrow and I think that you had better buy another if you can get a good one if Sam will let you have the Kimball cow. I think you had better get it, but he will have to wait till I get my pass for the money. Uncle Sam owes me six months' pay now (eighty-four dollars), and it may be two or four months before I get any. I shall have a pile when I do get it, but my paper is full, so good bye for this time. Kisses to all from your affectionate husband, Silas W. Haven.

Camp McClellan, Iowa, September 18, 1864[5]

Dear Jane,

I got to Davenport last Thursday night, and as it was too late to have a letter get to you before next Saturday, I put off writing till today. It got to that night after I left home pretty well tired out, and found them all well, except the baby, which had the flux. It was taxed the Friday before so that they could not go to the funeral. It was getting better. The next day, I went within six miles of Cedar Falls, and the next day I went to the falls and took the cars the same day and got to Laura's about five o'clock and found them all well. Frank Burdick and all his family were there. I went to Horace's the next day and found them all well, and Monday I footed it to Father's and found them all well, but father, he is not very well, but was hauling logs when I got there and worked so hard that he was pretty sick. The next day when I come away, I found Emily and Ida there. I came back to Dyersville with Ida and started to her house overnight, and Wednesday took the cars to Dubuque and put up at the soldier's home and the next day, I took the boat and came to Port Byron at the head of the rapids, and from there I took the cars and got into Davenport about 8 o'clock. My health is about the same. My hand don't pain me quite as bad as it did while I was at home and on my way here. I went to the Doctor this morning and am going to get some medicine at noon. I don't have anything to do yet and don't know but what I shall go to the regiment when they send off a squad. The regiment, I expect, is to Sulphur Springs, about 20 miles below St. Louis. The 44th was here when I got here, and company G was in the barracks just opposite. This is a very pleasant place. I would not mind much to stay here the balance of my time if I could get my pay. I had quite a good visit to Father's but expect that you will hear from them soon, and it may be that some of them will come out and see you soon. I think that you would enjoy a visit out there very much. They all want to see you very much. With love and kisses to you all, I bid you goodbye for this time. From your affectionate husband, Silas W. Haven.

Camp McClellan, Iowa, September 22, 1864

Dear Jane,

The 46th and 47th regiment, besides a number from other regiments whose time is up, are waiting here to be discharged. I don't know how long I shall stay here. They sent off a lot of recruits the other day, but don't send off any old soldiers. There is some talk that they are going to keep the old soldiers here till after the draft to guard the drafted men. The draft is going on here very quietly, and they are offering pretty large sums for substitutes (as high as fifteen hundred dollars). The fair is in operation here. I was down yesterday and took a look at it. There was quite a large crowd there, but did not have anything any nicer than they did at the Floyd County Fair. The regiment is at Jefferson Barracks now, and I expect they will stay there all winter.[6] They was paid off at Cairo so I can't draw any pay till November. If I can get a good position here, I shall stay, although I should have more duty to do than at the regiment, but I would rather be doing something than laying still as time drags heavy in camp with nothing to do. They had quite a time over at Rock Island last night, rejoicing over the recent news from the eastern army.[7] I think that before election, Grant will be in Richmond and am in hopes that before spring, the war will be closed up. I will close by hoping these few lines will find you all well and with love and kisses to all. I bid you goodbye for this time. From your affectionate husband, Silas W. Haven.

Camp McClellan, Davenport, Iowa, October 2, 1864

Dear Jane,

I received your letter yesterday and hasten to answer it. I was very glad to hear from you that you were all well, and also that you had been to Osage. I had been looking for a letter for four or five days, but yours was the first that I received. I some expected to have gotten it Friday, but it takes till Saturday for it to get here. I shall mail this tomorrow night so that you will get it Saturday. This is the fourth that I have sent. No. 2, I expect you got last Tuesday and No. 3 yesterday. I am sorry that you lost your blanket as it would have been so much use to you this winter. I should have bought some if I had had the money to share, and if I get my pay here, I will try and get three or four when the 48th is mustered out. My health is improving. I don't take any medicine now and have not had any duty to do. I drawed some clothes yesterday (2 shirts, 2 pair drawers, 2 pair socks, 1 blouse and one blanket).[8] I have also one woolen blanket, one oil cloth and a knapsack that belonged to a bounty jumper or deserter, which I expect to keep. Camp McClellan has on her Sunday suit today. We all went out on inspection that forenoon. There was about thirty old soldiers out and a company of recruits and one of drafted men, besides about one hundred and fifty drafted men and substitutes, which were inspected before their quarters. We have four classes of men here besides the invalid corps: old soldiers, new recruits, drafted men that reported promptly and drafted men and substitutes. The last are kept under guard. There is also a class of substitutes that [are] kept in the guard house. They take all their money away from them and keep it till they get to their regiments or send it home for them if they want. They do [it] that way to head off the bounty jumpers. I expect they will send off a lot tomorrow or the next day as the drafted men are coming in pretty [quickly] and the Invalid corps guard them. They had three or four tied up by their thumbs this morning. They are all quiet now. With love and kisses to you all, I will close for this time. From your affectionate husband, Silas W. Haven.

Private
Dear Jane,

I suppose you would like to know what we are staying here for and what the prospects are for the future. Well, they are detaining all the old soldiers here to guard the drafted men and conscripts. They use us for noncommissioned officers (sergeants and corporals), and I expect that they will keep us still after the drafted men are all in, and then such as are able to do field duty will be sent to their regiments, and the others will be either discharged or put into the invalids corps.[9] I expect that I probably will be one of the last if I don't get a permanent detail for something else, which I shall try to do. Two ladies, dressed in red, white and blue with McClellan badges, came into camp yesterday, and as one of the ladies' white skirt was rather dirty on the back, the boys hooted them out of camp. Write all the news and write often. From your husband, Silas W. Haven.

Camp McClellan, October 5, 1864, No. 5

Dear Jane,

As it is uncertain how long I shall stay here, I thought I would drop you a line so that you need not send the Miniatures till you get word from me again. They are sending off the recruits and drafted men, and they have some of the old soldiers go with them to guard them, so I am liable to be sent to my regiments any day, and if you send the miniatures here, they might get lost. I shall try to get a permanent detail here if I can. The drafted men are flocking in quite fast and the camp is pretty full now. There is quite a lot going away tonight, about two hundred, I believe. My health is about the same as when I left home. My hand has almost quit paining me, but my side troubles me some yet. We don't get very good rations here, only bread, meat (beef) and beans so that I have to buy the most of my living, which is not much. The butter that I started with from home all melted so I poured out about half of it, and the rest I brought here and it went real good. I buy potatoes and butter, which is the most of my living. I suppose you wonder where I get the money to buy with. Well, when I started to come away from Father's, they asked me how much money I had, and when they found out I had not got but little, Father gave me ten dollars and said I could pay him when I got my pay or when I got home as he did not want I should go (come) down here sick without I had money to pay my way, and it has come very good to me for I should have been clear down sick before this time. You wrote that Ella was sick, but did not say what was the matter. You did not say anything about Kitty. Did she go to Osage with you? But it is most mail time, so with love and kisses to you all, I will close this time. From your affectionate husband, Silas W. Haven.

Camp McClellan, Iowa, October 10, 1864, No. 6

Dear Jane,

I received your letter yesterday and was very glad to hear from you that you were all well. The time passes off very slow here. We don't have very good rations and are now kept pretty close. I expect that we shall be out of it soon, as the talk is that they are going to send us off tomorrow to our regiment. That writing on the back of that envelope was all right as there is no extension of furlough, but they have to send certificates back if they are not bale for duty, so my papers are all right. I think that I shall be very apt to get my pay the forepart of next month if I get to the regiment. The regiment is now at Jefferson Barracks near St. Louis, and expects to stay there this winter. I might have stayed at home longer, but it would have been better if I had come down two or three weeks sooner as then I should have got into the hospital, and before this time should have got a place as nurse. If I only had some money now, I would buy some blankets and clothing and send home as I can buy pretty cheap of the drafted men and substitutes, but I shall have to wait. Write what you think of going to father's a visiting this winter. I am on guard today and have to write this in a hurry. With love and kisses to you all, I will close for this time. From your affectionate husband, Silas W. Haven.

No. 7, Schofield Barracks, St. Louis, October 15, 1864

Dear Jane,

I left Camp McClellan on the 11th and got here last night. We had a pretty good time coming down, although it rained two nights. We had to come on the cars around the rapids above Keokuk and when we got there, we found no boat in, so we had to wait all day. Keokuk is a very pretty place. I found a number that I was acquainted with there. Three of my company (G. N. Potter, W. Decker, brother to one that was killed at Pleasant Hill, and J. R. Howdeshell. His wife is with him and has been with [him] ever since last spring).[10] I had one of my woolen blankets stole at Quincy. I expect that the boat hands got into Quincy and Alton are quite lively places. I have been over this town some today. It is quite a large place and has street railroads all over it. The streets are rather to narrow to suit me. The city is quite full of soldiers and they are sending lots of them, off very day to their regiments. I don't know how long I shall stop here as my regiment is out to Jefferson City. I am going to try to go to Jefferson Barracks to wait till the regiment comes in or sends for their sick and baggage, which is left in camp down there. My health is about the same, although I had the diarrhea pretty bad two days while I was coming down, but I am better now as long as I only eat one kind of food at a meal. I get along first rate, provided I don't have anything to do. I expect that they will put me into the invalid corps as soon as I get to the regiment, but I shall get some pay first. We have no special war news from the front as the movement of the troops is contraband. It is expected that if Price will fight, he will have a chance in a few days; if not, he has got the run pretty lively to get out of Missouri. But I have got my paper most full and have written nothing interesting, so I will close by sending love and kisses to all. From your affectionate husband, Silas W. Haven.

No. 8, Jefferson Barracks, October 20, 1864

Dear Jane,

As I don't know how long it will take for a letter to get from here to you, I thought I would write today and let you know how we are situated. There is about seventy of the regiment here in camp and I don't know how many there is in hospitals, probably as many more. Our camp is on the river bank, and the railroad runs about two rods on the other side so that it is quite business-like. My health is pretty good for me. I came here last Sunday and found the rations better than I have had since I left home. The regiment is out after Price, and as there was no communications with them, they let us come from St. Louis down here to stay. There is no telling when they will get back, probably not for a month. We are not very particular as we don't have anything to do, only to cook our grub and eat. I have a little tent to myself, partly filled with knapsacks, and if it want for my pay, I would not care how long we stayed here. The weather has been pleasant, only it is quite chilly nights, but we have plenty of blankets so that we got along quite comfortable. I don't expect to get any letters till the regiment gets back. Write everything you can think of that will be interesting, and I wish you would send me a St. Charles Paper so that we can find out who to vote for at election, as I am afraid that if the regiment don't get back that we won't have any printed tickets. With these few lines, I will close by sending love and kisses to you all. From your affectionate husband, Silas W. Haven.

October 20, 1864

I expect that you have read in the paper about one of our men (L. J. Treat) getting killed.[11] I will write a full (as far as I can find out) account of it. They arrested the man as a spy, and Treat and others were guarding him. They were on the cars coming up from Potosi and the cars stopped to let the troops get off as it was in the night and quite chilly. Treat spread his overcoat over the man as he only had his pants and shirt on when they stopped the man; [he] handed his coat back to Treat and as he took it, he stabbed him in the throat and cut his jugular vein off so that [Treat] bled to death in a very few minutes. He then jumbled off from the cars and stabbed four or five others before he was recaptured. He was pretty badly mauled as he had one gun broke and one bent over his head. They then tied his hands behind him and brought him up to the next station, but before he got there, the guards said he tried to roll off from the cars, so they stuck two bayonets through him, but did not kill him. The next morning when they reported it to Colonel Shaw, he told them to bury him. They told him that he was not quite dead. He said it made no odds. A woman came and looked at Treat as he was lying close by, and as she started to go off, she said "I've got a rope," so some of the boys went and got the rope, and in a few minutes they had [him] hanging on a tree and let him hang from four or five hours. The news this morning (21st) is good. Sheridan is given the rebs another thrashing. Price is leaving this state, but whether he will get out is doubtful. My impression is that he will. He may have to leave his train as our forces are after him pretty sharp, and the rumor is that Gen. Curtis is near the Kansas line with a large force; if so, Price will have to look out or he will get gobbled. His force is all mounted while ours is mostly infantry, so he can get around rather faster than our forces can. He has quite a large train and that may possibly be captured or he will have to destroy it. The Copperhead papers all say that the soldiers are all for Mac, but they will find out that where Mac get one, Lincoln will get five (some say ten).[12] We don't want the war closed up in the way that he would close it. That is, that the rebs were right and we are wrong so we go to Lincoln with a rush.

—

Gen. Phillip Sheridan, ordered by Grant to clean the Confederate soldiers out of the Shenandoah Valley, defeated Confederate Gen. Jubal Early at Cedar Creek, Virginia, on October 19, 1864. In Missouri, Gen. Sterling Price ordered Gen. Shelby to attack Union forces at Brush Creek, Missouri, near Kansas City, Missouri, on October 22, 1864. Union forces, commanded by Gen. Samuel Curtis and Gen. John Marmaduke, formed a strong position at Westport, in Kansas City. On October 23, 1864, Union forces defeated Shelby at Westport, and the Confederate retreat ended any further threats to Missouri from the Confederates for the duration of the war.

—

No. 9, Jefferson Barracks, October 26, 1864

Dear Jane,

There is a lot of boats go down and up every day, and as there is a sand bar opposite of us, some gets stuck and have to lay over. One got on the other day and it took still after dark to get it off, and then they had to lay over till morning. They have most everything to sell in St. Louis: all kinds of vegetables that we have up north in summer, besides fruit, nuts and persimmons, but as I did not have money to spare, I did not buy any when I was there. I traded watches since I got here and have got one that keeps time and got some "boat" (1.50 in Sutter checks), which I hope will keep me in tobacco till we are paid off, which I hope will be before long. I don't much expect that the regiment will be back for two or three weeks.

October 27

I waited till today to see if there was any particular news to write, but there is none, only our troops are getting the best of Price. They have taken two of his generals and have got all or nearly all of his artillery and expect to get his train; if they do, secession is dead in this part of Dixie. I don't have any idea of where our regiment will be posted. The corps have been reorganized and what part of it we belong to I don't know. It has been rumored that we shall winter in Chicago, but I guess that we shall stay. Guess that we shall stay somewhere on the Mississippi between here and Vicksburg. The fighting in this department is nearly done, I think. Two of our mess went to the hospital and one come back so we only have it six four companies here. I have not got any two-cent stamps yet so I will cut a piece out of the paper and send in this to fill up. I am in hopes that the regiment will get back so that we can get our pay by the middle of next month, for I expect that you need it very bad. Write how you get along husking corn. I expect that it will be all done before you get this and probably are having snow by this time, but I will close for this time by sending love and kisses to all. From your affectionate husband, Silas W. Haven.

No. 10, Jefferson Barracks, Missouri, November 3, 1864

Dear Jane,

It has been a very lonesome day for me today. We have not heard from the regiment for some time and can't give any guess when they will get back or where we shall go to when they do get back. My health continues good for me and I continue on the gain, but I am afraid that when we get on the move, I shall be down again. There is no particular news to write. Some of the Iowa boys have been sent from the hospital to Keokuk, and quite a lot of both Iowa and Illinois soldiers are getting furloughs.

November 4

There is no news the boys are all practically interested nowadays, and as we have but few McClellan men here. We can't raise no excitement as those that are for Mac will not say anything. We all feel sure that Lincoln will be elected and the Union preserved. I expect you will call this a dry letter, but it is a rather wet time. With these few lines, I will close by sending love and kisses to all. From your affectionate husband, Silas W. Haven.

No. 11, Jefferson Barracks, Missouri, November 11, 1864

Dear Jane,

I received your letter No. 6 last Sunday and was very glad to hear from you, but was sorry to hear that you had been unwell. I hope this will find you enjoying good health again. My health has been pretty good till yesterday. I had an attack of the diarrhea, but I kept quiet and did not eat anything till night and have got it checked up. I expect that it was brought on by the wet weather.

Election Day passed off very quiet here. We voted at the barracks. There was 168 for Lincoln to 12 for McClellan of the Iowa soldiers.[13] We all feel pretty well over the election, and things look pretty favorable to us that the war will soon close. Our regiment has not got here and we don't know as they will come here. They are now coming down the north side of the Missouri River, and we have heard that they were going to stop at St. Charles, about 24 miles from St. Louis, and that we are going to join them in a few days, and after they have rested, drawed some clothing (and pay, I hope). I expect that we shall go down the river to either Vicksburg or Memphis to winter. I don't think that we shall do much, only to garrison some place this winter. I have not heard from mother since I left Davenport. I expect to find a number of letters when I get to the regiment. I am glad to hear that Rockford is filling up, but I hope that they are not all Copperheads. I would like to be there with you this winter, but cannot. We have begun to count our time by months and it will soon wear away. I expect that you have plenty of butter. I have to pay sixty cents a pound if I get any. Direct your letters now to the regiment. With love and kisses to you all, I close for this time. From your affectionate husband, Silas W. Haven.

It is uncertain when we leave here as they have telegraphed not to come to St. Charles but to St. Louis. The Lieutenant is going tomorrow to St. Louis to send out. One of our men got a letter from the captain, which says we are going to get pay at St. Charles. Lieut. Granger has come to take the camp to St. Charles.

No. 12, Jefferson Barracks, November 17, 1864

Dear Jane,

I expect that we shall go to St. Louis tomorrow so I will write you a few lines today to let you know how we get along. I keep pretty well yet and hope this will find you all well. I did not get any letter from you last week, and now I don't much expect to get one till one comes to the regiment. It makes me feel lonesome to not get any mail when we are where mail can reach us. I also have not had any from mother since I come here. The last I heard from there, Father was sick. I went up to the office before breakfast, feeling pretty sure that I should have a letter, and was disappointed, and as the St. Louis paper did not come down, we are without news. They have been firing cannon up to St. Louis this morning for some good news, I expect. It was quite warm and cloudy yesterday and today, the sun shines some so we are quite comfortable. We have a squad of six and we put in five cents apiece and bought some potatoes, onions and cabbage and made some soup, and one of our men had a box from Floyd and we had soup, butter, cheese, bread and honey. So, you see, we had a first-rate dinner yesterday in advance of Thanksgiving. I don't sleep very well nights. I only got about four hours sleeping last night and can't think of anything to write so I will lay this by a short time.

November 18

We are going to St. Louis tomorrow. I heard that the regiment came in there today. I expect that we shall be paid soon. I am in hopes that the next time I write, I shall have some pay for you. Write how you all get along. I heard that you had snow up there. I expect that winter has sit in, in good earnest. By this time, I was in hopes that I should have got a letter from you before I left here as you wrote that you was sick when you wrote the last one I got. I have been afraid that you were not able to write. This state is complete by cleaned out of rebel soldiers, but there is some few bushwhackers, but they will soon play out as every paper speaks about the Union soldiers mustering them out. With love and kisses to you all, I remain your affectionate husband, Silas W. Haven.

No. 13, St. Louis, MO, November 24, 1864[14]

Dear Jane,

It is Thanksgiving today and I have been on detail all day drawing rations and only have a few minutes to write. I am pretty well at present. I joined the regiment Saturday and went on guard Sunday, and we were paid yesterday. The weather has been very cold and windy and our regiment was camped on the top of a hill, which made it very disgraceable, and we suffered some. Our regiment is embarked on the boat, ready to go down the river to Memphis probably and maybe to Vicksburg—anywhere but here will suit us, but must hurry. Write all the news and with love and kisses to all, I close this. From your affectionate husband, Silas W. Haven.

---

ON NOVEMBER 25, the 27th Iowa departed St. Louis and moved toward Smithland, Kentucky. The soldiers moved along the Cumberland River and headed to Nashville, Tennessee. The additional Union soldiers joined Gen. George Thomas's forces, who attempted to protect the city from an invasion from Confederate Gen. John Bell Hood, who moved rapidly northward from Atlanta in the fall of 1864.

---

At Cairo, IL, on board Steamer, November 28, 1864

Dear Jane,

We got to this place last evening and as we are under orders, we don't know how long we shall stay here. I improve this opportunity of writing you a few lines. My health is about as usual, although I don't have much appetite and don't sleep very well nights. I wrote you a letter Thanksgiving Day or night rather, in which I sent you some money. I shall put some in this as I want to mail it here as I can't get any time to express it. I guess it will go safe enough, at least it is the best I can do at present. You had better pay Fred and divide the rest as far as it will go. I will send you some more as soon as I can. I don't know where we shall go from here. The talk is that we are going to some place on the Cumberland, but nothing certain. I had rather go south, but I don't know as it makes any odds as it is all inside of ten months, but I must hurry and close or I may not get it mailed here. I will put thirty or forty dollars in this. I want to get some large bills as they paid me off all in ten dollar bills. With love and kisses to you, I bid you goodbye for this time. From your affectionate husband, Silas W. Haven.

No. 15, Near Nashville, Tennessee, December 2, 1864[15]

Dear Jane,

Here we are at Nashville, waiting for Hood to come in and take the place, which we have some objections to his having. We got here yesterday morning and came out about two miles to camp. I was with the wagons and before we got into camp, our company went out on picket and has not come in yet. I don't think that we shall have any fight here. It depends some on what Hood's intentions are if he tries to take this place. There will be a fight. It is supposed that he is threatening this place so as to get by here in to Kentucky and so open a passage to Richmond.[16] They had a fight out 17 miles from here day before yesterday, and we took one thousand prisoners and killed and wounded five or six thousand more, and it is supposed that he is falling back. I expect that we shall only stop here but a few days and then go down the river. I wrote you a letter from St. Louis and one from Cairo with money in it (Nov. 13 and 14). Write whether you get them all safe. I am pretty well for me at present. With love and kisses to you all, I close this from your affectionate husband, Silas W. Haven.

No. 16, Camp of the 27th, near Nashville, December 7, 1864

Dear Jane,

I seat myself on a hard tack box with a sheet forward on my knee to write a few lines to you. Our regiment moved out on the front line the night of the second, and we worked most all night, throwing up breastworks, and we have put in our spare time ever since making them stronger, and now we have got some pretty strong works, and if Hood undertakes to take Nashville, he will find more than he bargained for. It is supposed that Hood [has] some sixty or seventy thousand men, which he wants to cross Kentucky, and it is supposed that he will try to capture this place, but he is too late as we have got as large a force as he has and are well fortified, and I don't think that he will make a general attack on us, but try to get away from us and he has got to start pretty soon or he will have a force in his rear. There is continual firing on the picket line. I was out yesterday, but did not see any of the Johnnies near enough to hit so I did not fire. Once in a while the batteries send a shell amongst them and make them get. I will try to write you a better letter next time. My writing paper is all in my knapsack. This sheet is one that a man gave to me. The Christian Commission come around occasionally, giving paper, books, etc. With love and kisses to all, I close for this time. From your affectionate husband, Silas W. Haven.

December 12, 1864, Camp of the 27th, near Nashville

Dear Father and Mother,

I was pretty sure all day yesterday that I should get a letter from you and when the mail came in, sure enough it came and was read with much pleasure. I expect that you are anxious to know how we get along down here. Well, we got here the 1st and on the night of the 2nd, we formed a line and went to work, throwing up breastworks, and for a few days and nights, we kept as busy as gophers, and now we have got some pretty strong works and are ready for Hood if he wants Nashville, to attack us at any time he gets ready. Either day or night Hood's forces are estimated at sixty-five thousand, and as Thomas did not have half that number,[17] I expect that he thought that he could take Nashville and that would leave the road open for him to go to Kentucky, but Sherman knew what he was about when he left Thomas to take care of Hood, and now Hood is in a fix. If he makes an attack on us here, he will probably lose his whole army. If he tried to leave, he will be very apt to lose his trains and artillery and he can't stay here a great while longer or he will have a large army in his rear as well as in front. So it is uncertain what he will do. Our generals are prepared for any emergency and have force enough to back their plans and more coming every day. There has been some cannonading, just enough to make up the rebs. Our lines are fourteen miles around and well manned, so that quite a battle might be fought and we not know it. With these few lines, I will close in hopes that God in his providence will protect us and give us victory. This from your son, Silas W. Haven.

Well, mother, one sheet was hardly big enough to answer your letter and as I have a little more time, I will try another half sheet as Uncle Sam won't charge any more for carrying a full letter than a half one. The election has passed and the soldiers feel encouraged at the result and think that we are not fighting in vain. The Copperheads must feel pretty cheap on finding that so few of our soldiers could be found to vote for Little Mac. I wish some of them could be down here in front a spell. I would like to go out with them on picket and see how they would like their brother secesh when they had fired a few shots at them. It might possibly raise a smile to see them dodge when a shell went shrieking over their heads or a minie ball whistling by, but such time I hope are nearly over. It is pretty clearly demonstrated that Lee's and Hood's armies are the principal force that the rebs have, and the leading men are beginning to talk of peace and, I think, hope and trust, that before another seed time, we shall have such a peace as we have been fighting for. The deserters from Hood's army say they have not tents and as they are badly clothed, [in] this weather they must suffer a good deal. My paper is full and my fingers are cold so good bye for this time. Yours, with respect, S. W. Haven.

No. 17, Camp 27th Iowa, Nashville, December 14, 1864

Dear Jane,

I got a letter from you last night, dated November 28, also I got one Sunday, dated Nov. 14, and was very glad to hear from you. For the last fourteen days we have been in front expecting an attack, but Hood has thought that it was best for him to leave and so we are under orders to be ready to march in the morning to give him a chase. I don't know whether I shall start out with them or not. I was on picket today, but did not see nary reb, although I could hear the shoot once in a while. I got a letter from Mother [on] Sunday. They were well. I wish it was so that you could go there this winter. I was sorry that I could not express my money all at once as I do not dare to send it from here at present. If you get the other all safe and conclude to go to father's, you had better take all with you, as I think that Ella will be better off with you, especially this winter, but still, you can do as you think best. I am very glad to hear that you are having meetings there and rejoiced to hear that Ella has found her Savior. I hope that many in Rockford will turn to the Lord, but I must hurry and close. If I don't go out tomorrow, I will write some more. Captain Slocum got back a few days ago. He has been up north on furlough. I send the small change that I got when I drew my pay to the children for Christmas. With love and kisses to you all, I remain your affectionate husband, Silas W. Haven.

—

IN HIS REPORT on the performance of the 27th Iowa at the battle of Nashville, Col. James Gilbert wrote the following:

> We had advanced but a short distance when brisk skirmishing commenced. Our skirmishers were checked only a few minutes, however, and soon drove the enemy from his sheltered skirmish line back upon his reserves, and yet steadily back to within 400 yards of a strongly entrenched position. Here they were checked, but, being re-enforced, again advanced to within 200 yards of the rebel works, driving the enemy inside, and, finding good shelter behind trees and stumps, held this position until the main line was ready to charge, all the while doing excellent service in sharpshooting the gunners of a rebel battery in their immediate front. The approach of my command toward the rebel works was necessarily very slow, as it was nearest the pivot upon which the whole right wing of the army swung around upon the enemy's left flank. Heavy cannonading from the enemy occurred at times during the advance, but owing to the thick timber in front he failed to get range so as to do me material damage.[18]

—

No. 18, December 16, 1864, Camp of the 27th, Nashville

Dear Jane,

I wrote to you night before last and as you may be anxious to know how I get along, I wrote today to let you know I stood marching and what we did well. We started pretty early in the morning to go out to see what Hood was doing. Our Generals thought he had laid here long enough and would probably leave, so they thought that they would go out and get some of his artillery, wagon trains and as much of his army as they could as near as I can find out. We took eleven guns, about two thousand prisoners and quite a lot of wagons. One of our men that is in the wagon train was just here and said that there was thirteen ammunition wagons brought to their train after dark last night, so we have got so many certain. Our regiment was in front till most dark and then in closing around a battery, some other brigades got in front so we did not have any fighting to do; although the rebel shells come very close to us, quite a number passed over our heads and some Minnie balls whistled by us. Our forces did not have many men hurt as far as I can find out. There is one missing from Company B, but he may turn up all right as Company B was on the skirmish line, and he might get separated from them and there is so many troops out that it is hard work to find a regiment after getting separated from it. As we did not march very far at a time and did not have to double quick any, I got along very well till night, and then my side pained me some. This morning I was so lame that I could scarcely get around so I was sent back to camp. I saw some of the effects of the carnage as I came in: quite a number of dead horses and one rebel Lieutenant. They were killed by shells. They have been fighting all day so far and as I have been writing, they have made a grand charge. We could hear the musket volleys and the men hollowing as they always do when on a charge. I think that our men were successful as the firing is more distant. It is about five miles to the battlefield. It commenced to rain about noon and has rained slowly ever since. The hardest fighting so far has been done in the rain. I expect you will wonder why I started out on a march. I will tell you: the captain had just got back and have had no chance to tell him my situation, and I thought I would go as far as I could without injuring myself and if they double quicked any, I should have to fall out as I can't keep up. So the officers can't say but what. I have been willing to do all I can, and that is all that is required of any body. I expect that before this reaches you, the fighting in this part will be all done. We may possibly have to chase the rebs, but they will be in no situation to fight after leaving here. I can't say to you not to feel anxious about me for I know you will best put your trust in God for he has protected me so far and I feel assured that he will protect me to the end. With love and kisses to you all, I remain your affectionate husband, Silas W. Haven.

10 o'clock in the morning, December 17, 1864

Dear Jane,

We could hear no news from the battlefield last night so I waited till now to finish. The last we heard was that our brigade had made a charge, but with what success, we did not know. I have been on nettles ever since to hear from our regiment, and I have just heard [that] one of Company G (James McCanna) was wounded in the hand and only eleven in the regiment wounded, none killed.[19] Well, Jane, the battle of Nashville has been fought and won. How much our loss is we don't know yet. We have taken a number of guns and a large number of prisoners. I saw one of the first brigade of our division that come in with prisoners. He said that our corps had done the most of the fighting. You will get the account in the papers long before this reaches you. I got a letter this morning from you. It was sent out to the company yesterday. I was glad to hear that you were all pretty well. It rained all night last night and it has stopped now and is quite warm. I am in hopes that I can get a chance to send you some more money pretty soon, but I must close for this time. With love and kisses to all, I remain your affectionate husband, Silas W. Haven.

No. 19, Convalescent Camp, 27th Iowa near Nashville, December 25, 1864[20]
Dear Jane,

I went to town yesterday and got a supply of paper, envelopes and stamps and seat myself to write a few lines to you. Although I don't know as I can think of any special news to write. It has been over a week since the army has moved out after Hood and we don't get any reliable news from them. The rumor is that Hood's army is fleeing in all directions and our men are capturing large quantities of them. They have got all but two or three pieces of his artillery, and the most of his wagon trains and the fighting in this part is about done up. We don't look for our regiment back here as the talk is that they are going to Memphis or Vicksburg where they belong and go into winter quarters. We are having a pretty good time here as we have nothing to do, only to chop our wood and cook our grub. I walked through town yesterday and took a good look of the place that is three or four streets of it as I passed the prison. I saw a lot of Johnnies out front, waiting to be sent north. They were a hard-looking set and will suffer some up there. You write that everything is high up there. I don't know what you would think if you was down here. I paid 30 cents for ten sheets of paper and seven envelopes and provisions are clear up. I will send you a paper with the military prices in it. I expect you need some money pretty bad and I have had it, but did not dare to send it, but will risk some in this and will send some more soon. Up to December 5, I have got twelve letters from you. I keep a list of the number and dates of those I write to you. This is No. 19. I shall commence new Nos. the first of the year. With love and kisses to you all, I remain your affectionate husband, Silas W. Haven.

I wish you all a Merry Christmas. As this will reach you about January 1st, I will wish you all a happy New Year.

Millville, December 25, 1864[21]

Dear Silas,

We received your letter of the 12th date and we feel more anxious to hear from you again. We heard of the great battle near Nashville before we got your letter, and we feel to rejoice for the great victory obtained. But we feel that many hearts are made sad by the loss of friends and relatives that fell in battle, and we don't know but we are numbered with them. At present we are all well and hope to hear that you are enjoying the same blessing. The report is that Sherman has reached the sea coast and has invested Savannah, Georgia after marching throughout the state with little or no opposition.[22] Had a great battle near Savannah gaining a great victory. Now I expect that Grant will make a move to some purpose, and we hope it will be a peace move with a vengeance as the rebs want to be annihilated. Everything seems to be working right that pertains to the war. The mysteries of God are developing every day. The misty cloud that has hung over our national cause for years past begins to show a golden aspect, and we feel that brighter days are near at hand. But we must not get impatient. We showed too much of that in the beginning. We did not know what a rebellion was at first and rather resented it as an imposter and treated it as such. But now we find that it is a new thing and must be dealt with severity. The exposure of the northern Conspiracy is truly a providential disclosure, [and] that our cause is just is evident by the ways and means that God put in our way to frustrate the secret schemes of the enemy to destroy the Union and expose the rebel sympathizers in our midst. Surely we have great reason to praise God for his mercy endureth forever. Let us praise the God of Israel and worship him as our God who cometh for as in this day of great tribulation and rebellion. I suppose you would like to know how we are getting along about these times. Your father is taking things very easy, sit in house with me a good share of the time. With love and respect, please accept this from your mother. E. Haven

Convalescent Camp at the 27th Iowa near Nashville, Tennessee,
December 30, 1864

Dear Jane,

As I have quite a convenient place to write, I thought I would write you a few lines to let you know how I get along. I have not been very well this week as we had to move our camp inside the picket lines last Monday, and I got the diarrhea for a day and night, which put me back. I feel pretty well today and as we have got fixed up so that I can, I am going to take my pills regular and I think that they will fetch me out all right. Our officers are going to try to get our mail today. I hope they will as I want to hear from you real bad. The last I heard was you had got one of the money letters and I want to know whether the rest have got through safe. I shall not finish this till I find out whether they get the mail or not. We don't hear anything from the regiment. I expect that they are after Hood yet and I guess with some effort, as I just heard that they had sent in sixteen hundred prisoners today. I don't much expect that they will come back here but will go to Memphis or Vicksburg to winter and send for us to join them. Hood's army will nearly all depressed before they get through him so that the fighting in this part will be nearly done.

December 31

It made out to snow about two inches last night, and I started after I got my breakfast to town, and here I am in the Christian Commission rooms, finishing this. I feel pretty well today. I got a pretty good night's sleep, but it is so cold in camp that I guess that I shall stay here the most part of the day. Yesterday was the anniversary of our wedding day; for fifteen years, we have lived together, although for the past two years, I have been absent from home. Still, my thoughts have been with you and I hope that the time is not far distant when I shall be permitted to return to you again. This war, I think, is drawing to a close. The months rolls by pretty fast and soon after August will be here when our term of service closes. Still, we may have to stay till October, but your trust in God for he has protected me so far, and I feel assured that he will protect me to the end. With love, kisses and a happy New Year's to you all, I close for this time. From your affectionate husband, Silas W. Haven.

---

HAVEN WROTE A letter to his parents, dated December 30, 1864, which detailed the campaign around Nashville in a similar fashion to the correspondence with Jane. Haven summed up his impressions of the state of the war, noting, "It looks as if the 'anaconda' was going to draw the rebs all to Richmond and crush them in a heap. Their armies are dwindling down and Uncle Abraham is calling for more men to keep our ranks full. The secesh leaders begin to see the end and tremble. I wonder if they don't imagine a halter around their necks." Haven remained fervently committed to the idea of punishing the Confederacy for their actions as traitors and their involvement in the Civil War.

CHAPTER 7

# I Send This in a Rebel Envelope

## *1865*

For Pvt. Haven, during 1865, the final year of the war, he once again found himself recovering from illness. As the year progressed, he spent time in Mississippi, visited New Orleans, and traveled throughout Alabama, using his downtime to write several letters as the major military operations of the Civil War drew to a close. Haven participated in the military campaign to capture the city of Mobile in March and April 1865, before heading to Montgomery, Alabama, where he remained for the duration of the war. He eagerly anticipated the moment he would be discharged from military service, which took place on August 8, 1865, after a long journey home from Alabama. He used his final year of correspondence to remark on the end of the war, the assassination of President Lincoln, and his personal desire to be reunited with his family.

—

No. 1, Convalescent Camp of the 27th Iowa, near Nashville, Tenn.,
January 2, 1865[1]

Dear Jane,

I take my pen once more to commence a letter to you to let you know how I get along. My health is pretty good for me, although most [of] the time after eating I am sick to my stomach for a little while. Yesterday was New Year's and perhaps you would like to know how I passed it and what I had to eat. Well, I cooked a kettle of salt beef for three of us and cooked rations of beans and had bean soup for my dinner (or supper rather). I went to two the day before and bought a small can of oysters and had part for supper and the rest for breakfast yesterday. I spent the rest of [the] day in my tent reading some and writing a little, so you see what kind of a New Year's I had, rather better than last as I was on picket and it was a very cold day. The weather has been quite comfortable for a few days back. Our snow has most all gone off and left it muddy as usual. I expect that we shall leave here in a day or two to go to the regiment, whether at Memphis or some place on the Tennessee River. We don't know yet. I expect that we shall get a bunch of mail when we get there, and I am in hopes that we shall get paid again soon, but I will put this by for tonight and try to think of some news to finish.

January 6

Last Tuesday, we had orders to store our surplus things and be ready to go on the boat. We got already to start and our commissary went to town to draw our beef and find out what boat we was going on, and they told him to fetch the meat to camp as they had given no orders to move and had no boats for us. So we fixed up our tents again and here we are yet and probably shall stay till our troops get to Memphis and send after us. We are not fixed quite as comfortable as we were. I built a chimney last night and had to fix the fireplace this morning, as it smoked so that I could not stay in the tent. The weather has been quite comfortable for a few days back. It is some rainy today. Write how you get along, how your stove suits. Does Kitty go to school, what the children study, if you have got all the money I have sent you, and everything that is of interest to me. I will send you a paper if I can find something to stick it together. I have to pay ten cents apiece for them here. Pretty dear reading does your paper come yet. It is pretty near time to renew the subscription, I guess. Write all about the meetings there as I am quite interested in them as I can't think of anymore to write. I will close by sending love and kisses to all. From your affectionate husband, Silas W. Haven.

No. 2, Commission Rooms, Nashville, January 13, 1865

Dear Jane,

I am pretty well at present and we started yesterday for Eastport, Mississippi, where we expect to find the regiment. We got to the levee and the boat that was to take us was so heavy loaded that we had to stay, but we are to have a boat today. The last letter I wrote I kept five days before I could get it mailed, and then I brought it to town myself in the rain with mud ankle-deep and suck. Mud it would rub off when it got dry, about as well as the cold woman's grease. There is not many troops here; quite a lot of soldiers (cavalry) went through here to the front yesterday. We don't know what is going on out there. We hear that our corps is scattered from Eastport to Memphis on the railroad. It is very lonesome to be without news from home. If the regiment starts ours on another march, I expect to be in the same fit as they will have to leave me with the convalescents or carry me. With love and kisses to all, I bid you goodbye for this time. From your affectionate husband, Silas W. Haven.

No. 3, Camp of the 27th Iowa, Eastport, MS, January 22, 1865[2]

Dear Jane,

We had quite a time getting here as the boat was crowded. We changed boats twice, and I did not have any chance to wash my clothes and I got a few lice on me, which made it rather uncomfortable. The troops here have built winter quarters and I expect that we shall stop here a spell. I caught cold coming up and am not very well. I can eat my rations and work some. I worked all day yesterday. I got out shakes, blocks in the forenoon, and then a man came and claimed the lumber so I had my work for nothing in the afternoon. I put me up a tent and shall occupy till I can get out lumber for a shebang. The weather is warm but rainy. It rained nearly all day yesterday. I should have written before, but I had no place to write in and I have no ink so I have to write with a pencil. I am on guard today, but shall not have to stand tonight. I have worked all the spare time to get my tent ready, so that I can sleep tonight out of the hearing of swearing. Capt. Slocum was taken prisoner a few days ago. He went outside of the lines after lumber and the rebs got him. I am not glad that he is taken and I don't know but what it is wrong. I cannot feel sorry. Everything is very high here. I might have made a considerable if I had brought along something to sell, which I might as well as not (apples twenty five dollars a barrel). The town here is nearly all burnt up, only a few houses standing. We are camped on the west bank of Bear Creek, which is the line between Mississippi and Alabama, and Tennessee is the other side of the Tennessee River. I am in such a hurry that I can't think of anything to write; when I get fixed up, I will try to write something interesting if I can. With love and kisses to you all, I close for this time. From your affectionate husband, Silas W. Haven.

No. 4, Camp 27th Iowa, Eastport, MS, January 30, 1865

Dear Jane,

I can't do much at a time and it is hard work to get tools to work with. I worked one day last week and got out shake blocks enough and split out part of them, and someone stole the rest the next morning while I was on guard. It is rather uphill business to have to work all alone, but I guess that I shall get fixed after a while. I could not get an ax today, so I improve the time writing to you. We have been short for rations along back for some cause; they did not come up the river so we drew corn and hilled it once, and [had] Indian meal for two or three days. You ought to have heard the new recruits grumble. I got along very well, only I had to buy some coffee as that is my main stay. My health is not very good. I caught cold and cough a good deal nights. I went to the sutlers to get some honey, but they did not have any, and I shall go to the doctor's to get some medicine if my sugar that I drew don't stop it tonight. I have a little diarrhea at present, brought on by eating beef and cornbread. The weather has been quite cold but pleasant for a few days back. It is quite warm today. Capt. Slocum is a prisoner yet, but expected to be exchanged in a few days. The talk is that he will be court-martialed and discharged for going outside the lines. I shall not be very sorry if he is. Lt. Reiniger has resigned and I expect that he will go home in a few days. Lt. Hemenway of Company B has command of the company now, and I would like to have him command it while I stay with them.[3] Write whether you have ever had the doctor look at Kitty's throat, and write all the news you can think of. We don't get any news here very often. With love and kisses to you all, I remain your affectionate husband, Silas W. Haven.

No. 5, Camp of the 27th Iowa, Eastport, MS, February 5, 1865

Dear Jane,

I suppose you expect that by this time that I have got my shebang done so that I can write a good long letter, but I have not. I got the sides out last week, but could not get them hauled till Friday noon, and then I went to work and laid them three logs high and spread my borrowed tent over it, and have slept in it since, but as we expect to take the boats and leave for down the river every day, I am not going to do any more on it. It rained and sleeted some last night and is rather cold and disagreeable today. We don't know where we are going to from here. We are to report first to Cairo and I guess that from there, we shall go to Memphis and probably stay there long enough to get our pay, and then they will find something for the troops to do, maybe to go up the Red River again.[4] I can go with the regiment as long as they don't march and when they do, I shall be counted out. I don't know as we shall get our pay before next month. If we don't, we shall draw four months' pay. Capt. Slocum came back a few days ago and has taken command again; whether they let him come or he was exchanged, I don't know. I expect that there will nothing be done with him as he belongs to the Masons. There is nothing going on here and we don't get any news very often. I have three or four letters to write as soon as I can get time, or a place to write in convenience. We have a new chaplain to our regiment.[5] I have not been to see him yet. He preached to us last Sunday and

I like his appearance very well. My fingers are getting cold so I will close this and get my supper. With love and kisses to you all, I remain your affectionate husband, Silas W. Haven.

No. 6, On board steamer *Tarascon,* going down the river, February 12, 1865
Dear Jane,

I received two letters from you yesterday and was very glad to hear from you that you were all as well as you are, and had got my letters containing money all sage. My health is pretty good for me, but it costs me like everything to get things that I can eat so as to keep around when I eat my rations that I draw for a short time. My bowels get out of order and I soon get so that I can't eat anything without it hurting me, so I have bought some bread, occasionally some cheese and for quite a while, I bought butter so that I have had it all the while, but it costs high here. We left Eastport the 9th and we expect to go to New Orleans to take the place of some troops that have been there doing guard duty ever since the place was taken. We shall probably stay there till our time is out. I expect that we shall find it a little warmer than it is here. It has been quite cold for a number of days back, but as we were going to a warmer climate, I expressed my extra clothing yesterday. I was on guard and had to put them up in a hurry, and I did not have time to write or to look around to buy anything. I sent a blanket, overcoat, a pair of pants and a shirt (very dirty) besides some few trinkets and part of my ten days' rations of coffee. When we are on the move, it is very difficult to write so that they will go regular and when we are moving; don't look for letters till they come and then you won't be disappointed. There is a great many rumors about peace, but whether they will amount to much, it is uncertain. The majority of the Southern people are in favor of peace, but Jeff Davis and company want power so in the end, we shall probably have to fight it out, which will be pretty soon, as the army at Richmond is the only force that they have got to amount to anything, but I must close as my paper has run short out. With love and kisses to all, from your affectionate husband, Silas W. Haven.

No. 7, On board of Steamer *Tarascon* at Vicksburg, February 19, 1865
Dear Jane,

I did intend to write to you today in time for it to be mailed at this place, but for once I expect that I am foiled as I expect that we shall start from here tonight. We got to this place the 14th. The 16th the regiment went out four miles to camp. I stayed with the rations and did not go till the next day and yesterday, I tried nearly all day to get a kettle to wash and had to have it done after all so I did not write, and morning we had orders to march and I was detailed for guard, but when I got to the levee, I found that my guard duty was loading boats and I was to work all day, and it was now nine o'clock and I have just got into the cabin to write, and there is so much noise that I can't tell what to write. There is a piano going in the back part of the cabin, which helps to bother. My health is pretty good for me. We are in the dark as to our destination. I have thought all the while that we were going to try another Red River trip, but is rather uncertain. We shall have to change boats as ours are too large to go up the river. The general impression is that we are going to Mobile. It is either there or to New Orleans to take the place of other troops; either place will suit us to spend the rest of our time. I believe it is decided that we are to be mustered out the 22nd of August and we are to be in the state twenty days before that time, so six months longer will end our three years, which I think will be sufficient for me.[6] The impression in the army is that the war will close before long, as the South is nearly depopulated and are quarreling among themselves, while our armies are in good condition and are pressing them at every point, and if they don't cease fighting, they have found to be badly whipped at every point, and if they are so inclined, they will be exterminated. Write how the children get along to school. You did not write what Kitty studies. Give them all a kiss for me and tell them all to kiss you for me. With lots of love and kisses to you all, I will bid you goodbye for this time. From your affectionate husband, Silas W. Haven.

No. 8, Camp of the 27th Iowa, Six miles below New Orleans,
February 23, 1865

Dear Jane,

We got to this place day before yesterday and came into camp, and before we got to camp it rained and it has rained every little while since. I did not get to camp as quick as the regiment by half an hour (and we had two miles to march), and before I got in and my tent up, I got completely wet through, and I took a couple of pickets and laid down with my wet clothes on and slept what I could, which was not much. It don't look much like winter here. The grass is green, some fruit trees are in bloom and we landed opposite of an orange orchard. There was a lot of oranges on the trees and laying on the ground. They looked very nice and had a very pleasant smell, but they were sour and bitter and not fit to eat, but still the boys pitched into them and had great fun scrabbling for them. The country here is very level and they have ditches every five or six rods apart one way to drain the land, and if the river should run over the levee, the whole country would be flooded. The river is quite wide and deep and there is lots of shipping in the port. There was three (two quite large) sail ships towed up past us yesterday, which was quite a sight to the most of the boys as they had never seen any before. We are camped just below the battlefield, where Gen. Jackson fought the British in 1815.[7] There is a monument about a mile from here where fifteen hundred British were buried. There is a lot of boys gone to see it, but it is too muddy for me to go today. There is all kinds of rumors afloat. I think that if Mobile is not taken soon that we shall go there as soon as transportation is furnished. There was quite a lot (20,000, some say) of troops left here the day before we got here for Mobile, and the place is completely invested and our forces have got the first line of works; the place will be taken mostly by the batteries, I think, as we have not seen our batteries since we left Eastport, and we think that they have gone there. It is very uncertain what we shall do this summer, but one thing is certain. Six months more will finish up our three years' service for Uncle Sam, and a pretty hard three years too, but we shall not feel sorry that we have served our country, but proud that we came forward in the time that we did. It can't be said that we came for the big pay or big bounty; our hardships will be remembered as things in a dream. We have had no mail since we were at Cairo, but expect some today. I wrote to you from Vicksburg, but I don't expect that it went out till we got here, so this will follow pretty close, and if we leave here, it may be two or three weeks before I can get another to you. My health is pretty good for me. I am getting so that I rest pretty well nights, which is a great help to me. I drew a pair of pants and shoes and a dress coat at Vicksburg. With love and kisses to you all, I remain your affectionate husband, Silas W. Haven.

It still keeps wet and muddy and we don't get any mail yet. Col. Gilbert has been promoted to Brig. Gen.[8]

No. 9, Camp of the 27th Iowa near New Orleans, February 26, 1865

Dear Jane,

I received two letters from you Friday and take my pen today to try to answer them; one of them was written in January when the children were very sick. You speak about having ice up there. It has been rain all the time till today, since we got here Friday. I was one of four that was detailed to ditch the camp as the ground is so level that the mud and water was ankle-deep. I did not do hardly anything as there was only two spades and the one (John Hanchett) that I was to work with told me to stand and look on.[9] Yesterday morning, it rained very hard for about an hour. I began to think that we were going to have a flood, but it held up some and cleared off in the afternoon, and the mud dried up a considerable and today it is quite hot and the mud is fast disappearing. My health is quite good, yet getting wet did not do me any particular hurt, and I can eat my rations very well and am getting fat. It is not known yet where we are going, but I guess that if we are not needed at Mobile (and I don't think that we shall be) that as soon as we get reorganized that we shall go to Texas to watch the French either to Galveston or Brownville.[10] It looks very much like it now [that] secession is on its last legs now. The leaders are talking large just now, but it is the last flare-up of a candle, a bright flash and then sudden darkness. We don't have much of anything to do at present; have not had a roll call since we have been here. Tell Ella that I wanted to see her real bad when I heard that she was sick. I think that you must have had a hard time taking care of all three sick at once. Tell Emmett he must be careful about going on the river with his skates, as ice is not very strong in the spring. Tell Kitty that I will go with her to slide next winter and kiss them all for me. We are on the last half of the last year, and that will soon roll by and then, through the mercy of divine providence, I hope to meet you all again here on earth. With love and kisses to all, I remain your affectionate husband, Silas W. Haven.

No. 10, Camp of the 27th Iowa near New Orleans, March 1, 1865

Dear Jane,

We are still here and it rains as usual about every day so we have mud a plenty and my health keeps pretty good. Yesterday we were mustered and there is some prospect of getting our pay soon as they are paying the first division, and there is some prospect of our leaving here as they have got the corps nearly reorganized. It is uncertain yet where we got to, either to Mobile or Texas, probably the latter. We had orders yesterday to store all our surplus baggage and not to take anything, only a rubber, a woolen blanket, a piece of tent and a change of drawers and a shirt, and as I could not get a box to store my things in, I [wrapped] them up in a piece of rubber blanket and sent them by Parkers express to you. The package is marked Mrs. S. J. Haven, Rockford, Floyd County, Iowa, and will go to Waverly of its arrival. I was going to town today, but it was too muddy. I shall tomorrow if nothing happens. They have been firing some big guns today up to town, but whether for as a salute or for good news, we can't tell at present. They fired one hundred guns the other day on the receipt of the news from Charleston.[11]

No. 11, Camp of the 27th Iowa near New Orleans, March 6, 1865

Dear Jane,

We are already to leave here and I will try to write a few lines to you. I don't know where we are going, but as the first division has gone to Mobile, I expect that we are going there too, though there is a rumor that we are going to Knoxville, Tenn. I am pretty well. I went to the city last week and liked it very much, but would have liked it better if I had some money to buy some of the fruit, such as oranges, bananas and pineapples or some oysters. As it was, I only spent thirty-five cents for my fare on the cars and for my dinner. I had to walk about three miles, and then I got on the cars and rode about the same for which they charged five cents. New Orleans is kept clean and the streets are paved with blocks of marble or granite. The monument of Henry Clay is in the middle of one street, and the equestrian statue of Jackson is in the public square, which is ahead of the one at Memphis.[12] I went on top of the battle monument yesterday. It is a marble shaft about 12 feet square on top of brick work. There were thirty-six courses of brick high before the shaft commences. There are circular steps to the top (96 steps). I got pretty tired before I got to the top. It was never quite finished.[13] We are having quite a good time in the regiment. I think that our chaplain is a faithful minister and tries to do all the good he can. God grant that he may accomplish much good. With love and kisses to all, I close from your husband, Silas W. Haven.

No. 13, Dauphin Island, Alabama, March 17, 1865[14]

Dear Jane,

I got your letter No. 9 (dated Feb. 28) yesterday and was very glad to hear from you, as I had no mail since I left New Orleans.[15] I was sorry to hear that the children were sick. I hope they will be well before this reaches you. My health is pretty good. I feel as well as I ever did when I don't do anything, but as soon as I try to work or march, I find I am not of much account. We practiced firing at a target last Saturday, and my arm and wrist has been lame ever since some as it was when I left home, only it don't ache only when I use it. We have had a pretty easy time for over a month. The boys spend the most of the time getting and eating oysters when the weather is suitable. It rains pretty often and we have a chilly breeze with it so it is not very comfortable or pleasant wading in the water. I have only been once as I don't want to expose myself too often. I think I shall go again soon if we don't move as I am getting oyster hungry. The talk is that we shall move in two or three days. We are ready to move on a very short notice as all we have to do is to strike tents and pack up.

The time passes off very fast; this week is most gone and I don't know hardly where it has gone to. If we have to stay in our full-time, it won't be long, but the way things look now, we may possibly be at home the 4th of July, but if we don't, I shall not be disappointed as I expect to stay on full-time. I am glad to hear that the things got through all safe, and I hope those that I sent from New Orleans have got there before this reaches you.

March 18

We went down to the post and stood around awhile and rolled two caissons and a wagon about twenty rods, and then stood, lay and set around an hour or two, and then come back to our quarters, so we did not have very hard fatigue. The 13th corps crossed to Fort Morgan yesterday; probably it will reach us about tomorrow to move.[16] I will send the letter from mother in this if it don't make it too heavy. I have no more paper and shall put the last stamp on this, and don't know as I can get anymore. Write how you get along for money. With love and kisses to all, I close for this time. From your affectionate husband, Silas W. Haven.

No. 14, Camp near Spanish Fort, March 27, 1865[17]

Dear Jane,

It is rather uncertain when I can send a letter off, but as I had a little time, I thought I would commence so if I get a chance, I would send it along so that you could know how I get along. My health is about the same as usual. We left Dauphin Island a week ago this morning and came up the bay a little ways, and turned into fish river and came to David's landing, and stayed there till day before yesterday, and started for this fort. Our advance skirmished all day yesterday and day before, but we came right along. Our brigade was in the advance yesterday and I was where I could see our skirmishers. We got our reb early in the morning, but we could not get much out of him as he said he has just escaped from prison in Mobile and was making his way to us. Our skirmishers killed two or three on the march, and I heard that they killed two more and wounded some on the picket line last evening. We are about fifteen miles from Mobile on the east side of the bay, but if we have to go by land, we shall have to march about a hundred miles around. We come here to take this fort and capture the force that was on this part of the bay, but the report is that the fort is evacuated and the force gone to Blakely, and if they have not cropped the bay, to Mobile. We shall get the whole of them as we have got them cut off by land. I expect every moment to hear the cannon booming. The country here is wilderness. It is thick covered with pitch pine, which has been tapped to make rosin and turpentine off, and we can get any quantity of pine gum. It is very nice and I wish I could send you some. I went on picket and caught a little cold and my liver troubled some, so I went to the doctor and got some medicine, and when we left there, I was detailed as provost guard at Brigade headquarters as they thought it would be a little easier for me. I don't have much of anything to do and if we had our other team here, I could get along first rate, but is pretty hard work for me to carry all my things and keep up. We marched eight miles yesterday and also said before, and I kept along with them and feel pretty well today, only a little lame, so I guess that I shall get along here pretty well, rather better than in the company as I don't have any hard fatigue work to do or to double quick either. Our forces build breastworks every night. They are going on the slow and sure principal, and if the rebs don't find out how large a force is making for Mobile and evacuate, we shall get the whole of them. Our brigade is camped here to hold this point while the rest of the forces have gone out to hunt the rebs, and I guess that they have found them as I heard cannon just now. The big guns have been booming all afternoon, but with what effect we can't tell. It commenced raining about noon and we keep close in our tents. Our teams are hitched up so as to move in short notice if we are wanted, but I guess that we shall stop here tonight and it may be for a day or two.

March 29

We are still here in camp and the rebs have not seen fit to trouble us yet. Our division is guarding the rear of our force that are taking Spanish Fort, which the rebs are trying to hold. We have got it completely by invested and they are fighting pretty sharp this morning. The cannon and small arms have been going all the morning, and I should not be surprised if it was taken before night. Our brigade is guarding a principal point and has been expecting an attack, and has fortified pretty strong and is still at work, and it will take a pretty large force to drive us out. I am in hopes that we shall get a mail today and I shall put this in the office so if any goes out, it will go along. It looks like rain today with a pretty fresh breeze from the bay, but still it is quite pleasant and I feel pretty well, and if we don't have any hard marching to do, I think I shall get along first rate. With love and kisses to you all, and hoping soon to meet you, I remain your affectionate husband, Silas W. Haven.

No. 15, Camp of the 27th Iowa near Blakely, Alabama, April 5, 1865[18]

Dear Jane,

I received a letter from you yesterday and was very glad to hear from you, but was sorry that the children were sick. I was afraid that Kitty's throat would ulcerate. She will have to be very careful and not catch cold or she will have a bad time of it. You did not tell what the matter was with Ella and Emmett. I hope that they will all soon get well. I suppose that it is bad weather for colds up there. The weather here is quite nice and comfortable and agrees with me first rate. My health is pretty good, although I am some lame as I have had a little marching to do for the last three days back. I came back to the company last Friday, and Sunday our brigade was ordered out on a reconnaissance. We came out this way about two miles and a half, but did not find any rebs, but we found a torpedo, which killed two horses and stunned the officers (one an aide de camp and the other a Lieut. belonging to Gen. Gilbert's staff). Monday, we were assigned to Gen. Steele and march out here five miles to close the lines around Blakely.[19] We have got the rebs completely surrounded on the land side, and our troops have got them completely hemmed in at Spanish Fort and summons them to surrender, but they wanted a conditional surrender, so they bombarded them pretty lively last evening and kept up the firing pretty steady last night. Today, they only fire occasionally. It is some expected that they will surrender soon. I expect you would have been uneasy about me if you had known where I was when I got your letter. I was on picket and the rebs had a battery shelling us like fun. We did not care for their shells as we had holes dug in the ground, and when we heard them shoot, we laid low and their shelling did not trouble us. It was fun to see the boys hunt their holes when we heard the report of the cannon and then watch to see the shells burst. We were on the reserve through the day, as it was dangerous to go out on the picket line in day light. We went out after dark and staid on till about 5 o'clock. We had first-rate breastworks to stand behind, where they could not hit us with their shells or balls. The rebs were only about four hundred yards off, about as far as from our four to walkers. We kept watch that they did not advance their works, and the most of the boys kept shooting at them all night. I did not shoot any as it was useless waste of ammunition. We would match them and when their guns flashed, we would bob our heads below the works and the balls would go whizzing by and some would put on the pine trees behind us. We felt perfectly safe, but it was pretty hard on us to be up all night as most all of us was out of tobacco and got rather sleepy. I bought a pretty good supply at Dauphin Island, but the boys was all out and mine went in a hurry. I was so sleepy toward morning that I would go to sleep standing up. When I got to camp this morning, I found a dollar's worth that I had sent after and I have lent nearly half of that, but we shall have plenty in a few days as they are going to issue tobacco the same as clothing so we will be all right as far as tobacco is concerned. I am in hopes that our campaign is pretty near over if we get Spanish Fort with the troops that is in it in a day or two; their place (Blakely) will soon fall or be evacuated and Mobile will be ours as Spanish Fort and torpedoes was their main reliance, and our gunboat have taken up the torpedoes and cut the communication off the bayside.[20] Still, they may hold out for quite a spell, but it will eventually have to surrender, but I will leave the war question and try to full this up with something else. I am so sleepy, I can't think of anything to write, so with lots of love and kisses to all, I remain your affectionate husband, Silas W. Haven.

—

BRIG. GEN. JAMES GILBERT, in command at Blakely, stated, "At the command to advance the line raised a shout, pressed rapidly forward, reached and carried the enemy's works, and pursued the disconcerted enemy to the river-bank. . . . Officers and men throughout the entire command did their duty and did it well. . . . Too much praise cannot be bestowed upon them." In his report on the engagement at Blakely, Alabama, Lt. Col. Charles S. Hills, who commanded the 10th Kansas, described the battle, in which the 27th Iowa participated, as follows:

> The men, leaping over our entrenchments advanced on a run to the enemy's first line of rifle-pits, which were abandoned without much resistance as was also his second line. While descending the slope to the ravine which lay in my front the enemy opened with a galling fire of artillery and musketry, using shell, spherical case canister, and grape . . . but which, on reaching, I found to be enfiladed, and afforded no shelter whatever. For this reason no halt was ordered. . . . On gaining the high ground past the ravine the firing became more rapid, and had it been well directed would have been very destructive. No man in the line returned the fire but each one devoted his whole energy to reach the works as soon as possible climbed over fallen trees with scarce an effort, cleared each line of abatis at a single leap, and, scarcely noticing the ditch, mounted the parapets or poured through the embrasures at the recoil of the guns that their last discharge had opened for them, and their line was broken. Turning the left of my line (which after entering the embrasures had become a column) to the right, and being joined by those who had climbed the parapets, it swept down on their flank with fixed bayonets with scarcely any opposition, the men throwing down their guns and surrendering, officers waving their white handkerchiefs and delivering up their swords.[21]

—

No. 16, Blakely, Alabama, April 11, 1865

Dear Jane,

The smoke of the battle is over and I have just got my tent fixed and improve the opportunity of writing a few lines to you to let you know that I am safe and am enjoying pretty good health.[22] I expect that long before this reaches you, the papers will give you the particulars of our operations, but as they will not tell what part I participated in, I will write a full account [of] last Thursday. I was on picket and at night the relief that I was on advanced the picket line. I was left on the reserve to take care of the things; they got the lines advanced all safe and the rebs did not find it out till morning, and then they shelled us pretty sharp, but did no particular damage. They made one or two charges, but got repulsed last Sunday. I come on picket again and we was ordered to take thirty-six hours' rations as they were going to change the time of the relieving, but as they had taken Spanish Fort the night before, they got ready and at about 6 o'clock P.M. we charged on the works and took them. I don't know how many men we lost; only two of our regiment were wounded. I started on the charge, but as I could not run, they got into the works before I got halfway. We took about two thousand prisoners and the gunboat run up the white flag, but put out before we could take possession of her. My place on the picket line was near a battery and the shells come in pretty close, but could not hurt us as we would dodge under the works. We only had one man in our brigade hurt all day till the charge. Our brigade was the first in the works. The rumor is that Mobile is evacuated and also that Gen. Canby has orders from Grant to hold his position, but not to make any advance till further ordered.[23] The gunboats have ceased firing so that it may be true. The talk is that the rumor that we were going to be relieved is not true, so I guess that we shall stop here quite a while; so much for camp rumors. The rebel prisoners had the fun yesterday of digging up torpedoes. They had quite a lot put down, but our men charged over them and I don't think there was any exploding. I have heard a number explode yesterday and today, but have not heard of any ones getting hurt, and the rebs think that they do more damage to them than to us, as they have had a number of men hurt by them. We captured quite a lot of guns, ammunition, some hams and shoulders (very good), salt, beeves and sheep (rather poor and most starved) and lots of things too numerous to mention. They had some good breastworks and it was awful bad ground to get over to them, and it is a wonder that we did not lose more men than we did. I think that if we had been in here they could not have got in with twice the force that we came in with. They charged our skirmish (picket) line a few days ago with a line of battle and got repulsed. Our skirmish line (10th Kansas, about 250 strong, and Company K of our regiment) charged over the breastworks. They did not wait for our line to get up; they know that they would be supported so they rushed ahead, and I guess that the boys did not stop to think about torpedoes. The weather is quite pleasant and it is quite comfortable, neither too hot nor too cold as we get the breeze from the bay still with their torpedoes, centipedes, scorpions, tarantulas and rebs. It is not a very pleasant or safe place to live in. I think the folks around Mobile will not be very safe for a good while as the torpedoes may be run over a good many times and then explode at last, and the rebs have forgot where they put in part of them. Well, I went out a little while ago to stretch my legs and orders came for us to be ready to move at an early hour tomorrow morning, so I went down to the landing to see if I could hear any news, but could not and we can give no guess where or which way we are to go unless it is to Mobile as the report is that it is evacuated and we can see fires over there, like burning cotton, wherever we go. I hope it will be nearer home. I hardly know what to write to Ella about joining the church. I should like to have her go forward, but still I would not advise her to unless she could go with a clear conscience that she was doing right; perhaps if she waits awhile, she may see her way more clearly till she to pray for guidance from on high, and if she asks with faith, believing her way will be made plain to her. With love and kisses to you all, I remain your affectionate husband, Silas W. Haven.

P.S. I captured some rebel muster rolls so I write this on rebel paper with a rebel pen and have a rebel candle to give me light to write by.

No. 17, In camp 5 miles from Montgomery, Alabama, April 26, 1865[24]

Dear Jane,

I wrote to you after the battle of Fort Blakely and at that time we were under orders to move. We went to our cold camping ground before the fight and all the 16th corps got together and started the 13th for this place, marched 8 miles. I carried my knapsack, but could not keep up. The next day, I got back to the train and got my knapsack hauled. We marched 15 miles the 15th. I went to the company and got my knapsack on the wagon and have it carried every day since. We marched 12 miles that day and the 16th, 16 miles, the 17th, 18 miles, the 18th, 10 miles, the 19th, 10 miles and had a dispatch read that Lee had surrendered, and that our fighting was at an end.[25] The 20th, 14 miles, the 21st 6 miles in the rain, the 22nd, 8 miles and got to Greenville and 200 guns were fired as a salute for peace. The 23rd, 16 miles, the 24th, 18 ½ miles, and yesterday, 6 ½ miles and are camped here in the woods beside of a creek, waiting for orders. I expect that we shall be sent home as soon as they can get transportation. I guess that you will [be] glad; I know that I am, and all the army and the citizens here all appear to feel glad that the war is at an end and every[one] has a brighter face. I have stood the march better than I expected, although I could not keep up with the command, but at no time did I get behind of the division. Our regiment guarded the wagon train three or four days and I got along first rate them days. One day, I got to ride two miles, the only ride I have had on the march. The country below Greenville was a pine wilderness with but few plantations, and the roads were pretty bad and swampy. We have had two or three rainy days, which made it pretty hard about our getting along the country. Greenville is pretty good and the plantations are pretty close together. It is a timbered country, but it is different kinds of timber instead of pitch pine, and the soil here is clay. I don't know yet which way we shall go from here. Some say by transport around by New Orleans, some say by the cars to Vicksburg, others think that we shall march through Eastport on the Tennessee River. I think we shall go by railroad if the road is in order or by transports. I don't know when this will go out, but I think that we shall get some mail soon as we have been in the wilderness long enough to make us almost barbarians. We have been on the move so much that it has been hard work for mail to find us and almost impossible to keep clean. I have not changed my shirt since I left Fort Blakely, and today we are not certain but what we shall move, and the kettles were all packed, ready to put on the wagon. I took my shirt off and washed it in the creek and it is drying on the bushes, and I am in hopes it will get dry if it is clean, as the last time I had to put it on wet, but I have got the sheet full so I will close for this time, and I hope the next one will be dated on the way home. With love and kisses to all, I remain your affectionate husband, Silas W. Haven.

April 30

Dear Jane,

Our boats have just got here and I expect that I can send this off, so I will write a little more. We have had no news since we got here, only that Lincoln was assassinated.[26] The news by the boats partly confirms it and it has cast a gloom over the army. They had better not march this command through the country. If it is so, we have been short of rations, and had to live on Indian meal and fresh pork and poor beef for about a week. We have got along pretty well, although we did not have any knives, and maybe you would think it strange if I should tell you that we can beat the Southern people and darkies making corn cake. I have eat now that they have made that was as good as [what] we make and cook in our frying pans, but the boats are here and we shall have plenty of rations now. We was mustered for pay today; when we will get it is another thing. I was on fatigue today digging a well. We are camped about two miles from town. We marched seven miles through town the 27th and are in a thick woods, but we have made ourselves quite comfortable. I expect that I shall get some mail; if I do, I will write again. With love and kisses to all. From your affectionate husband, Silas W. Haven.

No. 18, Montgomery, Alabama, May 7, 1865

Dear Jane,

I saw a very imposing and mournful dress parade last Sunday evening. The mess came out with arms reversed. The band played the dead march and the men rested on arms while prayer was offered. It was done in respect to the dead. We don't have much news, but plenty of rumors. The idea that we shall march through the country has been discussed for the last two weeks, but is given up now pretty much and the time that we shall leave here is now the common talk. Some think we shall stay here till our time is nearly out, others not so long. I think that we shall be started on our way home in a very short time. I think that we shall spend the next Fourth of July at home. I went to town the other day and went on the top of the state house and took a good look at the city. It is a very pretty place and has a good many fine streets and buildings in it, although our cavalry burnt a great many machine shops, niter works. There was quite a stir in the streets. Our division were drawing rations. Lots of rebs coming in and giving themselves up, which they are doing as fast as they can. They are completely whipped and are glad of peace (aren't we, I reckon) still. We would go for them if it was necessary and it is not very healthy for us. This is rebel paper and envelope that I got from the Christian Commission, [but it is] not very good yet, I will say. I think of the President and Secretary of State. Their assassination has cast a gloom over the army, but still we are hopeful.

No. 19, Montgomery, Alabama, May 14, 1865

Dear Jane,

I went to the First Baptist Church in town today. I went pretty early and attended Sabbath school. They had an organ in the church. I suppose you would like to know how the ladies were dressed and as I did take some notice of their dresses, I will try and describe, but as you know, I am not a very good hand at description. I don't expect I could do justice to them. The most of them wore silk dresses without hoops, which looked rather odd; about half had coal scuttle bonnets with lots of artificial flowers. The rest had hats, narrow brim and flat, covered with flowers (artificial), which did not look very well. Very many are dressed in black, which is the case all through the South. I expect that you are wondering whether the women down South are pretty. I don't call myself a very good judge as I have heard that the ladies down here were handsome, but I have not seen but very few that I should call good looking. Their complexions are too white. I did not see but very few red cheeks today and they (I should judge) were artificial, painted. The girls from eight to twelve are pretty good looking. It appears to be a Southern characteristic that the girls have all small mouths and the women large, and all have white complexions, but I will leave this subject and would be glad to leave the climate as the North suits me the best in everything. The boys went to town the other day and got a lot of Confederate money and distributed out amongst the rest, and they have (some of them) been gambling with it pretty lively. I could not give any guess how much they got, but it must have been a considerable as everyone has a pretty good supply, and I saw some sold for 5 cents for a hundred dollars. I got 1.50 dollars and I will send part to you in this (one bill for each). We have lots of rumors, but nothing definite. The idea that we are going to march through to Vicksburg is about exploded. A small force may go through with the wagon train, but that won't be very hard as they can have their things hauled and ride part of the time. I think that when we leave here, it will be either on the cars or boat and direct to Iowa.

May 17

I seat myself to finish this as I expect that it will go out tonight. I was on fatigue duty Monday, went to town to draw rations, had to work about 15 minutes, but it was pretty hot going down and coming back yesterday. We had a general inspection and today [a] battalion drill so you see that we have to exercise a little. We had a high old time last night; a dispatch came in from Gen. Wilson that he had caught Jeff Davis and staff and some others of the head leaders of this rebellion.[27] It was not but a short time before the pine trees were loaded with candles and the boys were shouting, shooting, singing. They gathered around the regimental headquarters and had a lot of speeches and a good time and did not have nary drop of whiskey. All is quiet today, only the boys feel pretty well and sing occasionally "We'll hang Jeff Davis on a sour apple tree." We don't have any idea how long we shall stay here. The citizens want to have us stay as they like us pretty well, and they are afraid that when we go away that the Negro troops will take our place, and that is rather a bitter bill for them to swallow. I think that we shall stay here till we are mustered out, which I don't think will be long. I don't think that we shall get any pay till we are mustered out. I don't expect that the money I send in this will be worth any more up there than it is here, but it will do to keep for a curiosity, but with love and lots of kisses to you all, I close for this time. From your affectionate husband, Silas W. Haven.

—

ON MAY 21, 1865, Haven wrote a lengthy letter to his parents from Montgomery, Alabama. The letter echoed many of the sentiments Haven wrote to his wife in the previous letter. He discussed the weather, the physical landscape, and religion. Haven also took some time to enlighten his parents on his own thoughts about the current state of the war. He wrote:

> The first of last month's war, with all its horrors, was devastating this land and to human vision was likely to last for a indefinite period, but before the middle of the month, the rebel power was broken, their armies scattered and are hastening to their homes and to their allegiance to their rightful government, glad to escape with the boys of their property and slaves. Never more (I think) will they raise their hands against the old flag but will love and revere it and under it enjoy a prosperity never attained by them before, as they will have many settlers from the North and will enjoy the blessing of free labor.

At the same time, Haven shared some sentiments from his fellow soldiers among the ranks. He fervently stated:

> They have grown stronger throughout the scenes of carnage and bloodshed that I have praised through and my faith has never wavered, and I have always expressed the opinion that this war would come to a close quick; when it did close, something like the [falling] out of the bottom of a tub, and it did not surprise when events followed close upon each other that has broken the power of secession and today all that is thought of down here is the quickest way to get back into the Union. It is only a little over

> a month that the dispatch was read to that Lee had surrendered and since then, I have not heard an angry shot fired and I hope to never hear another.[28]

Haven then turned to the sadness that followed the death of Lincoln, but requested that faith remain with God, for he deserved trust and praise, even in the midst of hardship. He reflected again, as he had throughout his letters, about what punishment the Confederacy deserved for the war. He noted:

> I had always thought that the head leaders of this rebellion would escape to foreign lands, but since the assassination of our beloved president, I did not think that the assassins would escape, and as Jeff Davis, the arch leader of secession, has been reported to be one of them, I was prepared to hear of his arrest. And a few nights ago when the dispatch came in that he and others were arrested, you had ought to have seen our camp and heard the rejoicing; the pine trees were filled with candles, bonfires lighted, guns fired, speeches made at the various regiment headquarters and had a good time generally, and no whiskey to mar the festivities, and at about 11 o'clock all was quiet.[29]

Haven also explored the same ideas in a letter to his wife, also from Montgomery, dated May 23, 1865. He stated:

> I see by the papers that there is some folks that are foolish enough to express joy at the death of President Lincoln. They had better get over that before we get home as the soldiers have a summary way of dealing with such persons. It is a word and a blow and the blow will come first, and some down here have felt the blow, but did not hear the word. The rebel soldiers are coming in as fast as they can, all going home to fight no more. They speak very highly of Sherman and Sheridan and their men.[30]

—

No. 22, Camp of the 27th Iowa near Montgomery, Alabama, June 3, 1865
Dear Jane,

I seat myself to answer your letter, which I got day before yesterday, dated May 16th. I was glad to hear that you were all well and it found me enjoying pretty good health, although I don't feel very well today, as I had some diarrhea yesterday and caught cold, and my bowels are somewhat out of order, but a dose of pills will bring me all right. We had marching orders Tuesday, but they were countermanded and the first brigade went to Mobile in our place. We had a review Wednesday and it passed off fine. Gen. Smith spoke very highly of our division and our brigade.[31] Two of the regiments in our brigade are going to be mustered out immediately. Our regiment was two days behind to get out on the order as we were mustered on the 3rd of October, but they are trying to have us included as it was not our fault that we were not mustered in sooner, and the impression is that they will succeed, but still they may not. They might as well as we have nothing to do and there is plenty of veterans to do what is necessary. Our pickets were all relieved a day or two ago so we have nothing to do, only to guard our own camp. A number of the boys got their boxes that was sent to them from the North while we were at Eastport, but the most of the things were spoilt, especially the cakes and cookies, and the butter smells rather frowsy, but most of them had enough to pay the expenses as the tobacco was good. The weather is pretty warm here, but we have got pretty well used to it.

Rockford, June 4, 1865[32]

Dear Silas,

I take my pen to write you a few lines once more, hoping that we shall not have to write much longer, but we say what we wish to each other without writing. We are all pretty well and hope that this will find you well. There is a good many moving into town. I expect that Fred has sold his house and lot for two hundred and twenty dollars and is going to buy a piece of land.

June 5

Well, Silas, I left this last note to wait for the mail to come in to see if I could not hear from you, and I got a good long letter from you. I almost expected that it would be included at Davenport, but it was written May 14, way down in Alabama. It had the Confederate money in it. I was badly fooled for when I opened the letter, I thought that I had got some money in it, especially when I saw the green on the 50. I expect that I shall have to live pretty close until you get home or paid; since the talk has been that the soldiers were coming home, they begin to act as if they were afraid to let me have things. I went to Charles and traded some about three weeks ago. I got me a pair of shoes and some cloth to make Emmett some shorts.[33] I want you here so that you can know just what it costs to live. I work as hard as any lady can and try to save all I can. I do not hire anything and that I can possibly do myself. I even plastered the places where the plaster had got off. Emmett and I have been working in the garden some today. We have the beans this morning before school and the corn after. We felt well enough. We will clean the thing out pretty well tomorrow. We are giving a spell of dry weather just now and it is a good time to pull weeds.

June 6

I got so sleepy last night that I went to bed and did not finish writing, and I got up this morning and milked the cow and fed the pigs and got the breakfast started, and went out in the garden to hoe until Ella got the breakfast ready. I eat my breakfast and again hoed until it was time for the children to get ready for school, then I come in and helped them off, and I have got things started so that I can write a little more. It is showery this morning, but does not rain enough to do much good, but I have that it will before long for I want some water to wash with. I hardly know what to write before I commence. I can think of lots that I want to write about, but before I barely get going, I can't think of anything. I saw Mrs. Hanchett at the store the other day and she said that she had not had a letter for a long time.[34] I told her that he must be all right or you would have mentioned him. I wish that I could see you and talk with you. It seems as if you would be just as you were when you were at home last, but I must hurry. I shall not get my letter to the office in time to have it go out. If you could bring home two or three pieces of tent cloth without burning them too much, they would be very nice to make a stream bed. Fred wants you to hurry home so as to get rested by harvest time so you can help him harvest. I can't think of anything but you coming home. With lots of love to you, I will close for this time. Good bye from Jane.

Write often and tell me [what the] prospect of your coming is.

Waterloo, June 18, 1865[35]

Dear Brother,

After so long a time, I embrace the present opportunity to write to you to let you know that we have not forgotten you, not so, dear brother, there is not a day passes over without I think of you. I should have written as soon as I got your letter, only we talked of leaving Dubuque and I thought I would wait until we got to our new home. You see by the heading of this letter that we live a little nearer your home than we did if we had a team of our own. We do not get hold of a paper very often so I do not know much about what is going on in the world. We live only a little ways from the Depot west of it at the first crossing and the railroad runs nearer the house than Willow Creek did to father's house in Illinois. It is a very pretty place where we live. I hope you will give us a call when you come here. The cars run to Waverly now. I suppose that is nearer Rockford than Cedar Falls when they run to Rockford. I suppose this railroad is going through that place. I am a going to try and make Lane a visit. Oh how I will want to see her. I believe I think as much of her as though she was my own sister. I hope we shall soon see each other if she could only come here and meet you. I would be glad. The crops are very backward this year and everything around here looks discouraging to pain us. We had quite a storm night before last. The wind blew some, and it rained all that night and yesterday and part of last night. It rained some this morning, but has nearly cleared off now. I wish you were here to help us eat strawberries. We have quite a lot of them now in the garden. Harry is trying to farm this year, but is almost discouraged.[36] The prospects look bad. He is to work for another man and not farming on his own hook. He sends his best respects and well wishes to you and would write, only he has to work too hard that he is too tired so you must accept him. You must write to us and let us know when you will be [able] to [come] home. We are all enjoying pretty good health. My hands and arms trouble me some. They swell and pain me; I think it is the rheumatism. My health has been poor this spring, but is better now. You must excuse me for this rambling letter for I cannot collect my thoughts enough to compose a letter and as my hands pain me and as it is most milking time, I will close by asking you to write soon and subscribe myself, Your affectionate sister, Emily L. Henderson.

---

On June 23, 1865, from Montgomery, Alabama, James Gilbert issued a farewell statement to all of the soldiers under his command, including the 27th Iowa. His passionate and patriotic rhetoric reflected the sacrifices and the meanings of those sacrifices for every soldier. He said:

> After an association with many of you for nearly three long years, in camp and field, under those peculiarly trying circumstance which so generally bind heart to heart in friendship and in sympathy, a separation comes not without sadness. My brave officers and men, I shall never cease to remember how patiently you have endured all the hardships, privations, and exposes of the soldier on active duty, how heroically you have fought the enemy of our country upon many stubbornly contested fields, how uniformly you have fought to conquer. Such battle-fields as Prairie Grove, Little Rock, Fort de Russy, Pleasant Hill, Yellow Bayou, Tupelo, Oldtown Creek, Nashville, and Blakely, fought and bravely fought, won and nobly won, will ever be

monuments in history which shall tell to your children's children of your undaunted courage, your prowess in arms, your devotion to your country's cause. You have helped to bear the old flag on, on, until its proud folds once more kiss every breeze from the Lakes to the Gulf. Now, at last, no enemy is in arms, and the beams of peace have broken through the dark clouds of war. You will follow me, soon, to your happy friends and homes, to pursue again your former civil avocations. Be as good citizens as you have been soldiers. You will defend your country no longer by the bullet, but by the ballot. Stand by her cause always. But, alas! I cannot even bid good-bye to all of my brigade, for not a few of our comrades have paid the highest tribute of the patriot to his country. Let us fail not to cherish their memories as brothers, extend to their friends a soldier's sympathy, and drop for them a soldier's tear. Officers and soldiers, may Heaven's blessings rest upon you all. Farewell.[37]

—

No. 24, Camp of the 27th Iowa near Montgomery, Alabama, June 25, 1865[38]

Dear Jane,

After waiting for over four long weeks I got a letter from you last night and was glad to hear that you were all well. My health is not very good just now, although I am so as to be around, especially when there is any duty to do. I am troubled with the diarrhea. It ruins me pretty bad when I eat so I don't eat much, nor very often, sometimes twice, sometimes only once a day, and one day in about five days, I don't eat at all. I have not eaten anything yet today, but think that I shall have some coffee and flour porridge for dinner. I have lived mostly on fruit for a few days back as apples and berries are plenty, and peaches are getting ripe and they agree with me. We have plenty of rations. I don't draw near all of my bread and meat. I have traded off some tack and meat to get my washing. We draw two days' soft bread in every five, but I don't like it and it don't agree with me so I sell my part. I wish I could send my extra rations to you. It would be quite a help as I have a surplus of bread, meat, sugar, coffee and soap. We have no news of any account down here, hardly any camp rumors. Our regiment moved camp yesterday and we are pretty busy getting fixed up so as to live again. We are in a pleasant grove on pretty high ground and we supposed to be rather more healthy than it was at our old camp. We (that is, my bunkmate and myself) have got our tent fixed pretty good, partly shaded and the grass and brush hold up, and thought we would let the rest be till tomorrow, if we could as neither of us like to do anymore Sunday than we can help. We are now four miles from town, rather far for me to get to the church.

I have not been to town since I got my money and can't get any vegetables unless I do go so I shall try and go soon if it is not too hot and I feel well enough to walk then. I have been in hopes that we should have been ordered home before this time, but no order comes touching us yet, and the boys have made up their minds that we shall stay. I have not dared to risk any money in the present state of our mail, but hope that they will get it arranged in a few days so that I can send some as I have fifty dollars that is very inconvenient to carry in this hot weather, as I sweat so that it will get wet if I am not careful. We only draw four months' pay and have got four months (lacking five days) with us now. If I was discharged now, I should fetch home about two hundred dollars. I guess that it would be enough [to] pay up all of our debts and have enough to live on till I could get something to do to earn something to live on, and I hope the folks up there won't get afraid if they do have to wait sometime, as I am obliged to wait the motion of the government for my pay, and they can't expect me to pay up every two months when the government is behind from four to ten months, but if they will be patient a little while longer, I will either fetch or send enough to satisfy all demands. Tell Fred that he must not depend on my helping him harvest for if he does, he may get disappointed, as we are so far out in the wilderness that I expect the government will muster out the troops nearer home before they can take time to think of the 16th army corps, which was known by their fighting all over this part of the South. I knew you would be fooled when you saw the Confederate money, but I thought I would send some to keep to look at. There was about fifteen million here, but I must close. With love and kisses to you all, I will bid you goodbye for this time. From your affectionate husband, Silas W. Haven.

Rockford, June 25, 1865[39]

Dear Silas,

I improve this opportunity to write you a few lines. We are all well and hope this will find you well too. I did not get any letters from you last week. The last came in week ago last Friday and you said that it was rumored that you should go to New Orleans to be discharged, and the letter was three weeks old when I got it, so I have not went ten since but been looking for you home, and as you cannot come and I do not hear from you, I thought that I might as well write and see why you don't come. There is all sorts of rumors here about the soldiers coming home and I have heard that you would be here in a short time. I have heard several times that it had come in the papers that the regiment was going to be discharged.

June 27

Dear Silas,

I laid this by Sunday evening for I was so sleepy that I could not write. Ella went to the office yesterday and brought me a letter from you. We were very glad to hear from you, although it put a damper on our feelings to find that you were at gunnery, yet I think it will be too bad if you have to stay until the first of October. It seems a great ways off. I shall have to tell you that we have twenty-two little chickens; Kitty claims ten of them. I started to pack a crock of butter so as to have plenty when you come home. I can't think of anything more to write this time, so with lots of love to you, I bid you goodbye for this time. From your wife, S. J. Haven.

No. 25, Montgomery, Alabama, July 4, 1865

Dear Jane,

There is some talk that we are going to be mustered out soon. I think it is about time. I don't have anything to do as we was short of guns. I give mine up two weeks ago or more. I was intending to have written before, but waited for some mail till it was too late to send this yesterday. I will lay this by for a night as there is so much shooting going on and the bugs are awful thick.

July 5

Well, the sun is just coming up and it bids fair to be a very hot day, but still I think I shall try to go to the city. It was a very quiet fourth yesterday in camp and I guess that everything passed off first rate in town. They did not allow any liquor to be sold. Our orderly, J. E. Butler, has mustered as Lieutenant so we have got one commissioned officer to our company, although he is not very well at present, so Lieut. Peck retains command.[40] With love and kisses to you all and hoping soon to met you, I remain your affectionate husband, Silas W. Haven.

Rockford, July 9, 1865[41]

Dear Silas,

I take my pen to write you a few lines to let you know that we are all alive and all well, but Emmett, he has been having the ague for a day as too he did not have it to days. We have been having a spell of rainy weather and the river had been up so that it could not be forded. We have not had any mail for two weeks until Friday and there was none for me then. We had some very warm weather last week, but it has cooled off so that it is cool enough today. My hands are so cold that I can hardly write. They are so stiff with the cold. We had a heavy rain last night and this morning, and it is cloudy and cold. The fourth of July came and went and no soldiers came home to this place.

July 10

I did not finish this last night for I could not think of anything to write and thought that I would wait until the mail came in and see if I did not get some letters, and I got one from you and was very glad to hear from you, but sorry that you were not well. Emmett did not have ague yesterday nor today. The diphtheria is around near here. Two children died with it on Glove Creek. I wish that I would know whether to get any to put up hay for us or not. You wrote that you had got pay. I hope that you will get to send home what you can spare for I need it pretty bad, and I think if you try to send it in a letter, you had better not put a stamp on it if you had sent so many without any. The last letter I got before this one I got today had the enveloped greased all up so that you could read it. The envelope was cracked open. I have got my paper pretty well filled up and as I have only one sheet more, I guess that I will use it to write next time. S. J. Haven.

—

On July 15, the regiment received orders to move to Vicksburg. They had been merged with the 12th Iowa in preparation of their movement northward to be discharged. The group moved down the Alabama River from Montgomery to Selma, then traveled by train through Demopolis, Alabama, to Meridian, Mississippi, and then onward to Jackson, Mississippi. The group then marched overland to the Black River Bridge, where they boarded a train to Vicksburg to go by river back to Clinton, Iowa.

—

No. 26, Montgomery, July 16, 1865

Dear Jane,

If you don't get any more letters from me than I do from you, you must feel very anxious to hear from me as I have not had any for nearly three weeks and feel quite anxious to hear from you again, but I don't expect to get any more letters till I get home as the prospect is now that we shall leave here soon. We have been expecting to go all last week, but they had so much to do that we are here yet. We got the official order last night that we were relieved from duty and were to be mustered out immediately. We are now waiting for transportation to Selma. We may leave camp tonight as the boats went to Selma night before last and are expected back today. We are going by boats to Selma and by railroad to Vicksburg, and from there to Cairo by boats and I expect that we shall go to Clinton, Iowa, to be mustered out and paid off. My health is not very good, still I am improving. There is not any particular news to write. The new recruits don't go out with us, but are going to the 12th Iowa, and the 32nd Iowa don't go out now, as they are about six days behind and will have to serve their time out unless they get new orders. I will put this by and finish when I get a chance to send off, which will be when I get to Vicksburg.

Big Black River, MS, July 22

We are so far on our way and have been pretty successful in getting our transportation so far. We left Montgomery Sunday evening and got to Selma the next morning, and took a train and came through to Jackson. From Jackson to this place, we had to walk so some of the boys started the same night. Our company hired a team for twenty-five dollars to fetch our knapsacks through and we started at five Thursday morning, and I kept going till I got here, which was at about midnight. I did not have anything to carry but my canteen. The team got ahead of me afternoon, but I passed them in the night. I am pretty lame, but feel pretty well other ways. I found a secesh coat, which was all the bed I had night before last. The talk is that we are going up the river to be mustered out, which I hope is so as we shall get sooner and it is. We feel hot here. I expect that we shall either take the cars for Vicksburg today or tomorrow morning, but I must close this. With love and kisses to you all, from your husband, Silas W. Haven.

No. 27, On board Steamer, July 30, 1865

Dear Jane,

I improve this opportunity of writing a few lines to you to let you know how we get along. We got to Vicksburg the 23rd. The colonel got permission for us to come to St. Louis, which we were very glad to do as it was very hot there. We waited all day for a boat and got a good one and left at 8 o'clock P.M. and got to St. Louis night before last, and got permission to go to Iowa to be mustered out and discharged. We left St. Louis at 4 o'clock yesterday afternoon and are steaming up to Clinton as fast as we can. The boat that we are on (the *Canada*) is a small one and is heavily loaded, and has got two barges in tow so we don't get along very fast. I think that I shall get home but the 15th of August, and if the things belonging to the regiment that were left at New Orleans have good success in getting through quick, we may get home sooner, but I will lay this by for this time as I shall have time to finish before we get to Clinton.

August 1st

We expect to get to Davenport at 4 P.M. where we are going to stop and I hope that we can be speedily mustered out of service, as I am tired of laying around doing nothing. The boys all are in pretty good spirits, and we are having quite a pleasant time riding up the river and it seems that we had once more got into America. So with love and kisses to you all, I bid you goodbye for this time. From your affectionate husband, Silas W. Haven.

August 2

Arrived at Davenport 4 P.M., all got off from the boat and then re-embarked again and started for Clinton, where we expect to arrive at noon today. We stopped overnight. I shall fetch my money home when I come, as it won't be long.

—

THIS IS THE final letter in the collection. The regiment would be officially mustered out on August 8, 1865 in Clinton, Iowa.

EPILOGUE

# After the Guns Fell Silent

After his service to the United States concluded, Pvt. Silas W. Haven returned to Rockford on August 11, 1865. He arrived by train from Waverly, Iowa, in the early morning hours. Haven picked up where he left off before the war, worked as a carpenter, and became a prosperous furniture dealer. The town of Rockford quickly expanded in the years after the Civil War, with eight hundred residents by 1882, which added a large group of potential clients to Haven's customer base. Within fifteen years after the war, the town had a bank, a grain elevator, and a creamery that produced a thousand pounds of butter per day. Haven's furniture business flourished, allowing the family to amass, by 1870, a personal estate worth $300 and real estate worth $1,800.[1]

Even with some financial success, Silas Haven remained plagued by consistent pain from his military injury sustained during the charge at Fort DeRussy on March 14, 1864. Haven applied for a United States pension in the summer of 1866. He received a medical examination by Dr. J. W. Smith, who confirmed that he suffered from an inguinal hernia on his right side, acquired as a direct result from the military injury suffered in 1864. The doctor noted that the hernia remained small and "hardly apparent except upon coughing" and "lifting," and requested that he should wear a truss to ensure the possibility of "a complete cure." Since the injury did not completely prevent him from earning a living through manual labor, Haven got $4 a month. On April 3, 1884, he received an increase in his pension amount to $8 a month.[2]

In the decades following the war, Haven remained committed to his faith and working on the health and stability of the First Baptist church. In 1870, when the First Baptist church received legal incorporation, Haven received an appointment to serve as a member of the board of trustees for the church and remained on the board throughout his entire life in Rockford. Additionally, he accepted the positions of treasurer and clerk for the church.[3] In addition to his church service, Haven served as a township clerk for a decade and won election as a justice of the peace in 1878, a position he held through at least 1882.[4]

Haven also played an instrumental role in caring for the dead of Rockford. Rockford's Riverside Cemetery, where Haven purchased the family plot, started in the 1860s when John Harriman, a local resident, refused to bury his wife out on the prairie because he did not want the body left at a place "for the wolves to dig up." However, Harriman had the foresight to select an appropriate place high on a hill, where all of the other bodies buried near the town would be moved after the Civil War. Residents who wanted a plot in the cemetery, after it became officially organized in 1885, had to pay $15 for the lot and a yearly due fee of 25 cents (which later increased to $1) for the maintenance of the lot. Before its official incorporation, Silas W. Haven bought one of the four original blocks of the cemetery, block number 3. In addition to his furniture business, Haven worked as an undertaker for the community.[5]

The cemetery plot that Haven purchased included five spaces, but only three graves are filled: his own, his wife, and his youngest daughter, Laura Olive Haven, who died on January 30, 1866, just a few brief months after Haven returned from the war. On April 19, 1871, Silas Haven lost his beloved wife, Sarah Jane, at the age of forty-one years and nine months. Her rather brief obituary appeared in a local Iowa paper, with a poem following the announcement of her death. The poem reads:

> Leaves, flowers and birds are past away
> But buds and blooms shall yet be seen,
> And fields be gay, and hills be green,
> And streams all bright, and sweet birds sing;
> First, last, is spring.[6]

On June 15, 1892, Haven applied again for a pension increase due to his failing health. The hernia continued to plague him, and he could not wear a truss due to having bowel tenderness. Medically, his lungs, heart, stomach, and kidneys tested normal. Yet, he had an enlarged liver and spleen, was poorly nourished, appeared generally emaciated, and claimed he could no longer work. He received an increase in his pension to $10 a month. However, his health continued to deteriorate rapidly.[7]

For years, the date of Haven's death has remained a mystery. All published histories of Floyd County that include a brief biography of Haven have a question mark listed as his death date. A perusal of local histories at the Rockford

Historical Society and the cemetery records revealed the same thing: a question mark listed with his death date. Iowa did a Population Census Schedule in 1885. Haven appeared, working as a merchant, and residing on Church Street in Rockford, Iowa. Census records in 1900 had no record of Haven. Haven belonged to the Grand Army of the Republic, post no. 377 in Rockford, Iowa, a group he joined on December 27, 1884. The membership records of the organization indicated that Haven died on April 11, 1893 in Bristow, Iowa, one county over.[8]

As for the living descendants of Haven, his oldest daughter, Ella, at the age of thirty-two, married Sylvanus M. Fulghum, a twenty-seven-year-old thrasher, on October 31, 1882. The couple had a son, William K. Fulghum, who arrived on May 10, 1885, while still living in Floyd County. Within a few years after the birth of William, the couple relocated to Mason City, Iowa, and Ella Fulghum gave birth to a daughter named Charlotte and a son named Oliver Milton.[9]

Emmett, Haven's son, who attended school, according to the 1870 census records, eventually married a woman by the name of Sarah and the couple had six children: four sons named Glenn, Percy, Carleston, and Merille, and two daughters, Opal and Carrie. While Emmett Haven did not appear in the 1880 census (probably missed by the census taker, as was his father), the 1900 census indicated that he was living alone on Main Street in Laporte, Iowa. Ten years later, the census named all six children and indicates that the couple had been married twenty-eight years. They had rented a house in Black Hawk County, Iowa, and Emmett worked as a retail merchant.[10]

A decade later, all four of Emmett's sons had left home, married, and some of the couples had children. Merille, who married a woman by the name of Galeta, had a son named Galen and a daughter named Margaret. Percy married a woman named Elzina, and the couple had a son named Gilbert. Glenn had married a woman named Vera, and Carleston had a daughter named Beatrice with his wife Edna. According to the 1930 census, the final records currently open to the public, Emmett and his wife Sarah remained alive and well. The couple, then in their seventies, owned a home valued at $6,000, and Emmett Haven continued his work as a proprietor of a dry goods store in Black Hawk County, Iowa. Thus, Silas Haven's family flourished with a bounty of grandchildren and great-grandchildren, many of whom he never met.[11]

As the Haven family continued to flourish, the family members remained committed to remembering the legacy of a devoted soldier, father, and son. In 1965, William Burmeister (Haven's great-grandson through his daughter, Ella), residing in Mason City, Iowa, brought the local newspaper a pocket diary and prayer book used by Haven during the Civil War. In the newspaper interview, Burmeister shared several of the one-lined diary entries that line up with the letters presented in this volume. The prayer book, published by the YMCA in Chicago, came into Haven's possession while he was in the hospital in Memphis, Tennessee, on February 24, 1863. During World War I, Oliver Milton Fulghum, Haven's grandson, served in France and carried his grandfather's prayer book with him. The book arrived back to the family following Oliver's death in the war on July 15, 1918, in France. As the newspaper writer who interviewed the family member concluded, "Silas Haven's legacy may not be great as such things are measured. But they are intensely human and warm as viewed a century later by even the most casual observer."[12]

# Notes

INTRODUCTION

1. Oliver Wendell Holmes Jr., "The Soldier's Faith," *Speeches* (Boston: Little, Brown and Co., 1913), 58.

2. James McPherson, *What They Fought for, 1861–1865* (New York: Doubleday, 1995), 4.

3. The published collections of Iowa soldiers and civilians pale in comparison to other regions, especially the Confederacy, which received more noticeable attention in recent years. For some examples of Iowa collections, see Kathleen Davis, ed., *Such Are the Trials: The Civil War Diaries of Jacob Gantz* (Ames: Iowa State Univ. Press, 1991); Ted Genoways and Hugh H. Genoways, eds., *A Perfect Picture of Hell: Eyewitness Accounts by Civil War Prisoners from the 12th Iowa* (Iowa City: Univ. of Iowa Press, 2001); Mark Grimsley and Todd D. Miller, eds., *The Union Must Stand: The Civil War Diary of John Quincy Adams Campbell, Fifth Iowa Volunteer Infantry* (Knoxville: Univ. of Tennessee Press, 2000); Julie Holcomb, ed., *Southern Sons, Northern Soldiers: The Civil War Letters of the Remley Brothers, 22nd Iowa Infantry* (DeKalb: Northern Illinois Univ. Press, 2004); Tom Jewett, ed., *Failed Ambition: The Civil War Journals and Letters of Cavalryman Homer Harris Jewett* (College Station, Tex.: Virtualbookworm.com Publishing Co., 2004); Samuel Calvin Jones, *Reminiscences of the Twenty-Second Iowa Volunteer Infantry* (Iowa City: Camp Pope Bookshop, 1993); Orr Kelly and Mary Davies Kelly, *Dream's End: Two Iowa Brothers in the Civil War* (New York: Kodansha International, 1998); Richard L. Kiper, ed., *Dear Catherine, Dear Taylor: The Civil War Letters of a Union Soldier and His Wife* (Lawrence: Univ. Press of Kansas, 2002); Charles F. Larimer, ed., *Love and Valor: The Intimate Civil War Letters between Captain Jacob and Emeline Ritner* (Western Springs, Ill.: Sigourney Press, 2000); Benjamin F. McIntyre, *Federals on the Frontier: The Diary of Benjamin F. McIntyre, 1862–1864* (Austin: Univ. of Texas Press, 1963); Barry Popchock, ed., *Soldier Boy: The Civil War Letters of Charles O. Musser, 29th Iowa* (Iowa City: Univ. of Iowa Press, 1995); and Mildred Throne, ed., *The Civil War Diary of Cyrus F. Boyd, Fifteenth Iowa Infantry, 1861–1863* (Baton Rouge: Louisiana State Univ. Press, 1998).

4. *Des Moines Sunday Register,* Apr. 9, 1961, article accessed from the Floyd County Historical Society. See also Donald C. Elder III, ed., *A Damned Iowa Greyhound: The Civil War Letters of William Henry Harrison Clayton* (Iowa City: Univ. of Iowa Press, 1998), vii. Elder lists Iowa enlistments at 76,242.

5. There is only one other published set of recollections from the 27th Iowa, the regiment that Haven fought with through the duration of the war, and the book is actually a self-published volume. The volume is Edward Rolfe, *A Civil War Union Soldier Describes*

*His Army Life as Three Years of "Hard Marches, Hard Crackers, and Hard Beds, and Pickett Guard in a Desolate Country": The Three Year Adventure of an Iowa Farmer,* ed. Laurence Lillibridge (Prescot Valley, Ariz.: Lillibridge Publishing Co., 1993).

6. *History of Floyd County, Iowa; Together with Sketches of Its Cities, Villages, and Townships, Educational, Religious, Civil, Military, and Political History; Portraits of Prominent Persons, and Biographies of Representative Citizens* (Chicago: Inter-state Publishing Co., 1882), 914.

7. *Republican Intelligencer* (St. Charles City, Iowa), May 26, 1859; *History of Floyd County,* 889–91; Floyd County Land Records and Deeds, Vol. B and C, 1856, Floyd County Court House. The forty-acre plot of land sold to Melissa D. Rolfe on September 22, 1856, was valued at the time at $120.

8. *Republican Intelligencer* (St. Charles City, Iowa), May 26, 1859; *History of Floyd County,* 539–40, 890–94, and 899.

9. *Republican Intelligencer* (St. Charles City, Iowa), May 24, 1860, and Nov. 15, 1860; *History of Floyd County,* 364–65 and 890–94.

10. Bell Irvin Wiley, *The Life of Billy Yank: The Common Soldier of the Union* (Baton Rouge: Louisiana State Univ. Press, 1952), 39–40.

11. McPherson, *What They Fought for,* 2–7; Samuel L. A. Marshall, *Men against Fire: The Problem of Battle Command* (New York: William Morrow and Co., 1947), 160–61; Reid Mitchell, *Civil War Soldiers: Their Expectations and Their Experiences* (New York: Touchstone, 1988), 18; Gerald Linderman, *Embattled Courage: The Experience of Combat in the American Civil War* (New York: Free Press, 1989), 80; Gary Gallagher, *The Union War* (Cambridge, Mass.: Harvard Univ. Press, 2011); Chandra Manning, *What This Cruel War Was Over: Soldiers, Slavery, and the Civil War* (New York: Alfred A. Knopf, 2007), 4; Michael A. Flannery and Katherine H. Oomens, eds., *Well Satisfied with My Position: The Civil War Journal of Spencer Bonsall* (Carbondale: Southern Illinois Univ. Press, 2007), 10. For other works on the Union soldier, see James M. McPherson, *For Cause and Comrades: Why Men Fought in the Civil War* (New York: Oxford Univ. Press, 1997); Reid Mitchell, *The Vacant Chair: The Northern Soldier Leaves Home* (New York: Oxford Univ. Press, 1993); Earl J. Hess, *The Union Soldier in Battle: Enduring the Ordeal of Combat* (Lawrence: Univ. Press of Kansas, 1997); James I. Robertson, *Soldiers Blue and Gray* (Columbia: Univ. of South Carolina Press, 1988); Aaron Sheehan-Dean, *The View from the Ground: Experiences of Civil War Soldiers* (Lexington: Univ. Press of Kentucky, 2007).

12. Jason Phillips, "Prophecy among Civil War Soldiers: A History of the Future," (paper, Second Biennial Conference of the Society of the Civil War Historians, Richmond, Va., June 19, 2010); McPherson, *What They Fought for,* 4. McPherson argued that many soldiers remained active in politics and read the newspapers.

13. For more on the history of the 27th Iowa, especially when it comes to the role of Company G in the regiment, see Michael F. Vala, *The Story of Rockford: Its Origin, History, and Present Development* (Dubuque, Iowa: M. F. Vala Publishing, 1970).

14. McPherson, *For Causes and Comrades,* x.

### 1. KISS THE CHILDREN FOR ME

1. McPherson, *What They Fought for,* 58 (see Intro., n. 2).

2. This statement offers a clue as to the financial difficulties the Haven family faced at the start of the Civil War. The winter months proved cruel, in terms of having enough food, so Haven relied on the generosity of his parents to assist his family in surviving the

end of the winter. The dire financial straits of the family, and Haven's constant worry about getting paid and sending money to them, are reflected throughout his correspondence during the Civil War.

3. See Manning, *This Cruel War,* 145 (see Intro., n. 11). Manning argues that Union soldiers believed that once God had forgiven them for the sin of slavery, victory would be right around the corner. Manning wrote, "While fraught with more anxiety and a heightened sense of obligation compared to white Southerners' religious beliefs, Union soldiers' religious faith also assumed that eventual victory was certain because it was the will of God."

4. Ibid., 45. Manning noted that many Union soldiers accepted the premise that since slavery caused the Civil War, its destruction was necessary for the war to come to a conclusion.

5. McPherson, *What They Fought for,* 40–42. As James McPherson argued, some soldiers fought to punish Confederates for committing acts of treason and causing the Civil War. Haven's strong ideological viewpoint, made up of a desire for the destruction of slavery combined with punishment of traitors, helped drive him not only to enlist, but also to continue fighting the war until the end. McPherson explained that strong ideological motivation propelled some Union soldiers to fight through their entire enlistment, even when things got rough in the summer of 1864.

6. This seems to be a reference to Senator James Henry Lane, who served as brigadier general in the war until his commission was canceled because he could not serve as both a senator and a military officer. He held strong antislavery views and regularly engaged in violent acts as a jayhawker in Kansas. For more, see Bryce Benedict, *Jayhawkers: The Civil War Brigade of James Henry Lane* (Norman: Univ. of Oklahoma Press, 2009).

7. This is the only letter within the collection that exists before Silas Haven joined the 27th Iowa.

8. 27th Iowa Civil War Enlistments, State Historical Society of Iowa; *Roster and Record of Iowa Soldiers in the War of the Rebellion Together with Historical Sketches of Volunteer Organizations, 1861–1866,* Vol. 3 (Des Moines: General Assembly, 1910).

9. Under a proclamation issued by President Abraham Lincoln on July 2, 1862, the 27th Iowa came into existence, as companies moved to Camp Franklin, outside of Dubuque, Iowa, between July 30 and August 26, 1862. For more, see *Iowa Roster and Records of Iowa Solders in the War of the Rebellion* (La Crosse, Wis.: Brookhaven Press, 1908–11).

10. George Ball, a resident of Floyd County, Iowa, married Mary L. Cory on May 9, 1858. Although he wanted to serve in the army, he was rejected from military service on September 9, 1862. *Report of the Adjutant General Acting Quartermaster General of Iowa, January 1, 1863,* Vol. 1 (Des Moines: F. W. Palmer, State Printer, 1864), 976.

11. Frederick Muhm is Silas's best friend. Originally from Germany, Muhm resided in Rockford, Iowa, before joining the war effort. Muhm is one of the first twelve citizens from Rockford to join the war on August 22, 1861, with an enlistment that took place rather quickly, as Captain McClure visited on August 21 and the next day, the men left for war. Muhm would join the 27th Iowa on August 8, 1862 and was mustered out September 9, 1862.

12. The phrase "Kiss the children for me" is quite common among Civil War letters from both Union and Confederate soldiers. Haven used the phrase time and again throughout his correspondence.

13. William S. Raymond married Abigail Crowell on December 8, 1857.

14. This is his first specific reference to each of his children by name. Ella, born September 1850, is the oldest, followed by Emmett, born March 30, 1854, and Laura, whom Haven affectionately calls Kitty, is the youngest, born January 22, 1860.

15. Sylvester A. Haven, the brother of Silas, joined the 21st Iowa, Company C, in 1863 and served at the battles at Port Gibson, Champion Hill, Black River Bridge, Vicksburg (where he is wounded), as well as the siege of Spanish Fort. He will be mustered out in July 1865. Laura and Inez are Haven's sisters.

16. Otto Brodtbeck, from Switzerland, received an appointment later in the war to the position of quartermaster sergeant. The quartermaster sergeant oversaw supplies and stores for the soldiers of the company.

17. The 21st Iowa departed for St. Louis, Missouri.

18. Susan is Fred's wife.

19. The adjutant is Charles Comstock, originally from New York, who lived in Lansing, Iowa. He was appointed to the position of adjutant on September 16, 1862. There are many references throughout the collection of letters to Fred needing someone to write a letter for him because of his illiteracy. Haven wrote on behalf of Fred throughout most of the war.

20. Haven is referencing the Army of Northern Virginia's invasion into Maryland, which consequently resulted in the Battle of Antietam on September 17, 1862. For more on Antietam, see Stephen W. Sears, *Landscape Turned Red: The Battle of Antietam* (New York: Ticknor and Fields, 1983); Brian M. Jordan, *Unholy Sabbath: The Battle of South Mountain in History and Memory, September 14, 1862* (New York: Savas Beatie, 2012); James McPherson, *Crossroads of Freedom: Antietam* (New York: Oxford Univ. Press, 2002); and Gary W. Gallagher, ed., *The Antietam Campaign* (Chapel Hill: Univ. of North Carolina Press, 1999).

21. Originally from Pennsylvania, James N. Dennis, a resident of Clermont, Iowa, enlisted as a first sergeant on August 15, 1862, with the 38th Iowa.

22. Capt. Charles A. Slocum, from Charles City, Iowa, originally lived in New York. As a carpenter, he resided in Wisconsin, St. Louis, and Louisiana, where he restored plantation homes until the war broke out, forcing him northward to Iowa. The men elected him captain when the volunteer soldiers arrived in Charles City, Iowa, on August 21, 1862. After the war, he won election as a county auditor for Floyd County, representing the Republican Party. He also briefly owned the local newspaper, the *Republican Intelligencer,* in Charles City, Iowa, sold it, and then bought the *Floyd County Advocate* in April 1878, in order to decry against alcohol consumption. He emerged as one of the leading Republican Party advocates for prohibition.

23. Haven's experience as a soldier seems to parallel that of many other Union soldiers, whose experiences have filled several excellent historical works. For example, see Bell Irvin Wiley, *The Life of Billy Yank: The Common Soldier of the Union* (Indianapolis: Bobbs-Merrill, 1952); Reid Mitchell, *Civil War Soldiers: Their Expectations and Their Experiences* (New York: Touchstone, 1988); Gerald Linderman, *Embattled Courage: The Experience of Combat in the American Civil War* (New York: Free Press, 1989); Earl J. Hess, *The Union Soldier in Battle: Enduring the Ordeal of Combat* (Lawrence: Univ. Press of Kansas, 1997); Reid Mitchell, *The Vacant Chair: The Northern Soldier Leaves Home* (New York: Oxford Univ. Press, 1993); and McPherson, *For Cause and Comrades* (see Intro., n. 11).

24. One of the many amusing names for diarrhea, a common nuisance among Civil War soldiers.

25. Haven is referring to J. T. Graham, a prominent businessman living in Rockford. Graham had constructed several mills and was one of the early settlers in the community.

26. This is one of the few letters that is in poor condition as the rain bled much of the ink.

27. It is unclear who Haven is referring to here by the last names of Kimball and Harriman. Wyatt most likely refers to George Wyatt, one of the early settlers in Rockford, who ran a land office business and later opened a hotel.

28. Adj. Gen. Nathaniel Bradley Baker, born on September 29, 1818, grew up in New Hampshire and attended Harvard College. Having worked as a lawyer, Baker won election to the New Hampshire House of Representatives and served as speaker from 1850–51. Then Baker won the governorship of New Hampshire in 1854, served his term, and moved to Clinton, Iowa, where he practiced law. On July 25, 1861, Governor Kirkwood of Iowa appointed him adjutant general, a position he held through the duration of the war.

29. Webster was a neighbor of the Haven family who allowed some of his livestock to roam free and damage crops on the Haven farm.

30. A furlough, a temporary leave of absence from military duty, may be granted for either personal and family reasons or medical reasons during the war.

31. Many soldiers longed to have an image of a wife or children that they could hold on to during some of the most troublesome and lonely times in the war. Some soldiers held the image of their loved ones as they lay dying on the battlefield. As historian Drew Faust noted, soldiers used the images to have a final moment when they could commune with their loved ones before death. For more, see Drew Gilpin Faust, *This Republic of Suffering: Death and the American Civil War* (New York: Alfred A. Knopf, 2008), 10–12. Haven requested on several occasions for his wife to send a photograph of her and the children for him to look upon during his military service.

32. Oct. 14, 1862, John E. Sanborn Letters, Special Collections, Louisiana State University Libraries (LSUL). John E. Sanborn, born in New Hampshire and a resident of Epworth, Iowa, left behind approximately twenty letters, which are held in Special Collections at LSUL. Sanborn, appointed a surgeon on September 16, 1862, and mustered in on October 3, 1862, provided some keen insights that discuss similar observations as Haven during the war. In a letter dated October 14, 1862, Sanborn observed a problem among the men with whiskey, and that officers took action in order to keep the soldiers sober.

33. Throughout the war, Haven routinely sent gifts to other men for his wife to pick up, rather than to his wife directly.

34. Gen. John Pope, born in Kentucky and a veteran of the Mexican War, had early success in the Civil War as a Union commander in Missouri, at Corinth, Mississippi, and successfully took Island No. 10 in April 1862. His success warranted him a promotion and Lincoln appointed him to command the Army of Virginia, which experienced a resounding defeat at Second Manassas at the end of August 1862. Pope spent the remainder of the war commanding in the Department of the Northwest in Minnesota, which dealt mainly with Native Americans in the region.

35. Milaca is a community northwest of St. Paul. In the aftermath of the bloody Sioux uprising, one of the largest Indian uprisings in American history, Gen. John Pope sent expeditions of soldiers around the region to protect other friendly Native groups in the region. Sioux Indians, outraged at their living conditions on their reservation, massacred about three hundred whites in six weeks, from August 17 to September 23, 1862. After the rebellion was subdued, Pope had to secure the frontier so settlers could again return to the area. For more on the expedition, see *The War of the Rebellion: A Compilation of the Official Records of the Union and Confederate Armies* (Washington, D.C.: Government Printing Office, 1880-1901), Series 1, Vol. 13, p. 722. (hereafter cited as *OR*)

36. Oct. 22, 1862, John E. Sanborn Letters, LSUL. Sanborn did not travel with Haven on the mission to visit with the Native Americans. Instead, he remained back at Fort Snelling and took care of the sick, as several soldiers had measles.

37. Benjamin Stone Roberts served as assistant inspector general of the Northwest. Throughout his distinguished military career, he brought court-martial charges against Fitz John Porter in November 1862.

38. Col. Gilbert would receive orders to move toward Cairo, Illinois, after returning to Mille Lacs. Gilbert had taken only six companies on the expedition and would reunite with the other four, under the command of Maj. George W. Howard at Cairo.

39. John Spencer Childs moved to Rockford in March 1857. He worked in the mercantile business for several years and had five children with his wife, Lydia. F. Lyon.

40. Childs, a neighbor of the Havens', regularly served as someone who could be called on to help Jane receive and ship items to and from to her husband.

41. Fort Ripley is located about 120 miles northwest of St. Paul.

42. The reunited regiment remained at Cairo until November 20, 1862, when they departed down the Mississippi River to camp at Memphis, Tennessee.

43. Fort Pillow would later be the site of the infamous massacre of black Union troops by a Confederate force under the command of Gen. Nathan Bedford Forest. For more on Fort Pillow, see Andrew Ward, *River Run Red: The Fort Pillow Massacre in American History* (New York: Viking, 2005); and John Cimprich, *Fort Pillow, a Civil War Massacre and Public Memory* (Baton Rouge: Louisiana State Univ. Press, 2005).

44. Dec. 6, 1862, John E. Sanborn Letters, LSUL. Sanborn wrote about the expedition with Grant's army and explained that a rumor broke out in the army pertaining to the suspension of hostilities, and that peace had been declared in the entire Civil War. Although Sanborn admitted that the proclamation was only a rumor, he did express his desire to give the rebs "a tremendous thrashing."

45. A member of Company G, Isaac M. Fleenor enlisted on August 9, 1862. His father, Nicholas Fleenor, had come to Iowa in 1856 after spending part of his life in Virginia and Indiana. Isaac had ten siblings, including a brother, George, who died at Pacific, Missouri, on December 7, 1861, while serving with the Dubuque Battery. Isaac contracted typhoid fever and died in Cairo, Illinois, on December 19, 1862. S. Wise refers to Samuel Wise, an 18-year-old soldier from Floyd County, Iowa, who joined the regiment in August 1862. Of note, he contracted smallpox and died in Memphis, Tennessee, on January 8, 1863.

## 2. GUARDING THE RAILS

1. "Gen. Jackson" refers to Andrew Jackson, the hero of the battle of New Orleans during the War of 1812 and the seventh president of the United States.

2. The regiment was in Lexington, Tennessee, on January 1, 1863, in pursuit of Gen. Nathan Bedford Forrest's Confederate force. Forrest escaped across the Tennessee River at Clifton, Tennessee, resulting in no major military action for the regiment. They would then begin the march back to Jackson, Tennessee.

3. Gen. William T. Sherman had moved Union forces along the Yazoo River to the north of Vicksburg. Sherman's soldiers fought from December 27–29, 1862, including the battle at Chickasaw Bayou on December 29, where Union soldiers lost nearly 1,700 casualties. Sherman was forced to withdraw and Vicksburg remained safely in Confederate hands.

4. According to Civil War records, there is no trace of a Gen. Smith who died at this juncture of the war. The Rockford, Illinois, post of the Grand Army of the Republic would be named in honor of Gen. John B. Wyman, who commanded the 13th Illinois at the battles along the Yazoo River. Wyman, wounded by a musket ball that knocked him off his horse on December 28, 1862, yelled for his men to continue the attack as he was removed to the rear of the lines and died.

5. The rumor about Vicksburg is false, as Sherman had failed in his expedition.

6. The lieutenant colonel for the 27th Iowa was Jed Lake, from Independence, Iowa, who received his appointment as lieutenant colonel on August 11, 1862.

7. For more on religion and the Civil War, see Gardiner H. Shattuck Jr., *A Shield and Hiding Place: The Religious Life of Civil War Armies* (Macon, Ga.: Mercer Univ. Press, 1987); Randall Miller, Harry Stout, and Charles Wilson, eds., *Religion and the American Civil War* (New York: Oxford Univ. Press, 1998); Mark A. Noll, *The Civil War as a Theological Crisis* (Chapel Hill: Univ. of North Carolina Press, 2006); George Rable, *God's Almost Chosen People: A Religious History of the Civil War* (Chapel Hill: Univ. of North Carolina Press, 2010); and Steven E. Woodworth, *While God Is Marching on: The Religious World of Civil War Soldiers* (Lawrence: Univ. Press of Kansas, 2003).

8. Overton Hospital, in Memphis, Tennessee, had been a Confederate hospital for the early part of the Civil War until the city fell into the hands of the Union army on June 3, 1862. The hospital then transitioned to a Union hospital to care for the sick and wounded soldiers in the region.

9. Union and Confederate forces engaged in a brief skirmish in Memphis on February 17, 1863.

10. Medical inspectors during the Civil War evaluated hospital conditions and the competency of surgeons. During the Civil War, about half of the Union inspectors were political appointments, and the inspector had enough power to orchestrate sweeping changes in the hospital, if necessary. In Haven's case, he wanted Allen to give his medical opinion about Haven's health to determine if he deserved a discharge from military service or be assigned to another position, such as a desk job writing reports.

11. George W. Mahoney, a private in Company G with Haven, enlisted September 1, 1862 and died of disease on September 18, 1864, in St. Louis.

12. On March 4, 1863, Gen. Earl Van Dorn captured several Union regiments under the command of Gen. William Rosecrans near Spring Hill, Tennessee. The Confederate raiding parties, under the command of Van Dorn and Price, continued to threaten Union expeditions in Tennessee and Mississippi.

13. The regiment returned to Jackson on February 28 after spending a few weeks in Corinth, Mississippi, guarding a garrison in order to allow the soldiers who had been there to move on an expedition to Tuscumbia, Alabama.

14. The regiment never went on this expedition, as they would remain in Jackson until the end of May.

15. J. T. Graham was one of the prominent businessmen in Rockford, Iowa, and Haven's nearby neighbor.

16. The descriptive roll is the document a soldier receives upon his enlistment that detailed physical features, occupation, age, date of birth, and date of enlistment. Due to his illness, Haven had been marked for a discharge. However, when he forgot his paperwork, the new board of examiners decided not to accept the discharge and Haven remained in the military. Allen had the authority to determine Haven medically unfit for duty, but his absence ensured that Haven remained in the army.

17. The term "Copperheads" referred to the Peace Democrats or those members of the Democratic Party who wanted to end the war. For more on the Copperheads, see Jennifer L. Weber, *Copperheads: The Rise and Fall of Lincoln's Opponents in the North* (New York: Oxford Univ. Press, 2006).

18. For more on guerrillas during the Civil War, see Daniel Sutherland, *A Savage Conflict: The Decisive Role of Guerillas in the American Civil War* (Chapel Hill: Univ. of North Carolina Press, 2009).

19. George W. Mahoney, raised in Indiana, lived in Charles City, Iowa, the county seat of Floyd County, which is about ten miles northeast of Rockford.

20. In the western theater of the war, some infantry units were mounted on horses in order to quickly pursue guerrillas in the region.

21. According to the Clothing Book records for Silas Haven, he received a clothing ration worth $1.80 on April 6, 1863, which included a new pair of infantry pants.

22. Throughout their stay in Jackson, the regiment regularly traveled and guarded along the railroads in the region.

23. Apr. 11, 1863, John E. Sanborn Letters, LSUL. Sanborn echoed in this particular letter the medical issues that several Union soldiers faced in the region, including an accumulating number of amputees who would be sent home and be part of the "one legged brigade." Sanborn also explained the case of a man who shot himself through the wrist because he did not know the gun was loaded (this is the story that Haven tells). The man required amputation of his right arm. Another soldier fell into a tub of scalding water and died instantly.

24. Prescott, before the war, had been elected to call a meeting for the residents of Rockford to discuss a proposed property tax to build bridges in the county. In 1858, he won election as county surveyor.

25. Apr. 15, 1863, John E. Sanborn Letters, LSUL. Sanborn reflected on another rumor that the men would join the fight at Corinth. He also received orders to prepare to move, and the patients still recovering were sent to a general hospital in Jackson, Tennessee.

26. Ayers' pills, developed by drugstore owner James Cook Ayer in 1843, assisted in keeping the bowels regular and worked to end constipation and the headaches that came with irregular bowels. Ads for the pills regularly appeared in the St. Charles *Republican Intelligencer,* the paper for Floyd County, Iowa. For an example of an ad, see *Republican Intelligencer* (St. Charles City, Iowa), Sept. 25, 1856.

27. For the first six months of 1863, the 27th Iowa guarded the Memphis & Charleston Railroad connecting Memphis, Tennessee, to Corinth, Mississippi. The city of Corinth remained under threat by Confederate raiders throughout the war, especially after the Confederates lost at the second battle of Corinth on October 3–4, 1862. For more on Corinth during the Civil War, see Peter Cozzens, *The Darkest Days of the War: The Battles of Iuka and Corinth* (Chapel Hill: Univ. of North Carolina Press, 1997).

28. Apr. 21, 1863, John E. Sanborn Letters, LSUL. Sanborn went with the regiment to Corinth and prepared to fight some guerrillas in the region. He explained how the men enjoyed being linked to the 52nd Illinois.

29. Tullahoma, in southeast Tennessee, emerged as a six-month battle area following the battle of Stones River (Murfreesboro, Tennessee) over New Year's of 1863. Union Gen. William Rosecrans faced off against Confederate commander Braxton Bragg, who kept the Union forces at bay. Rosecrans eventually flanked Bragg in July 1863 and moved onward toward Chattanooga, Tennessee. Tullahoma is more than ten miles from Corinth.

30. Haven does not explain why he owes money to Gleason. Nathaniel Gleason later joined the war, but would die at Pleasant Hill, Louisiana, in April 1864.

31. The Dutch term *sutler* meant to undertake low offices. A sutler sold supplies to a soldier, such as newspapers, patent medicines, shoelaces, candy, tobacco, and fried pies. The sutlers followed the armies, but often faced accusations of fraud as they sold the goods at exorbitant rates and the items often were not in great condition. The sutlers ensured that they had a bounty of goods, especially when they knew the soldiers would receive their pay on a specific date.

32. A rather amusing remark from Haven, who only occasionally shows his sense of humor in the letters. Haven wanting a scolding from his wife reflects how much he misses both the good and bad times with her.

33. Soldiers continually marched and camped on previous battlefields and regularly encountered the dead. Historians John Neff and Drew Gilpin Faust have recently written extensive books on the meaning of death in the Civil War. See John R. Neff, *Honoring the Civil War Dead: Commemoration and the Problem of Reconciliation* (Lawrence: Univ. Press of Kansas, 2005); and Faust, *This Republic* (see Ch. 1, n. 31).

34. Northern soldiers burned large stores of cotton throughout the war because cotton provided the main source of revenue for the Confederacy. Confederate blockade runners tried to sneak some supplies of cotton out to be sold in other parts of the world. African American slaves, another resource for the Confederacy that Union armies targeted throughout the war, came about with the passage of the First Confiscation Act on August 6, 1861. The act allowed for the seizure of all property that assisted in aiding the rebellion, including slaves. Slaves captured and brought to Union lines worked in manual labor positions, such as fortification and road builders, cooks, and washers. The Union government clarified the policy in July 1862 with the passage of the Second Confiscation Act and the Militia Act, which stated that all captured slaves belonging to Confederate holders are forever free, and they could be used in military or naval service.

35. The chaplain for the regiment, Daniel N. Bordwell, grew up in New York before he moved to Iowa. Bordwell, appointed chaplain on October 3, 1862, remained in the position until he resigned on August 25, 1864. His replacement, Frederick F. Kiner, received appointment to chaplain on December 31, 1864.

36. The Memphis & Charleston Railroad.

37. Grand Junction, Tennessee, along the Memphis & Charleston Railroad, is northwest of Corinth, Mississippi, and nearby La Grange, Tennessee.

38. Toon's Station is a railroad station in southwestern Tennessee, between Jackson, Tennessee, and Corinth, Mississippi.

39. Gen. Joseph Hooker, commander of the Union Army of the Potomac, suffered a severe defeat at the hands of Confederate Gen. Robert E. Lee at Chancellorsville, Virginia, on May 1–5, 1863. For more on the battle of Chancellorsville, see Stephen Sears, *Chancellorsville* (New York: Houghton Mifflin, 1996) and Theodore Ayrault Dodge, *The Campaign of Chancellorsville: Maps, Sketches, and Plans* (New York: Da Capo Press, 1999).

40. See Dee Alexander Brown, *Grierson's Raid: A Cavalry Adventure of the Civil War* (Urbana-Champaign: Univ. of Illinois Press, 1954).

41. George Wyatt, whom Haven referenced in several earlier letters in 1863. James Haven, the brother of Silas, remained in contact with him for the duration of the war.

42. Albert C. Rupe served as the first lieutenant of Company G until his promotion to captain on April 30, 1865.

43. While a majority of Haven's correspondence went to his wife and family, he paused here to write to his small church congregation back in Rockford, Iowa.

44. The battle on the Rappahannock referred to the Union loss at Chancellorsville. The good news from Vicksburg could have referred to the Union victory at Champion's Hill or Grant's success in laying siege to the city, trapping the Confederate forces within it.

45. Haven placed this emphasis on the word "cow."

46. The Clothing Book for the 27th Iowa revealed that Haven got a clothing ration on June 3, 1863, valued at $5.35. He received an additional allowance at the end of the month, valued at $2.70. Items in the ration included woolen socks, a flannel shirt, and a blanket.

47. Edward Crowell, who enlisted in August 1862, Daniel Dean, who also enlisted in August 1862, and William C. Decker, all part of Company G, are the men referred to here. Crowell, one of the early settlers in Floyd County, worked as a farmer and owned a large

estate. He also won election as county coroner in 1865, representing the Republican Party, and later served as a county supervisor in 1870. Dean married Elmira Knouse on May 23, 1858, in Floyd County, one of twenty-seven couples to elope during that year in the county. Dean died during the war on February 26, 1864. Decker would die of a wound on April 9, 1864, at Pleasant Hill, Louisiana. Both Dean and Decker are buried in Floyd County, along with thirty-five other soldiers from the county who died during the war.

48. Julia Knapp is Jane's sister.

49. May 29, 1863, John E. Sanborn Letters, LSUL. Sanborn noted that the men would soon depart Jackson and head south. He also discussed the importance of taking Vicksburg and how he wanted the regiment to move south in order to "crush the rebels."

50. The regiment, with their evacuation from Jackson, traveled by rail to Grand Junction, then to La Grange, and marched to Moscow, Tennessee, by June 6, 1863.

51. Haven is correct in quashing this rumor. Black soldiers did fight at Milliken's Bend, along with the 10th Illinois Cavalry and the 23rd Iowa on June 7, 1863, just north of Vicksburg. The entire Union force lost only about six hundred casualties, not 7,000.

52. June 3, 1863, John E. Sanborn Letters, LSUL. In a brief letter, Sanborn observed that the community of Jackson, Tennessee, was overrun with secessionist supporters, which he called "secesh." Sanborn recalled that the soldiers in the regiment hated the Confederates and wanted to burn the city of Jackson, Tennessee, for daring to support the Confederacy during the war. Sanborn called the residents of Jackson "poison."

## 3. EVERYTHING IS QUIET IN CAMP TODAY

1. *OR*, Series 1, Vol. 24, pp. 387–88 (see Ch. 1, n. 35).

2. Albert G. Daniels, also originally from Vermont, served as a fourth sergeant in Company G.

3. For more on the Vicksburg Campaign, see David Martin, *Vicksburg Campaign: April 1862–July 1863* (New York: Da Capo Press, 2002); Michael Ballard, *Vicksburg: The Campaign That Opened the Mississippi River* (Chapel Hill: Univ. of North Carolina Press, 2004); and Jeffery Korn, *War on the Mississippi: Grant's Vicksburg Campaign* (New York: Time-Life Books, 1985).

4. The entire regiment gathered together in Moscow, Tennessee, and guarded the Memphis & Charleston Railroad there until August 20, 1863.

5. Despite his abolitionist leanings, Haven used racial terminology that many in the modern era would find offensive. Yet, the language is very typical of the nineteenth century, even from individuals who fought against slavery.

6. Jacob Knapp, the brother of Jane Haven, appeared frequently in the letters. Jacob, born in Illinois, moved to Rockford in 1856. As an artilleryman with the 3rd Iowa Battery, he fought at Arkansas Post, Helena, Pea Ridge, to name a few. After the war, Knapp married Cynthia DeWolf and the couple had three children. Knapp worked as a farmer after the war. See *History of Floyd County*, p. 917 (see Intro., n. 6).

7. Jacob R. Howdeshell, from Charles City, Iowa, arrived in Iowa from Pennsylvania, where he was born and raised. He was later transferred to the Invalid Corps in September 1863.

8. Historians have significantly chronicled the experiences of Northern women on the home front and their contributions to the war effort. For two superb examples, see Nina Silber, *Daughters of the Union: Northern Women Fight the Civil War* (Cambridge, Mass.: Harvard Univ. Press, 2005) and Judith Giesberg, *Army at Home: Women and the Civil War on the Northern Home Front* (Chapel Hill: Univ. of North Carolina Press, 2009).

9. At Vicksburg, the Union forces remained in position and used the siege with hopes of starving the Confederate soldiers and citizens out of the city. Johnston still had not attacked the Union forces.

10. Brig. Gen. James Ronald Chalmers served under Nathan Bedford Forrest and spent much of 1863 raiding Kentucky, north Mississippi, and west Tennessee. From Holly Springs, Mississippi, he returned to the state after the war and served in the state and the U.S. House of Representatives.

11. Gen. Lorenzo Thomas, in charge of the United States Colored Troops (USCT) in Tennessee, quickly raised nearly 3,000 black soldiers in the Memphis vicinity by June 1863. USCT in Tennessee recruited other black soldiers, guarded railroads, and engaged in some fierce battles, including at Moscow in December 1863 and at Fort Pillow in April 1864, where hundreds were murdered while trying to surrender. Tennessee would contribute nearly 23,000 black Union soldiers to the war effort. For more on black troops in the Civil War, see Benjamin Quarles, *The Negro in the Civil War* (Boston: Little Brown, 1953); Dudley Taylor Cornish, *The Sable Arm: Negro Troops in the Union Army, 1861–65* (New York: Norton, 1966); and Joseph Glatthaar, *Forged in Battle: The Civil War Alliance of Black Soldiers and Their White Officers* (New York: Free Press, 1989).

12. Germantown, Tennessee, is a suburb of Memphis and located east of the city.

13. Blue mass, a medicine produced in the 1800s, contained a large amount of mercury and rose honey. The mass had been prescribed for a large amount of ailments, including constipation, toothaches, and parasite infections. Spanish flies, or blister beetles, had been used by some apothecaries, who constructed a plaster from the wings of the insects to treat blisters.

14. Gen. Pemberton surrendered his Confederate army to Gen. Grant on July 3, 1863. The city officially fell into Union hands the following day, when a giant Union flag appeared above the courthouse.

15. Wiley, *The Life of Billy Yank*, 101–2 (see Intro., n. 10). Historian Bell Wiley chronicled several cases of Union soldiers making note of Southern women and their usage of tobacco. Several soldiers remarked of their apparent disgust at tobacco usage, especially in Memphis and Mississippi. Some soldiers even observed young girls (seven or eight years old) practicing the same habit.

16. Throughout his letters, Haven never writes of any affection for Southern women. In fact, he simply views all Southerners as a monolithic group who receive the finger of blame for both the war and the institution of slavery. Historian Chandra Manning argued that initially, Union soldiers viewed Southern women as the guardians of virtue on which the nation survived. However, as more Union soldiers traveled across the South and observed how white Southern women benefited from the system of slavery, their perceptions changed. Manning wrote, "Even white women who did not trudge out to the field every day seemed to have lost the decency on which the survival of republican society depended." Union soldiers connected the degradation of Southern women directly back to the "corrupt and festering curse of slavery." For more, see Manning, *This Cruel War*, 71–72 (see Intro., n. 11).

17. Many Confederate women forced to take a loyalty oath during the course of the war had a similar angry reaction. Emma LeConte, when she had to take the oath, called it a "tyrannical measure" forced upon the Southern people. LeConte, living in South Carolina, wished she could raise enough funds to flee the country. Instead, she remained behind, subject to horrific treatment at the hands of Yankee soldiers, according to her diary. She said, "They invade our country, murder our people, desolate our homes, conquer us,

subject us to every indignity and humiliation—and then we must offer our hands with pleasant smiles and invite them to our homes, entertain them perhaps with 'Southern hospitality'—all because sometimes they act with common decency and humanity!" For more, see Earl Schenck Miers, ed., *When the World Ended: The Diary of Emma LeConte* (Lincoln: Univ. of Nebraska Press, 1987), 108–9.

18. The regiment would never travel to Kentucky, as they remained in Moscow until moving to Memphis in August. The leadership did undergo some major changes. Col. James Gilbert received command of the 3rd Brigade on July 19, 1863, until Col. James True returned from a leave of absence on August 15, 1863. Maj. George Howard would command the 27th Iowa until the return of Gilbert.

19. Maj. Gen. Benjamin Prentiss and Brig. Gen. Frederick C. Salomon commanded the Union forces at the victory at Helena, Arkansas.

20. Haven mailed the letter from Jake back to Jane so she would have word from her brother.

21. The Enfield Rifle-Musket, from Great Britain, became the second largest weapon used in the Civil War, behind the Springfield Rifled Musket. The effective firearm could fire a lead projectile at speeds of 850–900 feet per second and could travel a distance of well over four hundred yards.

22. Confederate raider Gen. John Hunt Morgan had moved throughout southern Indiana and Ohio toward Pennsylvania in July 1863. Morgan hoped to divert resources from Union forces in Mississippi and Pennsylvania, and his men averaged twenty hours a day in the saddle. He expected Copperhead support to assist him in his raid, which failed to materialize. The men are captured on July 26, 1863, at New Lisbon, Ohio. Morgan spent time in the Ohio State Penitentiary before he escaped.

23. Abraham Lincoln had wanted the capture of Charleston since the beginning of 1863. After an earlier failed naval attempt, Union soldiers tried again at Charleston and attacked Battery Wagner for a second time on July 18, 1863 (the first failed attack had been a week earlier). The battle, made famous by the performance of the 54th Massachusetts, an all-black regiment under the command of Col. Robert Gould Shaw, ended with the fort remaining in Confederate hands.

24. The Invalid Corps, also known as the Veteran Reserve Corps, consisted of wounded Union soldiers during the Civil War who could no longer participate in a full combat capacity. Some of the wounded who could still use a gun served on guard duty. Others, who lost a limb or had a severe injury, worked as cooks or nurses for the duration of their enlistment.

25. The rumor proved false, as the men remained in Moscow until August 20, before they moved to Memphis.

26. Union Leagues, formed by patriotic, wealthy men to promote the Union, appeared in 1863 and 1864. The organizations raised money for the United States Sanitary Commission, an organization that cared for wounded Union soldiers. They remained an active force after the Civil War, especially as local groups registered black voters and supported the Republican Party.

27. In this letter, Pvt. Haven included a newspaper clipping. The clipping, from the Family Reading Section of an unknown paper, is a poem, entitled "The Old Ship Union," by Mrs. M. A. Denison:

> What do you see, O sailor!
> Looking out in the night?

I see the old ship Union,
And red in her binnacle light;
Onward she goes right cheerily
All sails set to the breeze;
There's never a stauncher old vessel
Rides over treacherous seas

28. A letter from Haven's mother.

29. Haven's parents are Solomon and Charlotte Haven.

30. Haven received some clothing items on August 9, 1863, valued at $3.85. The clothing allowance consisted of two shirts.

31. Frank Leslie's *Illustrated Weekly* and *Harper's Weekly* are two of the most popular newspapers read by Union soldiers throughout the war.

32. The 27th Iowa departed Moscow on August 20, 1863. The regiment spent a day in town before moving on to Helena and then Brownsville, Arkansas.

33. Albert C. Rupe was the first lieutenant of the 27th Iowa, Company G.

34. The brigade moved to Helena, Arkansas, on August 24, 1863, in order to link up with the Army of Arkansas, under the command of Maj. Gen. Frederick Steele.

35. Confederate Gen. Sterling Price, who had retreated to Little Rock since the loss at Helena in July 1863.

## 4. THE ARKANSAS EXPEDITION

1. Haven had moved into the interior of Arkansas because his commander, Gen. Frederick Steele, had been ordered to take control of the entire state. Steele moved the Army of Arkansas, which the 27th Iowa had joined, toward Little Rock, Arkansas.

2. The battle of Pea Ridge, on March 7–8, 1862, took place in northwest Arkansas. Confederate Gen. Earl Van Dorn surprised federal forces at Elkhorn Tavern, but the Union soldiers regrouped and won the battle. Confederate forces retreated to the Mississippi River and abandoned Arkansas and Missouri.

3. Jacob and Charles Knapp, who served with the 3rd Iowa Battery, were the brothers of Haven's wife Jane.

4. Tim Folger was killed in battle at Pleasant Hill, Louisiana, on May 4, 1864. Nathaniel Gleason also died at Pleasant Hill on April 21, 1864.

5. Haven wrote a similar letter with almost identical content to his son Emmett from Brownsville, Arkansas, on September 6, 1863.

6. According to the Clothing Book, this is the final clothing ration drawn by Haven during the war on September 7, 1863. The value of the goods was only 32 cents.

7. A letter from Haven's mother.

8. Confederate raider William Clarke Quantrill, who had been denied a commission by the Confederate government in 1862 because his actions were deemed too barbarous, rode into Lawrence, Kansas, on August 21, 1863. His band of more than four hundred raiders massacred 150 civilians, left thirty wounded, and the town obliterated by fires started by the raiders. In response to the massacre, Union commanders instituted a new policy in Kansas City, forcing anyone who may be sympathetic to the guerrillas out of their homes. For more, see Michael Fellman, *Inside War: The Guerilla Conflict in Missouri during the Civil War* (New York: Oxford Univ. Press, 1989).

9. Marcus Tuttle ultimately decided not to actively run, according to an article pub-

lished in the *The Union Sentinel* (Osceola, Iowa), August 15, 1863. His name still appeared on the ballot as he faced off against William Stone, the Republican.

10. Samuel Smith was a minister with the Methodist church and resided in Cedar Township within Floyd County.

11. While the 27th Iowa was active in the capture of Little Rock, no one in the regiment was killed, wounded, or missing. Haven would remain with the regiment in Little Rock until the middle of November 1863.

12. Casualty estimates for the battle at Bayou Forche, the major battle outside of Little Rock that led to the fall of the city, were seventy-two for the Union and an unknown number for the Confederates. Brig. Gen. John Davidson's cavalry successfully routed the Confederate soldiers entrenched on the other side of the Arkansas River.

13. Mahoney fought with the 3rd Iowa Battery.

14. Maj. Gen. James G. Blunt, the only general in the Civil War from Kansas, received an appointment to command the Department of the Frontier in 1863. Fort Smith, located in western Arkansas along the banks of the Arkansas River, was supposed to be the new command headquarters for the department. However, William Quantrill raided Blunt's men in October 1863, killing eighty of the one hundred escorts traveling with Blunt to Fort Smith. Blunt lost his command position, but redeemed himself by defeating Confederate cavalry in 1864 at the battle of Westport, in Kansas City, Missouri.

15. Charles Knapp, one of the first soldiers to join the war effort from Rockford on August 22, 1861, remained with the 3rd Battery for the duration of the war.

16. The captain whom Haven referred to was Charles Slocum.

17. This refers to Nathan Kimball, who commanded the Department of Arkansas.

18. Known as True's Brigade, the 27th Iowa remained with this group when they became part of the Army of Arkansas for the expedition to take Little Rock. In November, the soldiers were transferred to Gilbert's Brigade in the District of Memphis, part of the 5th Division, 16th Corps of the U.S. Army.

19. Sept. 23, 1863, John E. Sanborn Letters, LSUL. Sanborn talked about his positive impressions of Little Rock, Arkansas, which included the nice homes, beautiful trees, and the plentiful amount of Yankees from New England, New York, and Iowa all over the city.

20. Joseph C. Rich, originally from New York, lived in Charles City, Iowa, before the Civil War. He survived the war and died in June 1895.

21. "Arkansas quick step" refers to diarrhea.

22. The election data here represent the Iowa governor race in 1863 between William M. Stone, the Republican, and Marcus Tuttle, the Democrat. Stone won an overwhelming majority of the votes from the county, 568–206, which reflects the vote within the regiment. The regiment voted 371 for Stone and seventy-eight for Tuttle. Across Iowa, 10,770 soldiers voted for Stone, while only 2,093 soldiers voted for Tuttle. *Republican Intelligencer* (Charles City, Iowa), November 5, 1863; *History of Floyd Country,* 365 (see Intro., n. 6).

23. Gen. Theophilus H. Holmes commanded all of the Confederate forces at the battle of Helena. He took over command of the Department of Arkansas for the Confederacy on October 10, 1863.

24. True was in command of the 62nd Illinois and would remain in Little Rock after the 27th Iowa left for DeValls Bluff on November 15, 1863.

25. Charles Wood, originally from Pennsylvania, served with the regiment throughout the duration of the war and returned home to Floyd County, Iowa. Benjamin Parker, raised in Iowa, remained with the regiment until May 31, 1864, when he was transferred to the Veteran Reserve Corps.

26. Confederate Gen. John Marmaduke, a cavalry commander in the Trans-Mississippi West, accused a fellow commander, Maj. Gen. Lucius M. Walker, of being a coward. Walker challenged Marmaduke to a duel, which Walker subsequently lost and died on September 6, 1863.

27. The captain reference is to Charles A. Slocum.

28. This rumor was true, as the regiment headed back to Memphis on November 15, 1863.

29. Pine Bluff, Arkansas, is located along the Arkansas River, southeast of Little Rock. The Confederate forces, under Marmaduke, tried to attack the federals at Pine Bluff on October 25, 1863. Col. Clayton Powell held off Marmaduke, with the assistance of nearly three hundred black soldiers who used bales of cotton to construct a defensive position.

30. Val is Clement Vallandigham, an Ohio member of the Copperheads, who had unleashed critical rhetoric against the Lincoln Administration. On May 5, 1863, Union Gen. Ambrose Burnside, commanding the Department of Ohio, had Vallandigham arrested and he was deported to the Confederacy. Vallandigham made his way to Canada, where he unsuccessfully ran for governor of Ohio in 1863, losing to Republican and Unionist John Brough.

31. As Haven noted, after leaving Little Rock, the 27th Iowa headed for DeValls Bluff, where they started moving down the White River to eventually head up the Mississippi River and back to Memphis, where the regiment remained through January 1864.

32. Included with the letter was the following poem, entitled "Pleasures":

Of the pleasures of spring
With its birds and its flowers
But beautiful still is the rose in its bower
But beautiful, more beautiful are the pleasures of home
Oh I invite all ye who roam
To come and partake of
The pleasures of home
There is pleasure in winter when there is ice
And there is snow. There are pleasures to share
Which we all know and many are the
Pleasures we find below
There is pleasure in winter and summer
And spring and pleasure in contentment
Which wealth cannot bring
There are pleasures for many, there are
Pleasures for all. Among the pleasures are
Many which we can recall. There are
Pleasures beyond this world of care
Let us look above to the pleasures there.
Ella

33. Collierville, Tennessee, is just east of Memphis.

34. In the fall of 1863, Union Gen. Nathaniel Banks led an expedition into Texas in order to prevent French officials in Mexico from intervening on behalf of the Confederacy. Banks controlled the mouth of the Rio Grande River and several of the outer islands in Texas. Gen. Frederick Steele remained in command of Arkansas for all of 1864.

35. Haven wrote letters dated December 17, 23, 24, and 31. Dec. 25, 1863, John E. Sanborn Letters, LSUL. This is the final letter from Sanborn in the collection that provides any significant details about the war. Most of the letter entailed pensions, being homesick, and the need for religion in the camp. Sanborn and Haven shared similar sentiments throughout the war when it came to their opinions of Southern civilians, the abuse of alcohol, and religion.

## 5. THE MERIDIAN AND RED RIVER EXPEDITIONS

1. Cairo, Illinois, a base of Union operations on the Mississippi River.

2. Daniel M. Dean, a private in Company G, 27th Iowa Regiment, died on February 26, 1864.

3. *OR*, Series 1, Vol. 32, Part 2, p. 39 (see Ch. 1, n. 35).

4. Another letter from Haven's mother to her son.

5. Colesburg is located northwest of Dubuque, Iowa. Dyersville, west of Dubuque, is directly south from Colesburg.

6. Despite Union victories at the end of 1863 in Chattanooga, the Northern public remained restless with the war. Peace Democrats routinely tried to pass resolutions denouncing Lincoln and ending the war, but the Republicans defeated the measures on a regular basis. During the early months of 1864, there were several riots and a few violent outbreaks from the Copperheads in their quest to end the war.

7. Haven's rumor is confirmed when Col. Gilbert received orders to move the 27th Regiment to Vicksburg on January 28, 1864.

8. With Union forces in control of Chattanooga, Atlanta emerged as the next major target in the southeastern United States. Gen. William T. Sherman received command of the Union forces in Chattanooga when Grant received a promotion to lieutenant general in March 1864. Sherman invaded Georgia, with his sights set on Atlanta.

9. "Greenbacks" refers to U.S. paper money.

10. Maj. George W. Howard, originally from Maine, commanded the 27th Iowa throughout the war.

11. Shipp Island, Mississippi, west of Mobile, served as a base of operations for Union forces in the Mobile campaign. For more on the efforts to take Mobile Bay in August 1864, see Craig Symmonds, *Lincoln and His Admirals* (New York: Oxford Univ. Press, 2008); Jack Friend, *West Wind, Flood Tide: The Battle of Mobile Bay* (Annapolis, Md.: Naval Institute Press, 2004); and James P. Duffy, *Lincoln's Admiral: The Civil War Campaigns of David Farragut* (New York: John Wiley & Sons, 1997).

12. Union forces evacuated Corinth in order to consolidate forces in the west.

13. James H. Noble, a member of the 27th, would enlist in August 1862 and serve until the end of the war, despite a severe wound suffered at the battle of Pleasant Hill, Louisiana, on April 9, 1864.

14. The 27th Iowa participated in Gen. William T. Sherman's Meridian campaign in February and March 1864. The Union forces raided and destroyed the railroad at Meridian, in east-central Mississippi.

15. Haven refers here to Gen. John Alexander Logan, who served as commanding general of the U.S. Army of the Tennessee in 1864 and 1865. A lawyer and future congressman from Illinois, Logan fought during the Vicksburg campaign, where he was wounded in the thigh in June 1863, and served in the Georgia campaign until he received a wound in the left arm at Dallas, Georgia, on May 30, 1864.

16. Generals Pemberton and Grant met under a tree when they negotiated the surrender of Vicksburg on July 3, 1863.

17. Edward Reiniger, second lieutenant in Company G of the 27th Iowa, grew up in New York State and lived in Charles City, Iowa, after the war. A farmer and carpenter, he successfully ran for sheriff in 1881.

18. In a margin note, Haven estimated that the army had about 50,000 soldiers.

19. A letter to Haven from his mother.

20. Brierfield, Mississippi, is the former plantation home of Confederate President Jefferson Davis.

21. The regiment did not return to Corinth, but remained in Vicksburg before they headed to the Red River.

22. In a margin note, Haven assured his wife that he had not pillaged or "jayhawked" anything from the civilians.

23. On March 10, 1864, the 27th boarded transports and traveled to the Red River, disembarking at Simsport on the Atchafalaya River. The 27th participated in the maneuver with the 24th Missouri and the 14th and 32nd Iowa. Col. William T. Shaw commanded the expedition.

24. On March 10, 1864, Union Gen. A. J. Smith moved his force, including the 27th Iowa, out of Vicksburg and down the Mississippi River to the Red River. The Red River campaign, envisioned by Union Gen. Henry Halleck and commanded by Nathaniel Banks, was supposed to control Louisiana and eastern Texas. However, the three Union forces, one commanded by Gen. Sherman and another by Gen. Steele, failed to communicate with one another and failed in their efforts, as 30,000 Confederates, under Gen. Kirby Smith, protected the region. For more on the Red River campaign, see Ludwell Johnson, *Red River Campaign: Politics and Cotton in the Civil War* (Baltimore: Johns Hopkins Univ. Press, 1958); James G. Hollandsworth, *Pretense of Glory: The Life of General Nathaniel Banks* (Baton Rouge: Louisiana State Univ. Press, 1998); and Gary D. Joiner, *Through the Howling Wilderness: The 1864 Red River Campaign and Union Failure in the West* (Knoxville: Univ. of Tennessee Press, 2006).

25. *OR*, Series 1, Vol. 34, Part 1, p. 362 (see Ch. 1, n. 35).

26. Beck would actually die from his wounds on March 20, 1864, and was later buried in Floyd County. He had been with the 27th Iowa since its formation.

27. Hershel I. Perrin survived his injuries and would be mustered out in the summer of 1865. Born in New York, he lost his parents at a young age and moved to Vermont, then Minnesota, and ended up in Floyd County, Iowa, in 1857. After the war, he married and had five children, named Harriet, Alicia, Ephraim, Nora, and Ester.

28. The attack at Fort DeRussy near Simsport, Louisiana, had been successful, with the corps losing only thirty-eight killed and wounded on March 14, 1864. The soldiers moved toward Alexandria, Louisiana, following the engagement.

29. Herschel Perrin and Jacob Beck both served in Company G, 27th Iowa.

30. Pvt. Haven, as he explained, spilled ink on this letter and some large chunks have been edited out because of the inability to decipher the letter.

31. During the Meridian campaign, Sherman's men captured several slaves from Confederate plantations around Meridian, Mississippi.

32. Gen. A. J. Smith.

33. Since the battle at Pleasant Hill, the Union forces, under Gen. Nathaniel Banks, retreated to Grand Ecore, then Natchitoches, Louisiana, and ended up in Alexandria, Louisiana, until May 13, 1864, when the city underwent evacuation.

34. Slocum received a wound on April 9, 1864, when a piece of shell struck him at Simmesport, the last major engagement of the Red River campaign.

35. For additional details on the movement of the soldiers from Alexandria back to Vicksburg, see *OR*, Series 1, Vol. 34, Part 1, pp. 359–64 (see Ch. 1, n. 35).

## 6. COPPERHEADS ARE AS STILL AS MICE

1. Due to his illness, Haven missed an expedition, as the 27th Iowa moved toward Greenville, Mississippi, defeated a Confederate force under Gen. Marmaduke at Ditch Bayou, and then the soldiers moved back to Memphis on June 10 and remained there until June 24. Gilbert described the action in a report, which can be found in the *OR*, Series 1, Vol. 34, Part 1, pp. 980–81 (see Ch. 1, n. 35).

2. The rest of the regiment spent July 1864 in Tupelo, Mississippi, and then moved to Oxford for much of August, before heading back to Memphis on August 30, 1864. While in Tupelo, the regiment participated in the battle of Tupelo, July 14–15, 1864. James Gilbert chronicled the military actions and bravery in a report, available in the *OR*, Series 1, Vol. 39, Part 1, pp. 287–88, and the August maneuvers can be found in the *OR*, Series 1, Vol. 39, Part 1, pp. 380–81 (see Ch. 1, n. 35).

3. La Grange, Tennessee, east of Memphis.

4. Lt. Col. Jed Lake, originally from New York, received a promotion to full colonel on June 26, 1865.

5. There is no clear indication as to why there is a major gap in correspondence. It may be because the letters were not saved or have been lost, rather than Haven having nothing significant to say. During the gap in writing, Haven moved to Davenport, Iowa, to visit some family members and stayed at Camp McClellan. The regiment, after returning to Memphis, moved via the Mississippi River to Cairo, Illinois, on September 5. The men spent time at Jefferson Barracks, Missouri, for most of September 1864. Haven does not appear to have rejoined the regiment, having additional duties and responsibilities, while the army engaged bushwhackers in Missouri in October.

6. Jefferson Barracks, along the Mississippi River at Lemay, Missouri, sits just south of St. Louis.

7. In 1864, in the eastern theater of the war, Gen. Ulysses S. Grant, attached to the Army of the Potomac, led Union forces on a relentless series of battles known as the Overland campaign. Battles ensued at the Wilderness and Spotsylvania Court House outside of Fredericksburg, Virginia, and at Cold Harbor, outside of Richmond. Grant then laid siege to the city of Petersburg, Virginia, trapping Robert E. Lee within the city. In Georgia, Gen. Sherman captured the city of Atlanta after three months of maneuvers and battles that turned the tide of Northern morale across the United States.

8. The Clothing Book records with the adjutant general do not indicate Haven got any further clothing allowances because Haven is not with his regiment in Missouri.

9. The Invalid Corps, created by the Union Army, allowed wounded soldiers to continue service in the military, performing light work details rather than fighting on the front lines. Men performed guard duty, cooked, provided medical care, and worked as hospital orderlies.

10. George Potter, a native of Maine and resident of Charles City, Iowa; Wheeler Decker, the brother of William C. Decker, who died at Pleasant Hill, Louisiana, after a gunshot wound to the head; Jacob R. Howdeshell, a resident of Charles City, Iowa, had been with the Invalid Corps since September 13, 1863.

11. A Confederate prisoner, utilizing a pocket knife, murdered 4th Sgt. Lewis J. Treat on September 27, 1864, at the Big River Bridge in Missouri. Treat started the war at the rank of fourth corporal.

12. In the presidential election of 1864, Abraham Lincoln, representing the newly formed Union Party, ran against Democrat George McClellan, the former commander of both all Union forces and the Army of the Potomac. Historian Chandra Manning noted that many Union soldiers expressed resentment against the Copperheads, especially as the war progressed. See Manning, *This Cruel War*, 99–101 (see Intro., n. 11).

13. The election statistics among Haven's comrades seems rather typical, considering that Lincoln won 80 percent of the soldier vote over George McClellan.

14. The first letter after Haven rejoined his regiment, following over a five-month absence.

15. For more on the battle of Nashville, see Thomas Robson Hay, *Hood's Tennessee Campaign* (New York: Press of Morningside Bookshop, 1956); Stanley Horn, *The Decisive Battle of Nashville* (Baton Rouge: Louisiana State Univ. Press, 1956); James Lee McDonough, *Nashville: The Western Confederacy's Final Gamble* (Knoxville: Univ. of Tennessee Press, 2004); and Brian Craig Miller, *John Bell Hood and the Fight for Civil War Memory* (Knoxville: Univ. of Tennessee Press, 2010).

16. Hood designed the campaign in order to take Nashville, move into Kentucky, cross the Ohio River, and link up with Robert E. Lee's army, which was still under siege at Petersburg. If Hood had taken Nashville, it would have put pressure on Grant to either abandon Petersburg or recall Sherman, who had been marching to Savannah, to deal with Hood.

17. At the battle of Nashville, Hood had about 30,000 soldiers, compared to 55,000 under the command of Thomas.

18. *OR*, Series 1, Vol. 45, Part 1, p. 480 (see Ch. 1, n. 35).

19. Pvt. James McCanna, originally from New York, received a slight wound on his hand at Nashville, but recovered.

20. Several members of the regiment pursued the retreating Confederate forces to Lawrenceburg, Tennessee, where the pursuit ended on Christmas. Haven remained in Nashville due to his illness.

21. A letter from Haven's mother.

22. Sherman captured the city of Savannah on December 21, 1864, after his successful march from Atlanta.

## 7. I SEND THIS IN A REBEL ENVELOPE

1. The rest of the regiment pursued Hood's retreating Army of the Tennessee, followed him to the Tennessee River, and then headed to Eastport, Mississippi, where they remained until February 9, 1865.

2. After recovering from illness following the battle of Nashville, Haven joined the rest of his regiment, which had been in Eastport, Mississippi, since January 5, 1865, after an unsuccessful pursuit of Hood's army.

3. Samuel J. Hemenway, born in New York, moved to Lansing, Iowa, in 1855. He started the war as a captain and had the distinction of never missing a day of military service through leave of absence. Lt. Edward Reiniger resigned on February 3, 1865. Capt. Charles Slocum ended up discharged on February 8, 1865.

4. On February 9, 1865, the regiment moved via transport to Cairo, Illinois, and then headed to New Orleans.

5. The new chaplain, Frederick F. Kiner, joined the regiment on January 25, 1865. Before his time as chaplain, Kiner served as a first sergeant in the 14th Iowa and participated in battles at Shiloh, Columbus, Kentucky, Sherman's Meridian expedition, and the Red River campaign. Captured at the Hornet's Nest at Shiloh, Kiner spent six months in a prison camp in Macon, Georgia, before being exchanged for another prisoner.

6. The date the regiment was mustered out, August 8, almost matched the rumored date that Haven heard in February 1865. Haven enlisted to serve in the Union army for three years.

7. Chalmette, Louisiana, where Jackson fought British Gen. Packenham in the battle of New Orleans in January 1815, is located just east of the city of New Orleans.

8. Col. James I. Gilbert received his promotion several months after his wound at the battle of Pleasant Hill. His victory at Fort DeRussy and his gallant performance at Nashville secured his promotion to brigadier general. He now commanded the 117th Illinois, 27th Iowa, 32nd Iowa, 10th Kansas, and 6th Minnesota.

9. John Hanchett, originally from New York, lived in Ulster, Iowa, before the war and received a promotion to fifth corporal on June 25, 1865.

10. On June 7, 1863, a French army marched into Mexico City to collect a debt. Lincoln was worried that Napoleon III would annex Mexico as part of a new French empire and drag the United States into a conflict with France. Thus, it was important for the United States to have a military presence at the Rio Grande, near Brownsville, Texas, to prevent any blockade runners or French forces from invasion. The desire to keep an eye on the French emerged as one of the reasons why Lincoln approved of Nathaniel Banks's expedition up the Red River.

11. On February 16, 1865, Confederate Gen. William J. Hardee evacuated his men from Charleston after receiving reports that Sherman's army had arrived in Columbia, South Carolina. Hardee, without any chance of getting reinforcements due to Sherman's position, left the city on February 17.

12. The famous equestrian statue stands in Jackson Square in New Orleans, in the heart of the French Quarter.

13. The battlefield monument at Chalmette still stands today.

14. On March 17, the 27th Iowa received orders to travel on the steamer *Brown*. See *OR*, Series 1, Vol. 49, Part 2, p. 15 (see Ch. 1, n. 35).

15. The regiment left New Orleans on March 7, 1865 and headed to Dauphin Island, a barrier island off the coast of Mobile, where they stayed until March 20.

16. Gen. Edward R. Canby, in command of the Department of West Mississippi, led nearly 45,000 troops to attack the city of Mobile, which had about 10,000 Confederates inside to defend the city. Canby ordered that troops prepare to attack from the west. However, the main attack came from the east and the soldiers to the west had been used as a diversion.

17. Haven's regiment was part of the actual attack coming from the east. First, the Union soldiers lay siege to Spanish Fort to the east of Mobile on March 26, 1865.

18. During the fight at Blakely River on April 1, 1865, the Union ironclad *Rodolph*, hit a torpedo and sank in the river. Despite the loss of the ship, the Union forces laid siege to Fort Blakely on April 2.

19. When the regiment joined Gen. Steele, they participated in laying siege to Fort Blakely. The siege lasted six days, from April 4–9, with the Union forces successfully taking the fort and occupying it on April 10.

20. Union forces stormed Spanish Fort on April 8, 1865. Although the Confederates

repulsed the initial attack, the Union regrouped and took the fort. The Confederate soldiers inside the fort escaped under the cover of darkness.

21. *OR*, Series 1, Vol. 49, pp. 255 and 258–59 (see Ch. 1, n. 35).

22. The regiment suffered only three wounded men, in terms of casualties, at the battle of Fort Blakely.

23. On April 11, Confederate forces abandoned Fort Hugar and Fort Tracy, the final two forts protecting Mobile. The Confederates also left the city that evening.

24. After spending three days occupying the fort, the regiment headed to Montgomery, Alabama. The march took roughly two weeks and the regiment remained in Montgomery for the duration of the war.

25. Gen. Robert E. Lee surrendered the Army of Northern Virginia to Gen. Ulysses S. Grant at Appomattox Court House, Virginia, on April 9, 1865. For more on the surrender, see William Marvel, *Lee's Last Retreat: The Flight to Appomattox* (Chapel Hill: Univ. of North Carolina Press, 2005).

26. Actor John Wilkes Booth assassinated President Lincoln at Ford's Theater, in Washington, D.C., on April 14, 1865. For more on the assassination, see Edward Steers Jr., *Blood on the Moon: The Assassination of Abraham Lincoln* (Lexington: Univ. Press of Kentucky, 2005).

27. The 4th Michigan Cavalry captured Confederate President Jefferson Davis at Irwinville, Georgia, on May 10, 1865. For more on Davis and his capture, see Nina Silber, *The Romance of Reunion: Northerners and the South, 1865–1900* (Chapel Hill: Univ. of North Carolina Press, 1997) and William J. Cooper Jr., *Jefferson Davis and the Civil War Era* (Baton Rouge: Louisiana State Univ. Press, 2008).

28. Letter from Silas Haven to his parents, Montgomery, Alabama, May 21, 1865.

29. Letter from Silas Haven to his parents, Montgomery, Alabama, May 21, 1865.

30. No. 20, letter from Silas Haven to Jane, Montgomery, Alabama, May 23, 1865.

31. Gen. A. J. Smith.

32. A letter from Sarah Jane Haven to her husband. At the end of the war, the correspondence between Haven and his wife, written during a large amount of downtime when the war had been decided, remained largely intact.

33. Charles City, Iowa.

34. This is the wife of John H. Hanchet, a member of Company G in the 27th Iowa.

35. This is the only letter from Emily in the collection. It seems that Haven either kept the letter or mailed it to Jane for safekeeping. It appears that, as he noted, he destroyed many of the letters he read.

36. Harry Henderson is Emily's husband.

37. *OR*, Series 1, Vol. 49, p. 1030 (see Ch. 1, n. 35).

38. Haven wrote a letter to Jane from Montgomery on June 18, 1865. The letter contained basic details of camp life and only briefly explored his diet, the weather, and his current state of health, which entailed diarrhea.

39. These two short letters were from Sarah Jane to her husband.

40. John E. Butler, born in New York and living in Nashua, Iowa, received a promotion to captain on June 27, 1865.

41. This is the final letter from Sarah Jane to her husband in the collection.

## EPILOGUE

1. *Globe Gazette* (Mason City, Iowa), July 14, 1965, p. 29; *History of Floyd County,* 891, 894, and 914; Population Schedules of the Ninth Census of the United States, 1870, Iowa,

The National Archives, Washington, D.C., accessed at the Iowa State Historical Society, Des Moines, Iowa.

2. Silas W. Haven Pension File, Application no. 108264, Certificate no. 69927, National Archives, Washington, D.C.

3. Of note, the First Baptist church remains in Rockford, Iowa, today and stands as a small building on the Main Street, blending in among the storefronts.

4. *History of Floyd County,* 889 and 914.

5. *Nora Springs/Rockford Register* (Rockford, Iowa), July 23, 2009, p. 5; Vala, *The Story of Rockford,* 334 (see Intro., n. 13).

6. Undated newspaper clipping included among the collection of letters. I confirmed the date of her death by visiting her gravesite at Riverview Cemetery, Rockford, Iowa.

7. Silas W. Haven Pension File, Application no. 108264, Certificate no. 69927, National Archives, Washington, D.C.

8. Population Census Schedule of Iowa, 1885, State Historical Society of Iowa, Des Moines, Iowa; Grand Army of the Republic Post Records, Department of Iowa, Post no. 377, State Historical Society of Iowa, Des Moines, Iowa. The post records cited his daughter, Ella J. Fulghum, of Mason City, Iowa, as the source for information pertaining to his death.

9. Birth and Marriage Records, Floyd County, Iowa, accessed at the Floyd County Courthouse, Charles City, Iowa.

10. *The Globe Gazette* (Mason City, Iowa), July 14, 1965, p. 29; Population Schedules of the Twelfth Census of the United States, 1900, Iowa, The National Archives, Washington, D.C.; Population Schedules of the Thirteenth Census of the United States, 1910, Iowa, The National Archives, Washington, D.C. All census records accessed at the Iowa State Historical Society, Des Moines, Iowa.

11. Population Schedules of the Fourteenth Census of the United States, 1920, Iowa, The National Archives, Washington, D.C.; Population Schedules of the Fifteenth Census of the United States, 1930, Iowa, The National Archives, Washington, D.C. All census records accessed at the Iowa State Historical Society, Des Moines, Iowa.

12. *The Globe Gazette* (Mason City, Iowa), July 14, 1965, p. 29.

# Bibliography


### ARCHIVAL COLLECTIONS

Floyd County Courthouse, Charles City, Iowa
Death Records
Land Records and Deeds
Marriage Records
Floyd County Historical Society
Cemetery and Marriage Listings, Floyd County, 1880–1900
Special Collections, Louisiana State University Library (LSUL)
John E. Sanborn Letters
National Archives and Records Administration, Washington, D.C.
United States Pension Files, Silas W. Haven, no. 108264
Riverview Cemetery Records, Rockford, Iowa
State Historical Society of Iowa
Adjutant General Records, Iowa, Clothing Books
Civil War Volunteer Enlistments, Iowa Adjutant General's Office
Grand Army of the Republic Post Records, Department of Iowa, Post no. 377
Historical Sketch, 27th Regiment Iowa Volunteer Infantry
Population Census Schedule of Iowa, 1885
Population Schedules of the Ninth Census of the United States, 1870, Iowa
Population Schedules of the Tenth Census of the United States, 1880, Iowa
Population Schedules of the Twelfth Census of the United States, 1900, Iowa
Population Schedules of the Thirteenth Census of the United States, 1910, Iowa
Population Schedules of the Fourteenth Census of the United States, 1920, Iowa
Population Schedules of the Fifteenth Census of the United States, 1930, Iowa
Roster and Record of Iowa Soldiers in the War of the Rebellion

### PERIODICALS

*Des Moines Sunday Register*
*Floyd County (Iowa) Advocate*
*Mason City (Iowa) Globe Gazette*
*Nora Springs/Rockford (Iowa) Register*
*Osceola (Iowa) Union Sentinel*
*Rockford (Iowa) Shell Rock Valley Guard*
*St. Charles City (Iowa) Republican Intelligencer*

## BOOKS AND ARTICLES


Ballard, Michael. *Vicksburg: The Campaign That Opened the Mississippi River.* Chapel Hill: University of North Carolina Press, 2004.

*Battles and Leaders of the Civil War.* 4 vols. 1884. Reprinted, New York: South Brunswick, 1956.

Beard, W. E. *The Battle of Nashville: The Limit of the Last Aggressive Movement of the Armies of the Confederacy, Hood's Grand Maneuver Designed to Prevent Sherman's March to the Sea, Fought in the Southern Suburbs of Nashville, December 15–16, 1864.* Nashville: Nashville Industrial Bureau, 1913.

Benedict, Bryce. *Jayhawkers: The Civil War Brigade of James Henry Lane.* Norman: University of Oklahoma Press, 2009.

Bowman, John S., ed. *The Civil War Almanac.* New York: Bison Books, 1983.

Briggs, John E. "The Enlistment of Iowa Troops during the Civil War." *Iowa Journal of History and Politics* 15, no. 3 (July 1917): 323–92.

Brinsfield, John, William C. Davis, Benedict Maryniak, and James I. Robertson, eds. *Faith in the Fight: Civil War Chaplains.* Mechanicsburg, Penn.: Stackpole Books, 2008.

Brown, Dee Alexander. *Grierson's Raid: A Cavalry Adventure of the Civil War.* Urbana-Champaign: University of Illinois Press, 1954.

Byers, Samuel H. M. *With Fire and Sword.* New York: Neal Publishing, 1911.

Byers, S. H. M. *Iowa in War Times.* Des Moines: W. D. Condit, 1888.

Cimprich, John. *Fort Pillow, a Civil War Massacre and Public Memory.* Baton Rouge: Louisiana State University Press, 2005.

Clark, Olynthus. *The Politics of Iowa during the Civil War and Reconstruction.* Iowa City: Clio Press, 1911.

Cooper, William J., Jr. *Jefferson Davis and the Civil War Era.* Baton Rouge: Louisiana State University Press, 2008.

Cornish, Dudley Taylor. *The Sable Arm: Negro Troops in the Union Army, 1861–65.* New York: Norton, 1966.

Cozzens, Peter. *The Darkest Days of the War: The Battles of Iuka and Corinth.* Chapel Hill: University of North Carolina Press, 1997.

Davis, Kathleen, ed. *Such Are the Trials: The Civil War Diaries of Jacob Gantz.* Ames: Iowa State University Press, 1991.

Dodge, Theodore Ayrault. *The Campaign of Chancellorsville: Maps, Sketches, and Plans.* New York: Da Capo Press, 1999.

Dollar, Kent T. *Soldiers of the Cross: Confederate Soldier-Christians and the Impact of the War on Their Faith.* Macon, Ga.: Mercer University Press, 2005.

Duffy, James P. *Lincoln's Admiral: The Civil War Campaigns of David Farragut.* New York: John Wiley & Sons, 1997.

Eicher, John H., and David J. Eicher. *Civil War High Commands.* Stanford: Stanford University Press, 2001.

Elder, Donald C., III, ed. *A Damned Iowa Greyhound: The Civil War Letters of William Henry Harrison Clayton.* Iowa City: University of Iowa Press, 1998.

English, E. A. *Roster and Register of Iowa Soldiers in the War of the Rebellion.* 6 vols. Des Moines: Iowa Adjutant General's Office, 1908–1911.

Faust, Drew Gilpin. "Christian Soldiers: The Meaning of Revivalism in the Confederate Army." *Journal of Southern History* 53 (February 1987): 63–90.

———. *This Republic of Suffering: Death and the American Civil War.* New York: Knopf, 2008.

Fellman, Michael. *Inside War: The Guerilla Conflict in Missouri during the Civil War.* New York: Oxford University Press, 1989.

Flannery, Michael A., and Katherine H. Oomens, eds. *Well Satisfied with My Position: The Civil War Journal of Spencer Bonsall.* Carbondale: Southern Illinois University Press, 2007.

Friend, Jack. *West Wind, Flood Tide: The Battle of Mobile Bay.* Annapolis, Md.: Naval Institute Press, 2004.

Gallagher, Gary W., ed. *The Antietam Campaign.* Chapel Hill: University of North Carolina Press, 1999.

———. *The Union War.* Cambridge, Mass.: Harvard University Press, 2011.

Genoways, Ted, and Hugh H. Genoways, eds. *A Perfect Picture of Hell: Eyewitness Accounts by Civil War Prisoners from the 12th Iowa.* Iowa City: University of Iowa Press, 2001.

Giesberg, Judith. *Army at Home: Women and the Civil War on the Northern Home Front.* Chapel Hill: University of North Carolina Press, 2009.

Glatthaar, Joseph. *Forged in Battle: The Civil War Alliance of Black Soldiers and Their White Officers.* New York: Free Press, 1989.

Grimsley, Mark. *The Hard Hand of War: Union Military Policy towards Southern Civilians, 1861–1865.* Cambridge: Cambridge University Press, 1995.

Grimsley, Mark, and Todd D. Miller, eds. *The Union Must Stand: The Civil War Diary of John Quincy Adams Campbell, Fifth Iowa Volunteer Infantry.* Knoxville: University of Tennessee Press, 2000.

Gue, B. F. *History of Iowa from the Earliest Times to the Beginning of the Twentieth Century.* Vol. 2, *The Civil War.* New York: Century History, 1903.

Hay, Thomas Robson. *Hood's Tennessee Campaign.* New York: Press of Morningside Bookshop, 1956.

Hess, Earl J. *The Union Soldier in Battle: Enduring the Ordeal of Combat.* Lawrence: University Press of Kansas, 1997.

*History of Floyd County, Iowa; Together with Sketches of Its Cities, Villages, and Townships, Educational, Religious, Civil, Military, and Political History; Portraits of Prominent Persons, and Biographies of Representative Citizens.* Chicago: Inter-state Publishing Co., 1882.

Holcomb, Julie, ed. *Southern Sons, Northern Soldiers: The Civil War Letters of the Remley Brothers, 22nd Iowa Infantry.* DeKalb: Northern Illinois University Press, 2004.

Hollandsworth, James G. *Pretense of Glory: The Life of General Nathaniel Banks.* Baton Rouge: Louisiana State University Press, 1998.

Holmes, Oliver Wendell, Jr. *Speeches.* Boston: Little, Brown and Co.

Horn, Stanley. *The Decisive Battle of Nashville.* Baton Rouge: Louisiana State University Press, 1956.

Ingersoll, Lurton D. *Iowa and the War of the Rebellion: A History of the Troops Furnished by the State of Iowa to the Volunteer Armies of the Union, Which Conquered the Great Southern Rebellion of 1861–1865.* Philadelphia: J. B. Lippincott, 1866.

Iowa Adjutant General's Office. *Roster and Record of the Iowa Soldiers in the War of the Rebellion.* Des Moines: Emory H. English, 1910.

*Iowa Roster and Records of Iowa Soldiers in the War of the Rebellion.* La Crosse, Wis.: Brookhaven Press, 1908–11.

Jewett, Tom, ed. *Failed Ambition: The Civil War Journals and Letters of Cavalryman Homer Harris Jewett.* College Station, Tex.: Virtualbookworm.com Publishing Co., 2004.

Johnson, Ludwell. *Red River Campaign: Politics and Cotton in the Civil War.* Baltimore: Johns Hopkins University Press, 1958.

Joiner, Gary D. *Through the Howling Wilderness: The 1864 Red River Campaign and Union Failure in the West.* Knoxville: University of Tennessee Press, 2006.

Jones, Samuel Calvin. *Reminiscences of the Twenty-Second Iowa Volunteer Infantry.* Iowa City: Camp Pope Bookshop, 1993.

Jones, William. *Christ in the Camp: Or, Religion in Lee's Army.* Goodyear, Ariz.: Diggory Press, 2006.

Kelly, Orr, and Mary Davies Kelly. *Dream's End: Two Iowa Brothers in the Civil War.* New York: Kodansha International, 1998.

Kiper, Richard L., ed. *Dear Catherine, Dear Taylor: The Civil War Letters of a Union Soldier and His Wife.* Lawrence: University Press of Kansas, 2002.

Korn, Jeffery. *War on the Mississippi: Grant's Vicksburg Campaign.* New York: Time-Life Books, 1985.

Larimer, Charles F., ed. *Love and Valor: The Intimate Civil War Letters between Captain Jacob and Emeline Ritner.* Western Springs, Ill.: Sigourney Press, 2000.

Lendt, David L. "Iowa and the Copperhead Movement." *Annals of Iowa* 40 (Fall 1970): 412–26.

Linderman, Gerald. *Embattled Courage: The Experience of Combat in the American Civil War.* New York: Free Press, 1989.

Long, E. B. *The Civil War Day by Day: An Almanac.* Garden City, N.Y.: Doubleday, 1971.

Madden, David, ed. *Beyond the Battlefield: The Ordinary Life and Extraordinary Times of a Civil War Soldier.* New York: Simon & Schuster, 2000.

Manning, Chandra. *What This Cruel War Was Over: Soldiers, Slavery, and the Civil War.* New York: Knopf, 2007.

Marshall, Samuel L. A. *Men against Fire: The Problem of Battle Command.* New York: William Morrow and Co., 1947.

Martin, David. *Vicksburg Campaign: April 1862–July 1863.* New York: Da Capo Press, 2002.

Marvel, William. *Lee's Last Retreat: The Flight to Appomattox.* Chapel Hill: University of North Carolina Press, 2005.

McDonough, James Lee. *Nashville: The Western Confederacy's Final Gamble.* Knoxville: University of Tennessee Press, 2004.

McIntyre, Benjamin F. *Federals on the Frontier: The Diary of Benjamin F. McIntyre, 1862–1864.* Austin: University of Texas Press, 1963.

McMurry, Richard. *John Bell Hood and the War for Southern Independence.* Lexington: University Press of Kentucky, 1982.

McPherson, James M. *Crossroads of Freedom: Antietam.* New York: Oxford University Press, 2002.

———. *For Cause and Comrades: Why Men Fought in the Civil War.* New York: Oxford University Press, 1997.

———. *What They Fought for, 1861–1865.* Baton Rouge: Louisiana State University Press, 1994.

———. *The Negro's Civil War: How American Blacks Felt and Acted during the War for the Union.* 1965. Reprint, New York: Ballantine, 1991.

Meyer, Steve. *Iowans Called to Valor.* Garrison, Iowa: Meyer Publishing Company, 1993.

Miers, Earl Schenck, ed. *When the World Ended: The Diary of Emma LeConte.* Lincoln: University of Nebraska Press, 1987.

Miller, Brian Craig. *John Bell Hood and the Fight for Civil War Memory.* Knoxville: University of Tennessee Press, 2010.

Miller, Randall, Harry Stout, and Charles Wilson, eds. *Religion and the American Civil War.* New York: Oxford University Press, 1998.

Mitchell, Reid. *Civil War Soldiers: Their Expectations and Their Experiences.* New York: Touchstone, 1988.

———. *The Vacant Chair: The Northern Soldier Leaves Home.* New York: Oxford University Press, 1993.

Neff, John R. *Honoring the Civil War Dead: Commemoration and the Problem of Reconciliation.* Lawrence: University Press of Kansas, 2005.

Noll, Mark A. *The Civil War as a Theological Crisis.* Chapel Hill: University of North Carolina Press, 2006.

Phillips, Jason. "Prophecy among Civil War Soldiers: A History of the Future." Paper presented at the Second Biennial Conference of the Society of Civil War Historians, Richmond, Va., June 19, 2010.

Popchock, Barry, ed. *Soldier Boy: The Civil War Letters of Charles O. Musser, 29th Iowa.* Iowa City: University of Iowa Press, 1995.

Quarles, Benjamin. *The Negro in the Civil War.* Boston: Little, Brown, 1953.

Rable, George. *God's Almost Chosen Peoples: A Religious History of the American Civil War.* Chapel Hill: University of North Carolina Press, 2010.

Reid, Richard M. *Freedom for Themselves: North Carolina's Black Soldiers in the Civil War Era.* Chapel Hill: University of North Carolina Press, 2008.

*Report of the Adjutant General Acting Quartermaster General of Iowa, January 1, 1863,* Vol. 1. Des Moines: F. W. Palmer, State Printer, 1864.

Robertson, James I. *Soldiers Blue and Gray.* Columbia: University of South Carolina Press, 1988.

Rolfe, Edward. *A Civil War Union Soldier Describes His Army Life as Three Years of "Hard Marches, Hard Crackers, and Hard Beds, and Pickett Guard in a Desolate Country": The Three Year Adventure of an Iowa Farmer.* Edited by Laurence Lillibridge. Prescot Valley, Ariz.: Lillibridge Publishing Company, 1993.

Rosenberg, Morton M. *Iowa on the Eve of the Civil War: A Decade of Frontier Politics.* Norman: University of Oklahoma Press, 1972.

Sears, Stephen. *Chancellorsville.* New York: Houghton Mifflin, 1996.

Sears, Stephen W. *Landscape Turned Red: The Battle of Antietam.* New York: Ticknor and Fields, 1983.

Shattuck, Gardiner H., Jr. *A Shield and Hiding Place: The Religious Life of Civil War Armies.* Macon, Ga.: Mercer University Press, 1987.

Sheehan-Dean, Aaron. *The View from the Ground: Experiences of Civil War Soldiers.* Lexington: University Press of Kentucky, 2007.

Silber, Nina. *Daughters of the Union: Northern Women Fight the Civil War.* Cambridge, Mass.: Harvard University Press, 2005.

———. *The Romance of Reunion: Northerners and the South, 1865–1900.* Chapel Hill: University of North Carolina Press, 1997.

Smith, John David. *Black Soldiers in Blue: African American Troops in the Civil War Era.* Chapel Hill: University of North Carolina Press, 2002.

Steers, Edward, Jr. *Blood on the Moon: The Assassination of Abraham Lincoln.* Lexington: University Press of Kentucky, 2005.

Stout, Harry. *Upon the Altar of the Nation: A Moral History of the Civil War.* New York: Penguin, 2007.

Stuart, A. A. *Iowa Colonels and Regiments: Being a History of Iowa Regiments in the War of the Rebellion.* Des Moines: Mills and Company, 1865.

Sutherland, Daniel. *A Savage Conflict: The Decisive Role of Guerillas in the American Civil War.* Chapel Hill: University of North Carolina Press, 2009.

Sword, Wiley. *Embrace an Angry Wind: The Confederacy's Last Hurrah: Spring Hill, Franklin, and Nashville.* New York: HarperCollins, 1992.

Symmonds, Craig. *Lincoln and His Admirals.* New York: Oxford University Press, 2008.

Thirft, William. *Roster and Record of Iowa Soldiers in the War of the Rebellion.* Des Moines: E. H. English, State Printer, 1908.

Throne, Mildred, ed. *The Civil War Diary of Cyrus F. Boyd, Fifteenth Iowa Infantry, 1861–1863.* Baton Rouge: Louisiana State University Press, 1998.

Vala, Michael. *The Story of Rockford: Its Origin, History, and Present Development.* Dubuque, Iowa: M. F. Vala Publishing, 1970.

Wall, Joseph Frazier. *Iowa: A Bicentennial History.* New York: W. W. Norton, 1978.

War Department. *The War of the Rebellion: A Compilation of the Official Records of the Union and Confederate Armies.* Washington, D.C.: Government Printing Office, 1880–1901.

Ward, Andrew. *River Run Red: The Fort Pillow Massacre in American* History. New York: Viking, 2005.

Ware, E. F. *The Lyon Campaign in Missouri: Being a History of the First Iowa Infantry.* Topeka, Kans.: Crane and Co., 1907.

Warner, Earl J. *Generals in Blue: Lives of the Union Commanders.* Baton Rouge: Louisiana State University Press, 1964.

Watson, Samuel J. "Religion and Combat Motivation in the Confederate Armies." *Journal of Military History* 58 (January 1994): 29–55.

Weber, Jennifer L. *Copperheads: The Rise and Fall of Lincoln's Opponents in the North.* New York: Oxford University Press, 2006.

Weed, Cora Chaplin. *Handbook for Iowa Soldiers' and Sailors Monument.* 1897. Reprint, Iowa City: Press of the Camp Pope Bookshop, 1994.

Wiley, Bell Irvin. *The Life of Billy Yank: The Common Soldier of the Union.* Baton Rouge: Louisiana State University Press, 1971.

Williams, Kenneth P. *Grant Rises in the West: From Iuka to Vicksburg, 1862–1863.* Lincoln: University of Nebraska Press, 1956.

Woodworth, Steven E. *This Great Struggle: America's Civil War.* Lanham, Md.: Rowman & Littlefield Publishing Group, Inc., 2011.

———. *While God Is Marching on: The Religious World of Civil War Soldiers.* Lawrence: University Press of Kansas, 2003.

Wubben, Hubert H. *Civil War Iowa and the Copperhead Movement.* Ames: Iowa State University Press, 1980.

# Index